Learn Linux Quickly

A beginner-friendly guide to getting up and running with the world's most powerful operating system

Ahmed AlKabary

BIRMINGHAM - MUMBAI

Learn Linux Quickly

Commissioning Editor: Vijin Boricha
Content Development Editor: Ronn Kurien
Senior Editor: Shazeen Iqbal
Technical Editor: Soham Amburle
Copy Editor: Safis Editing
Project Coordinator: Neil Dmello
Proofreader: Safis Editing
Indexer: Rekha Nair
Production Designer: Aparna Bhagat

First published: August 2020

Production reference: 1200820

Published by Packt Publishing Ltd.
Livery Place
35 Livery Street
Birmingham
B3 2PB, UK.

ISBN 978-1-80056-600-2

www.packt.com

I dedicate this book to my mother, Safeya, and my beloved wife, Franka.
You both mean the world to me.

Pack<t>

I am also very grateful for the support I have had from the Linux Foundation; I was the recipient of the 2016 LiFT scholarship award, and I was provided with free training courses from the Linux Foundation that have benefited me tremendously in my career.

A big shoutout also goes to all my 150,000+ students on Udemy. You guys are all awesome. You gave me the motivation to write this book and bring it to life.

Last but not least, thanks to Linus Torvalds, the creator of Linux. You have changed the lives of billions on this earth for the better. God bless you!

Contributors

About the author

Ahmed AlKabary is a professional Linux/UNIX system administrator working at IBM Canada. He has over seven years of experience working with various flavors of Linux systems. He also works as an online technical trainer/instructor at Robertson College. Ahmed holds two BSc degrees in computer science and mathematics from the University of Regina. He also holds the following certifications: **Red Hat Certified System Administrator (RHCSA)**, **Linux Foundation Certified System Administrator (LFCS)**, AWS Certified DevOps Engineer – Professional, AWS Certified Solutions Architect – Associate, Azure DevOps Engineer Expert, Azure Solutions Architect Expert, and **Cisco Certified Network Associate Routing & Switching (CCNA)**.

I am very thankful to everyone who's supported me in the process of creating this book.

Mom, words can't describe how much I appreciate and love you. Thank you for all your hard work and for believing in me.

Dad, you are the real MVP of my life. I know you wanted me to go to medical school to be a doctor just like you; sorry pops! Computer science is the future.

Ihab AlKabary, thank you for being my role model in life. Ever since I opened my eyes to this world, I always looked up to you. I wish you nothing but happiness and more success in life; keep on shining, brother.

Eman AlKabary, you are truly my best friend! Thanks for always encouraging me to do my best. I have learned perseverance and dedication from you.

My coworkers, I'm very fortunate to be surrounded by a brilliant group of people who've made me smarter and wiser. A big shoutout goes to Brad Martin, David Nagel, Jason Liu, Robert Séguin, and Colin Campbell.

Packt is searching for authors like you

If you're interested in becoming an author for Packt, please visit `authors.packtpub.com` and apply today. We have worked with thousands of developers and tech professionals, just like you, to help them share their insight with the global tech community. You can make a general application, apply for a specific hot topic that we are recruiting an author for, or submit your own idea.

Table of Contents

Preface

Linux is in huge demand in the IT industry as it powers over 90% of the world's supercomputers and servers. Linux is also by far the most popular operating system in the public cloud. Linux is the backbone infrastructure of the world's top companies, like Amazon, Google, IBM, and Paypal. You need to start learning Linux right now! *Learn Linux Quickly, First Edition* was written over the course of two years, from May 2018 to May 2020. This book implements a modern approach to learning Linux, and you will most definitely get to appreciate its uniqueness and friendly tone.

Who this book is for

If you have always wanted to learn Linux but are still afraid to do so, this book is for you! A lot of people think of Linux as a sophisticated operating system that only hackers and geeks know how to use, and thus they abort their dream of learning Linux. Well, let me surprise you! Linux is simple and easy to learn, and this book is the ultimate proof! You may have stumbled across a variety of sources that all explain Linux in a complicated and dry manner. This book does exactly the opposite; it teaches you Linux in a delightful and friendly way so that you will never get bored, and you will always feel motivated to learn more. *Learn Linux Quickly* doesn't assume any prior Linux knowledge, which makes it a perfect fit for beginners. Nevertheless, intermediate and advanced Linux users will still find this book very useful as it goes through a wide range of topics.

What this book covers

Chapter 1, *Your First Keystrokes*. In this introductory chapter, you will learn about the history of Linux and the impact of Linux in today's world and how it may shape the future. You will also learn how to install a Linux virtual machine and run few simple commands.

Chapter 2, *Climbing the Tree*. In this chapter, you will learn how the Linux filesystem hierarchy is organized and explore various Linux commands that will help you in navigating the Linux directory tree.

Chapter 3, *Meet the Editors*. Most of what you do on Linux revolves around files! In this chapter, you will learn how to use popular text editors like nano and vi to view and edit Linux files. You will also learn some handy commands that will let you view files from the comfort of your own Terminal!

Chapter 4, *Copying, Moving, and Deleting Files*. In this chapter, you will learn how to perform various operations on files. You will learn how to copy, move, and delete files. You will also learn how to rename and hide files!

Chapter 5, *Read Your Manuals!* Let's be honest! You can't memorize all the Linux commands that exist; no one can! That's why in this chapter, you will learn how to utilize and make use of the various Linux help and documentation tools.

Chapter 6, *Hard versus Soft Links*. In this chapter, you will first understand the concept of a file inode. You will also learn how to create hard and soft links and how they are different from one another.

Chapter 7, *Who Is Root?* It's time to finally meet the root user! In this chapter, you will understand the limits of regular users, and will also realize how powerful the root user is; you will also learn how to switch between different users on the system.

Chapter 8, *Controlling the Population*. You can think of Linux as a big powerful country! In this chapter, you will learn how to populate Linux with various users and groups. You will learn how to modify user and group attributes. You will also learn how to change file permissions and ownership.

Chapter 9, *Piping and I/O Redirection*. In this chapter, you will learn how to use Linux pipes to send output from one command to the input of another command and hence achieve more sophisticated tasks. You will also learn how to do input and output redirection.

Chapter 10, *Analyzing and Manipulating Files*. In this chapter, you will explore an array of Linux commands that will help you in analyzing and manipulating files. You will learn how to view the differences between files, display line count, view file sizes, and much more!

Chapter 11, *Let's Play Find and Seek*. Don't know where a file is? No worries! In this chapter, you will learn how to use the locate and find command to search for files on your Linux system.

Chapter 12, *You Got a Package*. In this chapter, you will learn how to install, remove, search, and update software on your Linux system. You will understand the software terminology used in Linux, including *package*, *repository*, and *package management system*.

`Chapter 13`, *Kill the Process*. In this chapter, you will learn how to interact with Linux processes. You will realize the differences between child and parent processes. You will also understand how to run processes in the background. Furthermore, you will learn how to kill processes!

`Chapter 14`, *The Power of Sudo*. In this chapter, you will learn how to grant `sudo` access to users and groups so that they can perform administrative tasks. You will learn how to use the `visudo` command to edit the `sudoers` file and you will learn the proper syntax for adding `sudo` rules.

`Chapter 15`, *What's Wrong with the Network?* Your network is down! In this chapter, you will learn how to troubleshoot your network connectivity. You will learn how to view your IP address, DNS, Gateway, and Host configuration. Furthermore, you will learn how to restart your network interface.

`Chapter 16`, *Bash Scripting Is Fun*. In this chapter, you will learn how to create bash scripts. You will learn how to use conditional statements to add intelligence to your bash scripts. Furthermore, you will also learn how to loop and create bash functions.

`Chapter 17`, *You Need a Cron Job*. Don't want to be tied to your computer 24/7? `cron` jobs have got you covered! In this chapter, you will learn how to schedule tasks with `cron` jobs. You will also learn how to schedule one-time jobs with the `at` utility.

`Chapter 18`, *Archiving and Compressing Files*. In this chapter, you will learn how to group files into an archive. You will also learn how to use various compression tools to compress your archives and save some disk space.

`Chapter 19`, *Create Your Own Commands*. Do you want to define your own Linux commands? In this chapter, you will learn how to use aliases to create your own Linux commands. You will also learn how to create temporary and permanent aliases.

`Chapter 20`, *Everyone Needs Disk Space*. In this chapter, you will learn how to partition your hard disk. You will also learn how to create and mount filesystems. In addition, you will learn how to fix a corrupted filesystem. Moreover, you will learn how to use Linux LVM to create logical volumes.

`Chapter 21`, *echo "Goodbye my Friend"*. What could your next steps be? Let me give you some suggestions on what to do after reading this book.

To get the most out of this book

The only requirement of this book is basically any computer that works!

Software/hardware covered in the book	OS requirements
Any virtualization software such as VirtualBox, VMware Player, or VMware Fusion	Windows, macOS, or Linux

If you are using the digital version of this book, we advise you to type the commands and scripts yourself. Doing so will help you avoid any potential errors related to the copying and pasting of commands and scripts.

I am a big believer of the "practice makes perfect" principle. The more you practice with Linux, the more you will get comfortable with it. You can install Linux as your main OS on your computer; this way you get to work with Linux on a daily basis. If that's not an option for you, then why not get a cheap Raspberry Pi and start playing around with it?

Download the color images

We also provide a PDF file that has color images of the screenshots/diagrams used in this book. You can download it here: `http://www.packtpub.com/sites/default/files/downloads/9781800566002_ColorImages.pdf`.

Conventions used

There are a number of text conventions used throughout this book.

`CodeInText`: Indicates code words in text, database table names, folder names, filenames, file extensions, pathnames, dummy URLs, user input, and Twitter handles. Here is an example: "The `exit` and `cd` commands are two examples of a shell builtin command."

When we wish to draw your attention to a particular part of a code block, the relevant lines or items are set in bold:

```
[default]
exten => s,1,Dial(Zap/1|30)
exten => s,2,Voicemail(u100)
exten => s,102,Voicemail(b100)
exten => i,1,Voicemail(s0)
```

Any command-line input or output is written as follows:

```
$ mkdir css
$ cd css
```

Bold: Indicates a new term, an important word, or words that you see onscreen. Here is an example: "The **File Name** is a part of the inode data structure."

 Warnings or important notes appear like this.

 Tips and tricks appear like this.

Get in touch

Feedback from our readers is always welcome.

General feedback: If you have questions about any aspect of this book, mention the book title in the subject of your message and email us at customercare@packtpub.com.

Errata: Although we have taken every care to ensure the accuracy of our content, mistakes do happen. If you have found a mistake in this book, we would be grateful if you would report this to us. Please visit www.packtpub.com/support/errata, selecting your book, clicking on the Errata Submission Form link, and entering the details.

Piracy: If you come across any illegal copies of our works in any form on the Internet, we would be grateful if you would provide us with the location address or website name. Please contact us at copyright@packt.com with a link to the material.

If you are interested in becoming an author: If there is a topic that you have expertise in and you are interested in either writing or contributing to a book, please visit authors.packtpub.com.

Reviews

Please leave a review. Once you have read and used this book, why not leave a review on the site that you purchased it from? Potential readers can then see and use your unbiased opinion to make purchase decisions, we at Packt can understand what you think about our products, and our authors can see your feedback on their book. Thank you!

For more information about Packt, please visit `packt.com`.

Your First Keystrokes 1

I want to welcome you to the first chapter of this book. When you read this book, you will feel like you are reading a story, but this is not an ordinary story, it is the Linux story. In this chapter, you will learn about the origin of Linux and the impact of Linux on today's world. You will also learn how Linux is shaping the future of Computing. Finally, you will learn how to install Linux as a virtual machine on your computer. So without further ado, let's jump-start into it.

A little bit of history

The story of Linux began in 1991 when Linus Torvalds, who was a computer science student at the University of Helsinki in Finland, began writing a free operating system as a hobby! It is funny to realize now that his side hobby project became the world's biggest open-source project in history. Oh, and in case you haven't figured it out already, this free operating system was Linux. There are a lot of definitions out there on the web for open-source, and some of them are somewhat confusing for the inexperienced reader, so here is a simplified explanation:

WHAT IS OPEN-SOURCE?

An open-source project is a software project that has its source code made accessible for the public to view and edit.

The source code is simply the collection of code (programs) used to develop software; in the context of Linux, it refers to the programming code that built the Linux operating system. Now since you know what open-source means, it is easy to imagine what closed-source is:

WHAT IS CLOSED-SOURCE?

A closed-source project is a software project that has its source code NOT made accessible for the public to view and edit.

Linux is the ultimate most famous example of an open-source project. On the other hand, Microsoft Windows is the most famous example of a closed-source project.

Some people don't know what an operating system is, but don't worry; I got you covered. Here is a simple definition of an operating system:

WHAT IS AN OPERATING SYSTEM?

 An operating system is a software program that manages a computer's resources such as memory and disk space. It also allows a computer's hardware and software to communicate with each other. Operating systems may also include other applications: text editor, file manager, graphical user interface, software manager, etc.

There are a lot of different operating systems out there; here are a few examples:

- Linux
- Android
- macOS
- Microsoft Windows
- Apple iOS
- BlackBerry

Keep in mind that this list is very short and is in no way comprehensive. There is a massive number of operating systems out there, and it is hard even to count them all.

When talking about operating systems, we have to mention the kernel, which is the core of any operating system.

WHAT IS A KERNEL?

 A kernel is simply the core of any operating system. It is the part of the operating system that organizes access to system resources like CPU, memory, and disk.

Notice that in the definition, I said the kernel is a part of the operating system. And the following figure can help you visualize the difference between a kernel and an operating system.

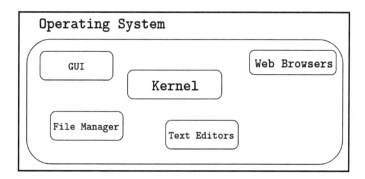

Figure 1: Operating System vs. Kernel

Unlike Microsoft Windows or macOS, Linux has a lot of different flavors; these flavors are called distributions, and they are also referred to as distros for short.

WHAT IS A LINUX DISTRIBUTION?

Since Linux is open-source, many people and organizations have modified the Linux kernel along with other components of the Linux operating system to develop and customize their own flavor of Linux that suits their needs.

There are literally hundreds of Linux distributions out there! You can go to www.distrowatch.com to check out the enormous list of Linux distros.

The good thing about distrowatch.com is that it shows you the popularity ranking of all the Linux distros in the world. You will even see that some Linux distros are designed with a specific purpose in mind. For example, Scientific Linux is a popular Linux distro among many scientists as it contains a lot of scientific applications preinstalled, which makes it the number one Linux choice among the scientific community.

Linux today and the future

In 1991, Linux was just a little baby. But this baby grew massively, and it became so popular. Today, Linux powers over 90% of the world's top supercomputers. And to add to your surprise, you may have been using Linux for years without noticing. How? Well, if you ever used an Android smartphone, then you have used Linux, and that's because Android is a Linux distribution! And if you still don't believe me, go to `distrowatch.com` and search for Android.

On a more serious matter, the majority of government servers run Linux, and that's why you will see a lot of government technical jobs requiring Linux-skilled individuals. Also, big companies like Amazon, eBay, PayPal, Walmart, and many others rely on Linux to run their advanced and sophisticated applications. Furthermore, Linux dominates the cloud as more than 75% of cloud solutions run Linux.

The Linux story is truly inspiring. What was once a hobby is now literally dominating the internet, and the future even looks more promising for Linux. Famous car manufacturers and automakers like Lexus and Toyota are now adopting Linux technologies like **Automotive Grade Linux** (**AGL**). You can find more information on `www.automotivelinux.org`.

Linux also runs on many embedded devices and is the backbone of the popular Raspberry Pi, Beagle Bone, and many other microcontrollers. You may even be surprised to know that some washing machines run on Linux! So every time you go and wash your clothes, take a moment, and be thankful for having Linux in our lives.

Installing a Linux virtual machine

There are a variety of ways to install a Linux system. For example, if you are currently running Windows as your primary operating system, then you may be able to dual boot Linux alongside Windows, but this method is not beginner-friendly. Any error in the installation process may cause you a lot of headaches, and in some cases, you won't even be able to boot Windows anymore! I want to save you a lot of pain and agony, so I am going to show you how to install Linux as a virtual machine.

WHAT IS A VIRTUAL MACHINE?

A virtual machine is simply a computer running from within another computer (host). A virtual machine shares the host resources and behaves exactly like a standalone physical machine.

You can also have nested virtual machines, which means that you can run a virtual machine from within another virtual machine.

The process of installing a virtual machine is straightforward; you only need to follow the following steps:

1. Install VirtualBox (or VMware Player).
2. Download an ISO image of any Linux distribution.
3. Open up VirtualBox and begin the installation process.

The first step is to install VirtualBox, which is a cross-platform virtualization application that will allow us to create virtual machines. VirtualBox is free, and it works on macOS, Windows, and Linux. A quick Google search: VirtualBox download will get the job done. If you are feeling a bit lazy, you can download VirtualBox at the following link: `www.virtualbox.org/wiki/Downloads`.

After you have installed VirtualBox, you now need to download an ISO image of any Linux distribution. For this book, you will be using Ubuntu, which is arguably the most popular Linux distribution among beginners. You can download Ubuntu at the following link: `www.ubuntu.com/download/desktop`.

I recommend that you download the latest Ubuntu **LTS** (**Long Term Support**) version as it is well tested and has better support.

For the last step, you need to open VirtualBox and create a Linux virtual machine with the Ubuntu ISO image you have downloaded from *Step 2*.

When you open VirtualBox, you have to select **New** from the menu bar.

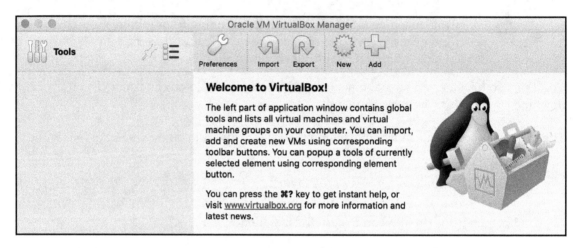

Figure 2: Creating a New Virtual Machine

Then you need to choose the name and type of your new virtual machine.

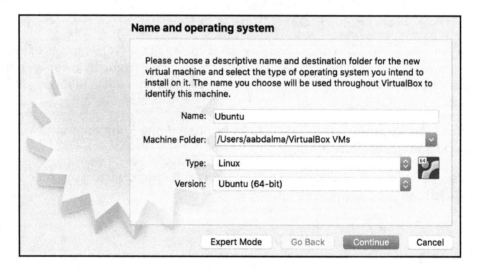

Figure 3: Choose Name and Type

After that, click on **Continue** and select how much memory you want to give to your virtual machine. I highly recommend 2 GB (gigabytes) or more. For example, here in the following screenshot, I chose to give my virtual machine 4096 MB of memory (RAM), which is equivalent to 4 GB.

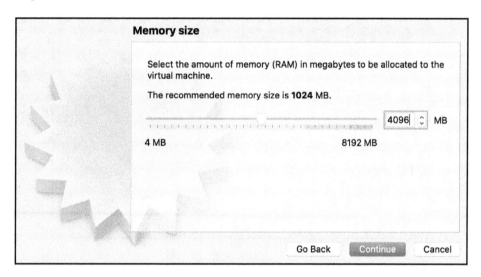

Figure 4: Choose Memory Size

After that, click on **Continue** and make sure that **Create a virtual hard disk now** is selected, as shown in the following screenshot, then click on **Create**.

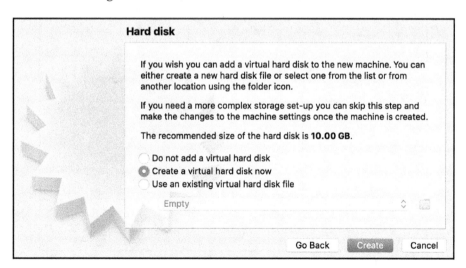

Figure 5: Create a Hard Disk

After that, choose **VDI (VirtualBox Disk Image)** as shown in the following screenshot, then click on **Continue**.

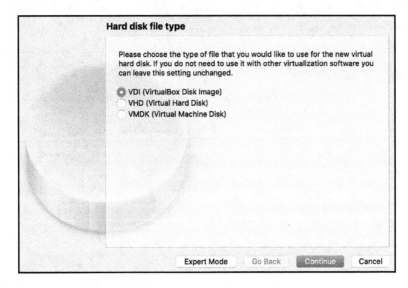

Figure 6: Hard Disk File Type

Now select **Dynamically allocated**, as shown in the following screenshot, then click on **Continue**.

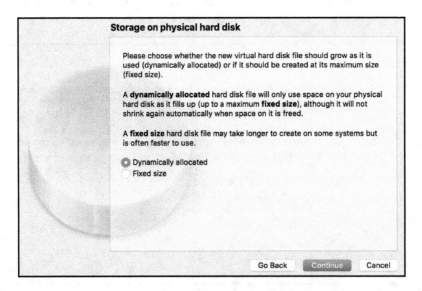

Figure 7: Storage on Physical Hard Disk

Now you can select the hard disk size of your virtual machine. I highly recommend you choose 10 GB or higher. Here in the following screenshot, I chose 20 GB for my virtual machine.

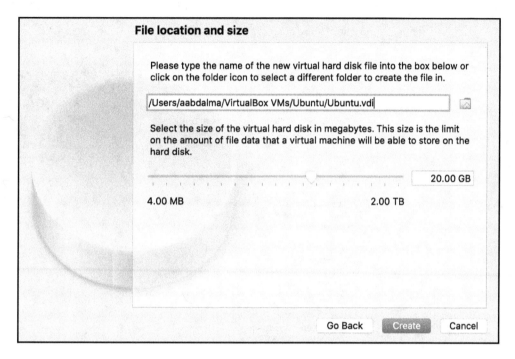

Figure 8: Hard Disk Size

After selecting the hard disk size, click on **Create** to finish creating your virtual machine.

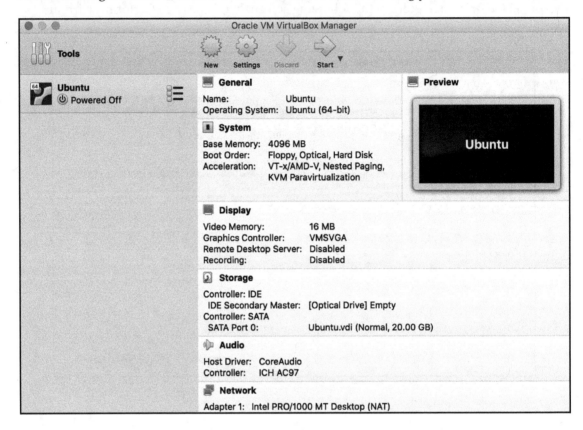

Figure 9: Virtual Machine Is Created

You can click on the green **Start** button to launch your virtual machine. You will then have to select a start-up disk, as shown in the following screenshot.

Figure 10: Select Start-Up Disk

Choose the Ubuntu ISO image that you have downloaded and then click on **Start** to launch the Ubuntu Installer, as shown in the following screenshot.

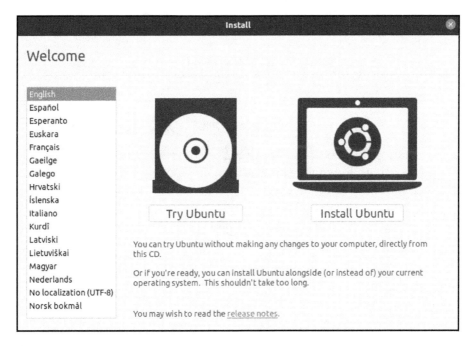

Figure 11: Ubuntu Installer

You can now select **Install Ubuntu**. Next, you will have to choose the language and the keyboard layout. After that, you should keep accepting the defaults.

You will eventually come to the step of creating a new user, as shown in the following screenshot.

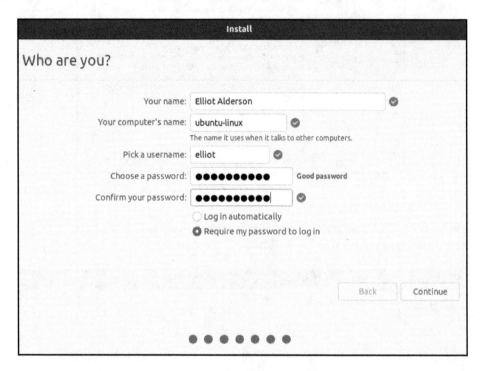

Figure 12: Create a New User

I chose the username `elliot` because I am a big fan of the TV Show Mr. Robot and for the fact that Elliot was using Linux while he was casually hacking E Corp! I highly recommend you choose `elliot` as your username as it will make it easier for you to follow along with the book.

You can then click on **Continue**, and the system installation will begin, as shown in the following screenshot.

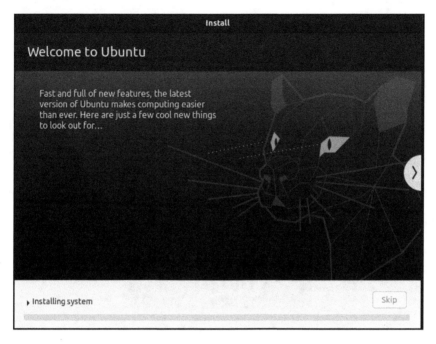

Figure 13: System Installation

The installation process will take a few minutes. Hang on there or make yourself a cup of coffee or something while the installation finishes.

You will have to restart your virtual machine when the installation is complete, as shown in the following screenshot.

Figure 14: Installation Complete

You can click on **Restart Now**. After that, it may ask you to remove the installation medium, which you can do by selecting **Devices -+ Optical Drives -+ Remove disk from virtual drive**.

Finally, you should see your **Sign In** screen, as shown in the following screenshot.

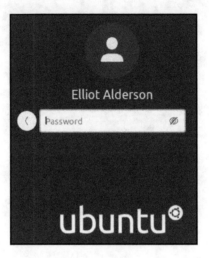

Figure 15: Ubuntu Sign In

You can now enter your password and hooray! You are now inside of a Linux system.

There are other ways you can use to experiment with a Linux system. For example, you can create an account on **AWS** (**Amazon Web Services**) and launch a Linux virtual machine on an Amazon EC2 instance. Likewise, you can create a Linux virtual machine on Microsoft Azure. So consider yourself lucky to be living in this day and age! Back in the day, it was a painful process to get up and running with Linux.

Terminal versus Shell

The **graphical user interface** (GUI) is pretty self-explanatory. You can easily get around and connect to the internet and open up your web browser. All of that is pretty easy, as you can see in the following screenshot.

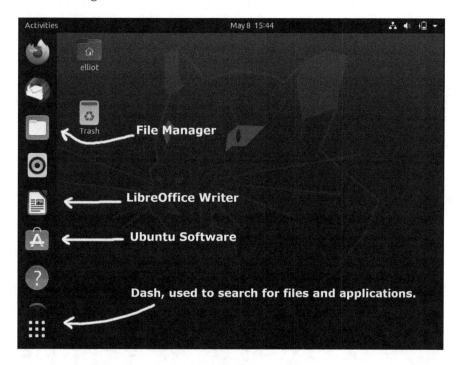

Figure 16: The Graphical User Interface

You can use **Ubuntu Software** to install new software programs on your system.

You can use **Dash** the same way you would use the Start menu on Microsoft Windows to launch your applications.

LibreOffice Writer is an excellent word processor that has the same functionality as Microsoft Word with only one difference; it's free!

Right now, you can be a casual Linux user, which means you can use Linux to do the basic tasks that everyday users do: surfing YouTube, sending Emails, searching Google, etc. However, to be a power user, you need to be proficient at using the Linux **Command Line Interface**.

To access the Linux **Command Line Interface**, you need to open the **Terminal Emulator**, which is often referred to as the **Terminal** for simplicity.

WHAT IS A TERMINAL EMULATOR?

A Terminal Emulator is a program that emulates (mimics) a physical Terminal (Console). The Terminal interacts with the Shell (the Command Line Interface).

Ok, now you might be scratching your head, asking yourself: "What is a Shell?"

WHAT IS A SHELL?

The Shell is a command-line interpreter, that is to say, it is a program that processes and executes commands.

Alright, enough with all the theory here. Let's walk through an example to understand and tie everything together. Go ahead and open the Terminal by clicking on the Dash and then search `Terminal`. You can also use the shortcut *Ctrl+Alt+T* to open the Terminal. When the Terminal opens, you will see a new window, as shown in the following screenshot.

Figure 17: The Terminal

It looks kind of similar to the **Command Prompt** on Microsoft Windows. Alright, now type `date` on your Terminal and then hit *Enter*:

```
elliot©ubuntu-linux:~$ date
Tue Feb 17 16:39:13 CST 2020
```

Now let's discuss what happened, `date` is a Linux command that prints the current date and time, right after you hit *Enter*, the Shell (which is working behind the scenes) then executed the command `date` and displayed the output on your Terminal.

You shouldn't be confused between the **Terminal** and the **Shell**. The Terminal is the window you see on your screen where you can type in your commands while the Shell is responsible for executing the commands. That's it, nothing more and nothing less.

You should also know that if you type any gibberish, you will get a **command not found** error as shown in the following example:

```
elliot©ubuntu-linux:~$ blabla
blabla: command not found
```

A few simple commands

Congratulations on learning your first Linux command (`date`). Now let's keep learning more!

One would usually display the calendar after displaying that date, right? To display the calendar of the current month, you can run the `cal` command:

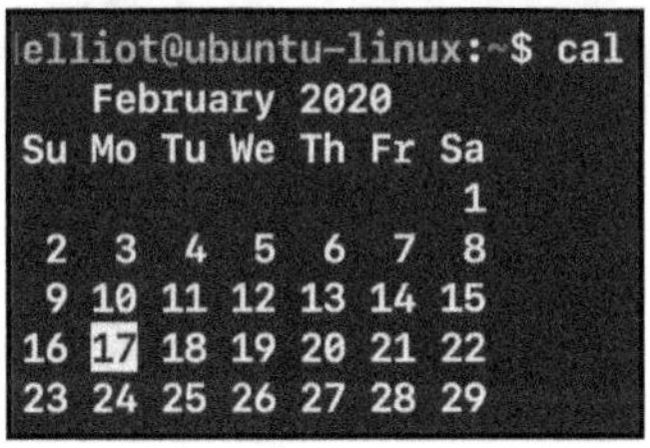

Figure 18 : The cal command

You can also display the calendar of the whole year, for example, to get the full 2022 calendar, you can run:

```
elliot@ubuntu-linux:~$ cal 2022
                            2022
      January               February               March
Su Mo Tu We Th Fr Sa  Su Mo Tu We Th Fr Sa  Su Mo Tu We Th Fr Sa
                   1         1  2  3  4  5         1  2  3  4  5
 2  3  4  5  6  7  8   6  7  8  9 10 11 12   6  7  8  9 10 11 12
 9 10 11 12 13 14 15  13 14 15 16 17 18 19  13 14 15 16 17 18 19
16 17 18 19 20 21 22  20 21 22 23 24 25 26  20 21 22 23 24 25 26
23 24 25 26 27 28 29  27 28                 27 28 29 30 31
30 31

       April                  May                   June
Su Mo Tu We Th Fr Sa  Su Mo Tu We Th Fr Sa  Su Mo Tu We Th Fr Sa
                1  2   1  2  3  4  5  6  7            1  2  3  4
 3  4  5  6  7  8  9   8  9 10 11 12 13 14   5  6  7  8  9 10 11
10 11 12 13 14 15 16  15 16 17 18 19 20 21  12 13 14 15 16 17 18
17 18 19 20 21 22 23  22 23 24 25 26 27 28  19 20 21 22 23 24 25
24 25 26 27 28 29 30  29 30 31              26 27 28 29 30


        July                 August              September
Su Mo Tu We Th Fr Sa  Su Mo Tu We Th Fr Sa  Su Mo Tu We Th Fr Sa
                1  2      1  2  3  4  5  6               1  2  3
 3  4  5  6  7  8  9   7  8  9 10 11 12 13   4  5  6  7  8  9 10
10 11 12 13 14 15 16  14 15 16 17 18 19 20  11 12 13 14 15 16 17
17 18 19 20 21 22 23  21 22 23 24 25 26 27  18 19 20 21 22 23 24
24 25 26 27 28 29 30  28 29 30 31           25 26 27 28 29 30
31

      October               November              December
Su Mo Tu We Th Fr Sa  Su Mo Tu We Th Fr Sa  Su Mo Tu We Th Fr Sa
                   1         1  2  3  4  5               1  2  3
 2  3  4  5  6  7  8   6  7  8  9 10 11 12   4  5  6  7  8  9 10
 9 10 11 12 13 14 15  13 14 15 16 17 18 19  11 12 13 14 15 16 17
16 17 18 19 20 21 22  20 21 22 23 24 25 26  18 19 20 21 22 23 24
23 24 25 26 27 28 29  27 28 29 30           25 26 27 28 29 30 31
30 31
```

Figure 19: The cal command for the year 2022

You can also specify a month, for example, to display the calendar of February 1993, you can run the command:

```
elliot@ubuntu-linux:~$ cal feb 1993
   February 1993
Su Mo Tu We Th Fr Sa
    1  2  3  4  5  6
 7  8  9 10 11 12 13
14 15 16 17 18 19 20
21 22 23 24 25 26 27
28
```

Figure 20: The cal command for February 1993

You now have a lot of output on your Terminal. You can run the `clear` command to clear the Terminal screen:

Figure 21: Before clear

This is how your Terminal will look after running the `clear` command:

Figure 22: After clear

You can use the `lscpu` command, which is short for **List CPU**, to display your CPU architecture information:

```
elliot©ubuntu-linux:-$ lscpu
Architecture:           x86_64
CPU op-mode(s):         32-bit, 64-bit
Byte Order:             Little Endian
CPU(s):                 1
On-line CPU(s) list:    0
```

```
Thread(s) per core:       1
Core(s) per socket:       1
Socket(s):                1
NUMA node(s):             1
Vendor ID:                GenuineIntel
CPU family:               6
Model:                    61
Model name:               Intel(R) Core(TM) i5-5300U CPU© 2.30GHz Stepping:  4
CPU MHz:                  2294.678
BogoMIPS:                 4589.35
Hypervisor vendor:        KVM
Virtualization type:      full
Lid cache:                32K
L1i cache:                32K
L2 cache:                 256K
L3 cache:                 3072K
NUMA node0 CPU(s):        0
Flags:                    fpu vme de pse tsc msr pae mce cx8 apic sep mtrr
```

You can use the uptime command to check how long your system has been running. The uptime command also displays:

- The current time.
- The number of users that are currently logged on.
- The system load averages for the past 1, 5, and 15 minutes.

```
elliot©ubuntu-linux:-$ uptime
18:48:04 up 4 days, 4:02, 1 user, load average: 0.98, 2.12, 3.43
```

You might be intimidated by the output of the uptime command, but don't worry, the following table breaks down the output for you.

18:48:04	The first thing you see in the output is the current time.
up 4 days, 4:02	This is basically saying that the system has been up and running for 4 days, 4 hours, and 2 minutes.
1 user	Only one user is currently logged in.
load average: 0.98, 2.12, 3.43	The system load averages for the past 1, 5, and 15 minutes.

Table 1: uptime command output

You probably haven't heard about load averages before. To understand load averages, you first have to understand system load.

WHAT IS SYSTEM LOAD?

In simple terms, system load is the amount of work the CPU performs at a given time.

So the more processes (or programs) running on your computer, the higher your system load is, and fewer processes running leads to a lower system load. Now, since you understand what a system load is, it's easy to understand load averages.

WHAT IS LOAD AVERAGE?

The load average is the average system load calculated over a given period of 1, 5, and 15 minutes.

So the three numbers that you see at the very end of the uptime command output are the load averages over 1, 5, and 15 minutes respectively. For example, if your load averages values are:

```
load average: 2.00, 4.00, 6.00
```

Then these three numbers represent the following:

- 2.00 --+: The load average over the last minute.
- 4.00 --+: The load average over the last five minutes.
- 6.00 --+: The load average over the last fifteen minutes.

From the definition of load average, we can conclude the following key points:

1. A load average of value 0.0 means the system is idle (doing nothing).
2. If the 1-minute load average is higher than the 5- or 15-minute averages, then this means your system load is increasing.
3. If the 1-minute load average is lower than the 5- or 15-minute averages, then this means your system load is decreasing.

For instance, load averages of:

```
load average: 1.00, 3.00, 7.00
```

Shows that the system load is decreasing over time. On the other hand, load averages of:

```
load average: 5.00, 3.00, 2.00
```

Indicates that the system load is increasing over time. As an experiment, first take note of your load averages by running the uptime command, then open up your web browser and open multiple tabs, then rerun uptime; you will see that your load averages have increased. After that, close your browser and run uptime again, you will see your load averages have decreased.

You can run the reboot command to restart your system:

```
elliot©ubuntu-linux:-$ reboot
```

You can run the pwd command to print the name of your current working directory:

```
elliot©ubuntu-linux:-$ pwd
/home/elliot
```

The current working directory is the directory in which a user is working at a given time. By default, when you log into your Linux system, your current working directory is set to your home directory:

```
/home/your_username
```

WHAT IS A DIRECTORY?

In Linux, we refer to folders as directories. A directory is a file that contains other files.

You can run the ls command to list the contents of your current working directory:

```
elliot©ubuntu-linux:-$ ls
Desktop Documents Downloads Music Pictures Public Videos
```

If you want to change your password, you can run the passwd command:

```
elliot©ubuntu-linux:-$ passwd
Changing password for elliot.
(current) UNIX password:
Enter new UNIX password:
Retype new UNIX password:
passwd: password updated successfully
```

You can use the hostname command to display your system's hostname:

```
elliot©ubuntu-linux:-$ hostname
ubuntu-linux
```

You can use the `free` command to display the amount of free and used memory on your system:

```
elliot©ubuntu-linux:-$ free
              total      used     free    shared  buff/cache  available
Mem:        4039732   1838532   574864     71900     1626336    1848444
Swap:        969960         0   969960
```

By default, the `free` command displays the output in kilobytes, but only aliens will make sense out of this output.

You can get an output that makes sense to us humans by running the `free` command with the `-h` option:

```
elliot©ubuntu-linux:-$ free -h
              total     used     free    shared  buff/cache  available
Mem:           3.9G     1.8G     516M       67M        1.6G       1.7G
Swap:          947M       OB     947M
```

That's much better, right? The `-h` is short for `--human`, and it displays the output in a human-readable format.

You may have noticed that this is the first time we ran a command with an option. The majority of Linux commands have options that you can use to change their default behavior slightly.

You should also know that command options are either preceded by a single hyphen (–) or a double hyphen (––). You can use a single hyphen if you are using the abbreviated name of the command option. On the other hand, if you are using the full name of the command option, then you need to use a double hyphen:

```
elliot©ubuntu-linux:-$ free --human
              total     used     free    shared  buff/cache  available
Mem:           3.9G     1.8G     516M       67M        1.6G       1.7G
Swap:          947M       OB     947M
```

As you can see, the previous two runs of the `free` command yielded the same output. The only difference is that the first time, we used the abbreviated command option name `-h`, and so we used a single hyphen. In the second time, we used the full command option name `--human`, and so we used a double hyphen.

You have the freedom of choice when it comes to using the abbreviated command option names versus the full command option names.

You can use the `df` command to display the amount of disk space available on your system:

```
elliot©ubuntu-linux:-$ df
Filesystem      1K-blocks      Used     Available     Use%      Mounted on
udev              1989608         0       1989608       0%            /dev
tmpfs              403976      1564        402412       1%            /run
/dev/sda1        20509264   6998972      12445436      36%               /
tmpfs             2019864     53844       1966020       3%        /dev/shm
tmpfs                5120         4          5116       1%       /run/lock
tmpfs             2019864         0       2019864       0%  /sys/fs/cgroup
/dev/loop0          91648     91648             0     100% /snap/core/6130
tmpfs              403972        28        403944       1%   /run/user/121
tmpfs              403972        48        403924       1%  /run/user/1000
```

Again you may want to use the human-readable option –h to display a nicer format:

```
elliot©ubuntu-linux:-$ df -h
Filesystem      Size      Used     Avail     Use%      Mounted on
udev            1.9G         0      1.9G       0%            /dev
tmpfs           395M      1.6M      393M       1%            /run
/dev/sda1        20G      6.7G       12G      36%               /
tmpfs           2.0G       57M      1.9G       3%        /dev/shm
tmpfs           5.0M      4.0K      5.0M       1%       /run/lock
tmpfs           2.0G         0      2.0G       0%  /sys/fs/cgroup
/dev/loop0       90M       90M         0     100% /snap/core/6130
tmpfs           395M       28K      395M       1%   /run/user/121
tmpfs           395M       48K      395M       1%  /run/user/1000
```

Don't worry if you can't understand everything you see in the output, as I will explain everything in detail in the following chapters. The whole idea of this chapter is to get your feet wet; we will dive deep later with the sharks!

The `echo` command is another very useful command; it allows you to print a line of text on your Terminal. For example, if you want to display the line `Cats are better than Dogs!` on your Terminal, then you can run:

```
elliot©ubuntu-linux:-$ echo Cats are better than Dogs!
Cats are better than Dogs!
```

You might be asking yourself, "How on earth is this useful?" Well, I promise you that by the time you finish reading this book, you would have realized the immense benefits of the echo command.

You can spend a great amount of time on your Terminal, punching in commands. Sometimes, you may want to rerun a command, but you may have forgotten the name of the command or the options that you have used, or you are simply lazy and don't want to type it again. Whatever the case may be, the history command will not let you down.

Let's run the history command and see what we get here:

```
elliot©ubuntu-linux:~$ history
1 date
2 blabla
3 cal
4 cal 2022
5 cal feb 1993
6 clear
7 lscpu
8 uptime
9 reboot
10 pwd
11 ls
12 passwd
13 hostname
14 free
15 free -h
16 free --human
17 df
18 df -h
19 echo Cats are better than Dogs!
20 history
```

As expected, the history command displayed all the commands that we ran so far in chronological order. On my history list, the lscpu command is number 7, so If I want to rerun lspcu, all I need to do is run !7:

```
elliot©ubuntu-linux:~$ !7
lscpu
Architecture:          x86_64
CPU op-mode(s):        32-bit, 64-bit
Byte Order:            Little Endian
CPU(s):                1
On-line CPU(s) list:   0
Thread(s) per core:    1
Core(s) per socket:    1
Socket(s):             1
```

```
NUMA node(s):           1
Vendor ID:              GenuineIntel
CPU family:             6
Model:                  61
Model name:             Intel(R) Core(TM) i5-5300U CPU @ 2.30GHz
Stepping:               4
CPU MHz:                2294.678
BogoMIPS:               4589.35
Hypervisor vendor:      KVM
Virtualization type:    full
Lid cache:              32K
L1i cache:              32K
12 cache:               256K
13 cache:               3072K
NUMA node0 CPU(s):      0
Flags:                  fpu vme de pse tsc msr pae mce cx8 apic sep mtrr
```

UP AND DOWN ARROW KEYS

You can scroll up and down on your command line history. Every time you hit your *up arrow* key, you scroll up one line in your command history.

You can also reverse and scroll down with your *down arrow* key.

You can use the `uname` command to display your system's kernel information. When you run the `uname` command without any options, then it will print just the kernel name:

```
elliot©ubuntu-linux:~$ uname
Linux
```

You can use the `-v` option to print the current kernel version information:

```
elliot©ubuntu-linux:~$ uname -v
#33-Ubuntu SMP Wed Apr 29 14:32:27 UTC 2020
```

You can also use the `-r` option to print the current kernel release information:

```
elliot©ubuntu-linux:~$ uname -r
5.4.0-29-generic
```

You can also use the -a option to print all the information of your current kernel at once:

```
elliot©ubuntu-linux:-$ uname -a
Linux ubuntu-linux 5.4.0-29-generic #33-Ubuntu SMP
Wed Apr 29 14:32:27 UTC 2020 x86_64 x86_64 x86_64 GNU/Linux
```

You can also run the lsb_release -a command to display the Ubuntu version you are currently running:

```
elliot©ubuntu-linux:-$ lsb_release -a
No LSB modules are available.
Distributor ID: Ubuntu
Description: Ubuntu 20.04 LTS
Release: 20.04
Codename: focal
```

Finally, the last command you are going to learn in this chapter is the exit command, which terminates your current Terminal session:

```
elliot©ubuntu-linux:-$ exit
```

A COOL FACT

 You may have already observed by now that Linux command names pretty much resemble what they do. For instance, the pwd command literally stands for **Print Working Directory**, ls stands for **List**, lscpu stands for **List CPU**, etc. This fact makes it much easier remembering Linux commands.

Congratulations! You made it through the first chapter. Now it's time for your first knowledge check exercise.

Knowledge check

For the following exercises, open up your Terminal and try to solve the following tasks:

1. Display the whole calendar for the year 2023.
2. Display the memory information of your system in a human-readable format.
3. Display the contents of your home directory.
4. Change your current user password.
5. Print the line "Mr. Robot is an awesome TV show!" on your Terminal.

True or false

1. The command DATE displays the current date and time.
2. To restart your Linux system, you simply run the restart command.
3. There is no difference between running the free -h and free --human commands.
4. The system load is increasing over time if your load averages values are:

    ```
    load average: 2.12, 3.09, 4.03
    ```

5. The system load is decreasing over time if your load averages values are:

    ```
    load average: 0.30, 1.09, 2.03
    ```

2
Climbing the Tree

In this chapter, you will climb a very special tree, which is the Linux filesystem. During this climbing journey, you will learn:

- The Linux filesystem hierarchy.
- What is the root directory?
- Absolute versus Relative paths.
- How to navigate the Linux filesystem.

The Linux filesystem

Alright, you are at the root of the tree and ready to climb up. In Linux, just like an actual tree, the beginning of the filesystem starts at the root directory. You can use the `cd` command followed by a forward slash to get to the root:

```
elliot@ubuntu-linux:~$ cd /
```

The `cd` command is short for **Change Directory** and is one of the most used commands in Linux. You can't move around in Linux without it. It's like your limbs (arms and legs), can you climb a tree without your limbs?
The forward slash character represents the root directory. Now to make sure you're at the root directory, you can run `pwd`:

```
elliot@ubuntu-linux:~$ pwd
/
```

And sure enough, we are at the root of the Linux filesystem. Whenever you are lost and you don't know where you are, `pwd` is here to rescue you.

Alright, while we are still at the root directory, let's see what's in there! Run the `ls` command to view the contents of the current directory:

```
elliot@ubuntu-linux:/$ ls
bin etc lib proc tmp var boot
dev home opt root sbin usr
```

To have a better view of the contents, you can use the long listing `-l` option with the `ls` command:

```
elliot@ubuntu-linux:/$ ls -l
drwxr-xr-x    2 root root         4096 Dec 28 15:36 bin
drwxr-xr-x  125 root root        12288 Jan  1 11:01 etc
drwxr-xr-x   21 root root         4096 Dec 26 23:52 lib
dr-xr-xr-x  227 root root            0 Jan  3 02:33 proc
drwxrwxrwt   15 root root         4096 Jan  3 02:35 tmp
drwxr-xr-x   14 root root         4096 Jul 24 21:14 var
drwxr-xr-x    3 root root         4096 Dec 29 07:17 boot
drwxr-xr-x   18 root root         4000 Jan  3 02:33 dev
drwxr-xr-x    3 root root         4096 Dec 26 23:47 home
drwxr-xr-x    3 root root         4096 Dec 27 15:07 opt
drwx------    4 root root         4096 Dec 29 09:39 root
drwxr-xr-x    2 root root        12288 Dec 28 15:36 sbin
drwxr-xr-x   10 root root         4096 Jul 24 21:03 usr
```

This output gives you a lot of valuable information that we will discuss in detail in the upcoming chapters. But for now, we focus on the first letter in the first column of the output. Take a look at the first column of the output:

```
drwxr-xr-x
drwxr-xr-x
drwxr-xr-x
drwxr-xr-x

  .
  .
  .
  .
```

You will see that the first letter is d, which means that the file is a directory. The first letter reveals the file type. The last column of the output displays the filename.

OTHER FILES!

 You will have more files under your root (/) directory. I have only chosen the most important and common ones that should exist on every Linux distribution. So don't freak out when you see way more files than those listed in this book.

Now each one of these directories has a special purpose, as you can see in the following table:

/	This is the root of your filesystem, where everything begins.
/etc	This directory contains system configuration files.
/home	This is the default home directory for all users (except the root user).
/root	This is the home directory for the root user.
/dev	This is where your devices such as your hard disks, USB drives, and optical drives reside on your system.
/opt	This is where you can install additional 3rd party software.
/bin	This is where essential binaries (programs) reside on your system.
/sbin	This is where system binaries (programs) that are typically used by the system administrator are stored.
/tmp	This is where temporary files are stored; they are usually deleted after a system reboot, so never store important files here!
/var	This directory contains files that may change in size, such as mail spools and log files.
/boot	All the files required for your system to boot are stored here.
/lib	This directory contains libraries needed by the essential binaries in the /bin and /sbin directories. A library is basically a set of precompiled functions that can be used by a program.

/proc	This is where information about running processes is stored.
/usr	This directory contains files and utilities that are shared between users.

Table 2: Linux Directories Explained

You can also run the man hier command to read more about the Linux filesystem hierarchy:

```
elliot@ubuntu-linux:/$ man hier
```

Alright, now let's do further climbing on the Linux directory tree. Take a look at *figure 1*, and you will understand why we choose a tree to describe the structure of the Linux filesystem.

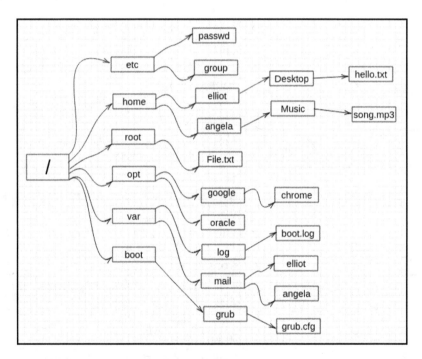

Figure 1: The Linux directory tree

The preceding figure only features very few files and by no means is a representation for the whole directory tree, as the Linux filesystem literally contains thousands of files. So you can think of the preceding figure as a subtree of the actual Linux directory tree.

Navigating through the directory tree

Alright, let's do more climbing. For example, let's climb to the /home directory to see how many users we have on the system. You can do that by simply running the cd /home command:

```
elliot@ubuntu-linux:~$ cd /home
elliot@ubuntu-linux:/home$
```

Notice how your command prompt changes as it's now showing that you are at the home directory.

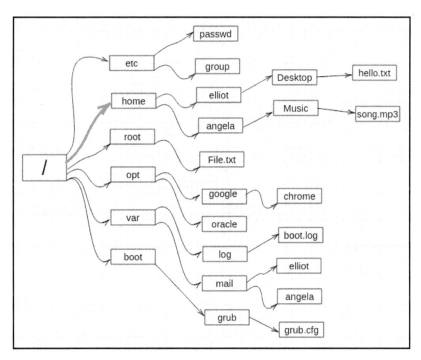

Figure 2: You are now at /home

Now let's run `ls` to view the contents of the `/home` directory:

```
elliot@ubuntu-linux:/home$ ls
angela elliot
```

These are the two users on my system (besides the root user). The `/root` is the home directory for the root user. You probably have only one user in `/home`; you will learn later in the book how to add other users to your system.

WHO IS ROOT?

The root user is a superuser who is allowed to do anything on the system. The root user can install software, add users, manage disk partitions, etc. The home directory of the root user is `/root`, which is NOT to be confused with `/` (the root of the filesystem).

If you want proof that you are currently at the `/home` directory, you can run the `pwd` command:

```
elliot@ubuntu-linux:/home$ pwd
/home
```

Sure enough! We are at the `/home` directory. Now let's climb to the home directory of user `elliot`. Now, believe it or not, there are two ways to navigate to `elliot`'s home directory. You can simply run the `cd elliot` command:

```
elliot@ubuntu-linux:/home$ cd elliot
elliot@ubuntu-linux:~$ pwd
/home/elliot
```

Or you can run the `cd /home/elliot` command:

```
elliot@ubuntu-linux:/home$ cd /home/elliot
elliot@ubuntu-linux:~$ pwd
/home/elliot
```

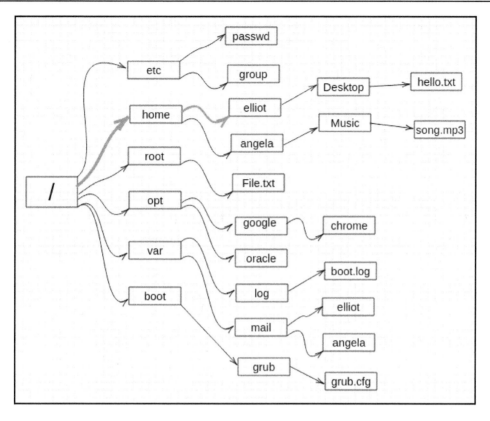

Figure 3: Now you are at /home/elliot

Notice that both commands have landed us in `elliot`'s home directory. However, running `cd elliot` is much easier than running `cd /home/elliot`, of course.

Well, think about it, we were initially at the `/home` directory, and that's why we were able to run `cd elliot` to land in `/home/elliot`.

However, in other situations, we would be forced to use the full path (absolute path) /home/elliot to reach our destination. To demonstrate, let's first change to the /etc directory:

```
elliot@ubuntu-linux:~$ cd /etc
elliot@ubuntu-linux:/etc$ pwd
/etc
```

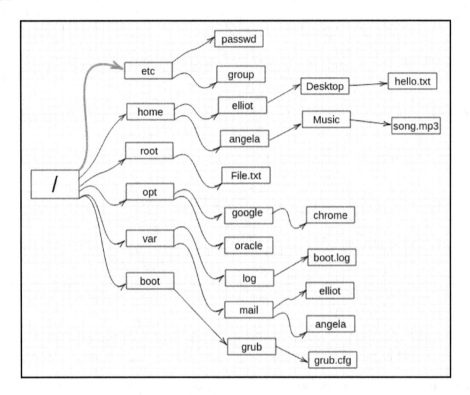

Figure 4: Now you are at /etc

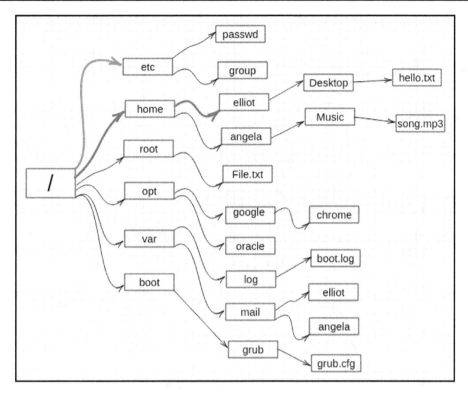

Figure 5: You want to go to /home/elliot

Figures 4 and *5* help you visualize it. You are at /etc and you want to go to /home/elliot.
To get to elliot's home directory, we can no longer use a short path (relative path) by
running the cd elliot command:

```
elliot@ubuntu-linux:/etc$ cd elliot
bash: cd: elliot: No such file or directory
```

As you can see, the Shell got mad and returned an error bash: cd: elliot: No such
file or directory. In this case, we have to use the full path (absolute
path)/home/elliot:

```
elliot@ubuntu-linux:/etc$ cd /home/elliot
elliot@ubuntu-linux:~$ pwd
/home/elliot
```

In case you haven't noticed by now, we have been using the forward slash (/) as a directory separator.

THE DIRECTORY SEPARATOR

In Linux, the forward slash (/) is the directory separator or sometimes referred to as the path separator. In Windows, it's the other way around because a backward slash (\) is used instead as a directory separator. However, be careful since the leading forward slash is the root of our filesystem. For example, in `/home/elliot/Desktop`, only the second and third forward slashes are directory separators, but the first forward slash represents the root of the filesystem.

It's crucial to realize the difference between absolute paths and relative paths.

ABSOLUTE VERSUS RELATIVE PATHS

An absolute path of a file is simply the full path of that file and, it **ALWAYS** begins with a leading forward slash. For example, `/opt/-google/chrome` is an example of an absolute path.

On the other hand, a relative path of a file never starts with the root directory and is always relative to the current working directory. For example, if you are currently at `/var`, then `log/boot.log` is a valid relative path.

As a rule of thumb, if you want to distinguish between a relative path and an absolute path, look and see if the path starts with the root directory (forward slash); if it does, then you can conclude the path is absolute, otherwise, the path is relative.

The following diagram shows you the relative path `Desktop/hello.txt` and will only work if your current working directory is `/home/elliot`.

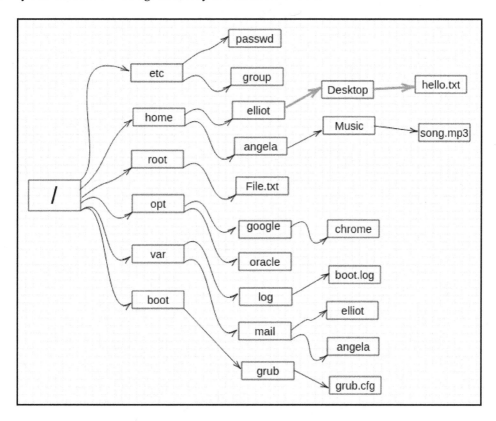

Figure 6: This Is a Relative Path

The following image shows you the absolute path `/home/elliot/Desktop` and will always work regardless of your current working directory.

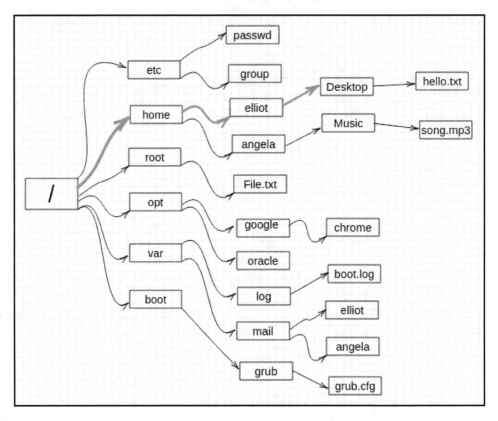

Figure 7: This Is an Absolute Path

Now let's climb to Elliot's `Desktop` directory to see what he has there. We will use an absolute path:

```
elliot@ubuntu-linux:/$ cd /home/elliot/Desktop
elliot@ubuntu-linux:~/Desktop$ pwd
/home/elliot/Desktop
```

We follow it with a `pwd` to confirm that we are indeed in the desired directory. Now let's run `ls` to view the contents of Elliot's desktop:

```
elliot@ubuntu-linux:~/Desktop$ ls
hello.txt
```

Notice that the file `hello.txt` is on Elliot's desktop, so we can actually see it right there on the desktop.

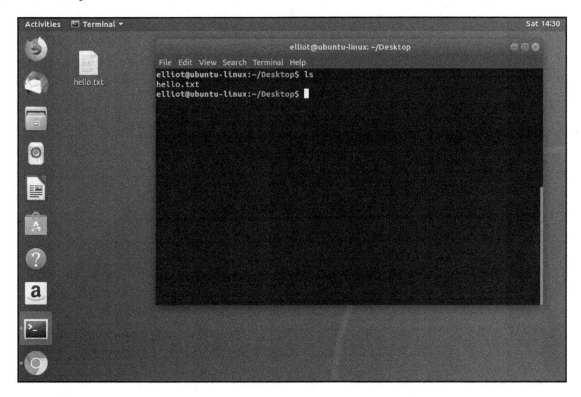

Figure 8: Elliot's desktop

As you can see in the preceding image, there is a file named `hello.txt` on Elliot's desktop. You can use the `cat` command to view the contents of a text file:

```
elliot@ubuntu-linux:~/Desktop$ cat hello.txt
Hello Friend!
Are you from fsociety?
```

If you open the file `hello.txt` on the desktop, you will see the same contents, of course, as you can see in the following screenshot.

Figure 9: The contents of hello.txt

Parent and current directories

There are two special directories under every directory in the filesystem:

1. Current working directory represented by one dot (.)
2. Parent directory represented by two dots (. .)

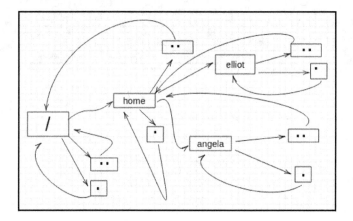

Figure 10: Visualizing Parent and Current Directories

It's easy to understand both directories by going through a few examples. To demonstrate, let's first change to /home/elliot so that it becomes our current working directory:

```
elliot@ubuntu-linux:~/Desktop$ cd /home/elliot
elliot@ubuntu-linux:~$ pwd
/home/elliot
```

Now run the `cd .` command:

```
elliot@ubuntu-linux:~$ cd .
elliot@ubuntu-linux:~$ pwd
/home/elliot
```

As you would expect, nothing happened! We are still at /home/elliot, and that is because one dot (.) represents the current working directory. It's like if you told someone, "Go where you are!"

Now run the `cd ..` command:

```
elliot@ubuntu-linux:~$ cd ..
elliot@ubuntu-linux:/home$ pwd
/home
```

We moved back one directory! In other words, we changed to the parent directory of /home/elliot, which is /home.

Let's run another `cd ..`:

```
elliot@ubuntu-linux:/home$ cd ..
elliot@ubuntu-linux:/$ pwd
/
```

Indeed we keep going back, and now we are at the root of our directory tree. Well, let's run `cd ..` one more time:

```
elliot@ubuntu-linux:/$ cd ..
elliot@ubuntu-linux:/$ pwd
/
```

Hmmm, we are at the same directory! Our path didn't change, and that's because we are at the root of our directory tree already, so we can't go any further back. As a result, the root directory (/) is the only directory where the **parent directory = current directory**, and you can visualize it by looking at *figure 10*.

You can also insert the directory separator `cd ../..` to move back two directories at once:

```
elliot@ubuntu-linux:~$ pwd
/home/elliot
elliot@ubuntu-linux:~$ cd ../..
elliot@ubuntu-linux:/$ pwd
/
```

You can also run `cd ../../..` to move back three directories and so on.

Moving around quickly

Now I will show you some cool tricks that will make you fast and efficient in navigating the Linux directory tree.

Go back home!

Let's change to the /var/log directory:

```
elliot@ubuntu-linux:~$ cd /var/log
elliot@ubuntu-linux:/var/log$ pwd
/var/log
```

You can now run the cd ~ command to go to your home directory:

```
elliot@ubuntu-linux:/var/log$ cd ~
elliot@ubuntu-linux:~$ pwd
/home/elliot
```

WOW! Let's do it again, but this time, we switch to user angela. In case you don't know, the character is called tilde and should be located next to your number *1* key on your keyboard:

```
elliot@ubuntu-linux:~$ whoami
elliot
elliot@ubuntu-linux:~$ su angela
Password:
angela@ubuntu-linux:/home/elliot$ whoami
angela
```

Notice here I used two new commands. The whoami command prints the name of the currently logged-in user. I also used the switch user su command to switch to user angela. You can use the su command to switch to any user on your system; you just need to run su, followed by the username.

Now, as user angela, I will navigate to the /var/log directory:

```
angela@ubuntu-linux:/home/elliot$ cd /var/log
angela@ubuntu-linux:/var/log$ pwd
/var/log
```

Then I run the `cd ~` command:

```
angela@ubuntu-linux:/var/log$ cd ~
angela@ubuntu-linux:~$ pwd
/home/angela
```

Boom! I am at Angela's home directory. Regardless of your current working directory, running the `cd ~` command will land you straight to your home directory.

Take me back!

Now, what if `angela` wants to go back as quickly as possible to her previous working directory?

Running the `cd -` command is the fastest method that will land `angela` back to her previous working directory:

```
angela@ubuntu-linux:~$ pwd
/home/angela
angela@ubuntu-linux:~$ cd -
/var/log
```

Cool! `angela` is back in `/var/log`. So anytime you want to go back to your previous working directory, just run the `cd -` command.

Hidden Files

The current directory `.` and the parent directory `..` exist under each directory in the Linux filesystem. But how come we can't see them when we run the `ls` command?

```
elliot@ubuntu-linux:~/Desktop$ pwd
/home/elliot/Desktop
elliot@ubuntu-linux:~/Desktop$ ls
hello.txt
elliot@ubuntu-linux:~/Desktop$ ls -l
total 4
-rw-r--r-- 1 elliot elliot 37 Jan 19 14:20 hello.txt
```

As you can see, I even tried to run `ls -l` and still can't see the current directory or the parent directory.

You need to use the `-a` option with the `ls` command as follows:

```
elliot@ubuntu-linux:~/Desktop$ ls -a
.  ..  hello.txt
```

Hooray! Now you can see all the files. The `-a` option shows you all the files, including hidden files and of course you can use the full option name `--all`, which will do the same thing:

```
elliot@ubuntu-linux:~/Desktop$ ls --all
.  ..  hello.txt
```

It turns out that any filename that starts with . (a dot) is hidden.

Hidden filenames start with .

Any filename that starts with a dot is hidden. That's why current and parent directories are hidden.

To demonstrate further, go to your user home directory and run the `ls` command:

```
angela@ubuntu-linux:~$ ls
Music
```

Now run the `ls -a` command:

```
angela@ubuntu-linux:~$ ls -a
.  ..  .bash_logout  .bashrc  Music  .profile
```

You can now see the hidden files in your home directory! Notice all the hidden filenames start with a dot.

Passing command arguments

So far, we ran the `ls` command only on the current working directory. However, you can list the contents of any directory without having to change to it. For example, if your current working directory is `/home/elliot`:

```
elliot@ubuntu-linux:~$ pwd
/home/elliot
```

You can list all the files in `/home/angela` by running the `ls -a /home/angela` command:

```
elliot@ubuntu-linux:~$ ls -a /home/angela
.  ..  .bash_history  .bash_logout  .bashrc  Music  .profile
elliot@ubuntu-linux:~$ pwd
/home/elliot
elliot@ubuntu
```

I was able to list the contents of `/home/angela` while still being in `/home/elliot`. This is possible because the `ls` command accepts any file as an argument.

WHAT IS AN ARGUMENT?

An argument, also called a command-line argument, is simply any filename or data that is provided to a command as an input.

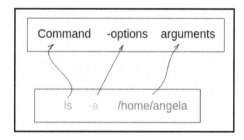

Figure 11: Linux Command Structure

You can see in the preceding image the general structure of a Linux command.

In Linux terminology, we use the verb **pass** when talking about command options and arguments. To use the correct Linux terminology, for example, in the preceding image, we say, "We passed the `/home/angela` directory as an argument to the `ls` command."

You will often find Linux users very keen on using the right terminology. Moreover, using the proper terminology can help you pass a job interview and land your dream job!

Notice in the preceding figure, we used the plural nouns *options* and *arguments*. That's because some commands can accept multiple options and arguments.

For example, we can do a long listing for all the files in /home/angela by running the ls -a -l /home/angela command:

```
elliot@ubuntu-linux:~$ ls -a -l /home/angela
total 28
drwxr-xr-x 3 angela angela 4096 Jan 20 13:43 .
drwxr-xr-x 9 root   root   4096 Jan 17 04:37 ..
-rw------- 1 angela angela   90 Jan 20 13:43 .bash_history
-rw-r--r-- 1 angela angela  220 Apr  4  2018 .bash_logout
-rw-r--r-- 1 angela angela 3771 Apr  4  2018 .bashrc
drwxrwxr-x 2 angela angela 4096 Jan 19 19:42 Music
-rw-r--r-- 1 angela angela  807 Apr  4  2018 .profile
```

So now you see a long listing of all the files in /home/angela including the hidden files, also notice that the ordering of the options doesn't matter here, so if you run the ls -l -a /home/angela command:

```
elliot@ubuntu-linux:~$ ls -l -a /home/angela
total 28
drwxr-xr-x 3 angela angela 4096 Jan 20 13:43 .
drwxr-xr-x 9 root   root   4096 Jan 17 04:37 ..
-rw------- 1 angela angela   90 Jan 20 13:43 .bash_history
-rw-r--r-- 1 angela angela  220 Apr  4  2018 .bash_logout
-rw-r--r-- 1 angela angela 3771 Apr  4  2018 .bashrc
drwxrwxr-x 2 angela angela 4096 Jan 19 19:42 Music
-rw-r--r-- 1 angela angela  807 Apr  4  2018 .profile
```

You will get the same result. This was an example of passing two commands options, what about passing two arguments? Well, you can do a long listing for all the files in /home/angela and /home/elliot at the same time by passing /home/elliot as a second argument:

```
elliot@ubuntu-linux:~$ ls -l -a /home/angela /home/elliot
/home/angela:

total 28
drwxr-xr-x 3 angela angela 4096 Jan 20 13:43 .
drwxr-xr-x 9 root   root   4096 Jan 17 04:37 ..
-rw------- 1 angela angela   90 Jan 20 13:43 .bash_history
-rw-r--r-- 1 angela angela  220 Apr  4  2018 .bash_logout
-rw-r--r-- 1 angela angela 3771 Apr  4  2018 .bashrc
drwxrwxr-x 2 angela angela 4096 Jan 19 19:42 Music
-rw-r--r-- 1 angela angela  807 Apr  4  2018 .profile

/home/elliot:
total 28
drwxr-xr-x 3 elliot elliot 4096 Jan 20 16:26 .
```

```
drwxr-xr-x 9 root    root    4096 Jan 17 04:37 ..
-rw------- 1 elliot elliot    90 Jan 20 13:43 .bash_history
-rw-r--r-- 1 elliot elliot   220 Dec 26 23:47 .bash_logout
-rw-r--r-- 1 elliot elliot  3771 Dec 26 23:47 .bashrc
drwxr-xr-x 2 elliot elliot  4096 Jan 19 14:20  Desktop
-rw-r--r-- 1 elliot elliot   807 Apr 4   2018 .profile
```

So now, you can see the contents of both the /home/elliot and /home/angela directories at the same time.

The touch command

Let's do a long listing for all the files in /home/elliot one more time to discuss something very important:

```
elliot@ubuntu-linux:~$ ls -a -l /home/elliot
total 28
drwxr-xr-x 3 elliot elliot 4096 Jan 20 16:26 .
drwxr-xr-x 9 root   root   4096 Jan 17 04:37 ..
-rw------- 1 elliot elliot   90 Jan 20 13:43 .bash_history
-rw-r--r-- 1 elliot elliot  220 Dec 26 23:47 .bash_logout
-rw-r--r-- 1 elliot elliot 3771 Dec 26 23:47 .bashrc
drwxr-xr-x 2 elliot elliot 4096 Jan 19 14:20  Desktop
-rw-r--r-- 1 elliot elliot  807 Apr  4 2018 .profile
```

Focus on the last two columns of the output:

Jan 20 16:26	.
Jan 17 04:37	..
Jan 20 13:43	.bash_history
Dec 26 23:47	.bash_logout
Dec 26 23:47	.bashrc
Jan 19 14:20	Desktop
Apr 4 2018	.profile

Table 3: Last Two Columns of ls -a -l /home/elliot

You already know that the last column of the output (2nd column of `Table 3`) shows the filenames, but what about all these dates that are displayed in the preceding column (1st column of `Table 3`)?

The dates in the first column of `Table 3` represent the last modification time of each file, which is the last time a file was modified (edited).

You can use the `touch` command to change the modification time of a file.

To demonstrate, let's first get the modification time on `elliot`'s `Desktop` directory, you can do that by running the `ls -l -d /home/elliot/Desktop` command:

```
elliot@ubuntu-linux:~$ ls -l -d /home/elliot/Desktop
drwxr-xr-x 2 elliot elliot 4096 Jan 19 14:20 /home/elliot/Desktop
```

Notice we used the `-d` option, so it does a long listing on the directory `/home/elliot/Desktop` instead of listing the contents of the directory.

The last modification time is shown to be: `Jan 19 14:20`.

Now if you run the `touch /home/elliot/Desktop` command:

```
elliot@ubuntu-linux:~$ touch /home/elliot/Desktop
elliot@ubuntu-linux:~$ ls -l -d /home/elliot/Desktop
drwxr-xr-x 2 elliot elliot 4096 Jan 20 19:42 /home/elliot/Desktop
elliot@ubuntu-linux:~$ date
Sun Jan 20 19:42:08 CST 2020
```

You will see that the last modification time of the directory `/home/elliot/Desktop` has now changed to `Jan 20 19:42`, which reflects the current time.

Of course, you will get a different result on your system because you will not be running the command at the same time as me.

Ok, great, so now we understand that the `touch` command can be used to update a file's modification time. Can it do something else? Hmmm, let's see.

What if we try to update the modification time of a file that doesn't exist? What will happen? The only way to know is to try it. Notice that user `elliot` has only one visible (not hidden) file in his home directory, which happens to be the `Desktop` directory:

```
elliot@ubuntu-linux:~$ pwd
/home/elliot
elliot@ubuntu-linux:~$ ls -l
total 4
drwxr-xr-x 2 elliot elliot 4096 Jan 20 19:42 Desktop
```

Now watch what will happen when user `elliot` runs the `touch blabla` command:

```
elliot@ubuntu-linux:~$ touch blabla
elliot@ubuntu-linux:~$ ls -l
total 4
-rw-r--r-- 1 elliot elliot    0 Jan 20 20:00 blabla
drwxr-xr-x 2 elliot elliot 4096 Jan 20 19:42 Desktop
```

It created an empty file named `blabla`.

You can do two things with the `touch` command:

1. You can update the last modification and access times of existing files.
2. You can create new empty files.

The `touch` command can only create regular files; it cannot create directories. Also, notice that it updates modification and access times, so what is the difference?

- Modification Time > Last time a file was changed or modified.
- Access Time > Last time a file was accessed (read).

By default, the `touch` command changes both the modification and access times of a file. I have created three files in `elliot`'s home directory: `file1`, `file2`, and `file3`:

```
elliot@ubuntu-linux:~$ ls -l
total 8
drwxr-xr-x 6 elliot elliot 4096 Jan 25 22:13 Desktop
drwxr-xr-x 3 elliot elliot 4096 Jan 25 22:18 dir1
-rw-r--r-- 1 elliot elliot    0 Feb 29  2004 file1
-rw-r--r-- 1 elliot elliot    0 Apr 11  2010 file2
-rw-r--r-- 1 elliot elliot    0 Oct  3  1998 file3
```

Now to change only the modification time of `file1`. We pass the `-m` option to the `touch` command:

```
elliot@ubuntu-linux:~$ touch -m file1
elliot@ubuntu-linux:~$ ls -l
total 8
drwxr-xr-x 6 elliot elliot 4096 Jan 25 22:13 Desktop
drwxr-xr-x 3 elliot elliot 4096 Jan 25 22:18 dir1
-rw-r--r-- 1 elliot elliot    0 Jan 25 23:08 file1
-rw-r--r-- 1 elliot elliot    0 Apr 11  2010 file2
-rw-r--r-- 1 elliot elliot    0 Oct  3  1998 file3
elliot@ubuntu-linux:~$
```

As you can see, the modification time of `file1` has now changed. I promised you I would only change the modification time, right? If you pass the `-u` option along with the `-l` option to the `ls` command, you will get the last access times instead of the modification times:

```
elliot@ubuntu-linux:~$ ls -l
total 8
drwxr-xr-x 6 elliot elliot 4096 Jan 25 22:13 Desktop
drwxr-xr-x 3 elliot elliot 4096 Jan 25 22:18 dir1
-rw-r--r-- 1 elliot elliot 0    Jan 25 23:08 file1
-rw-r--r-- 1 elliot elliot 0    Apr 11  2010 file2
-rw-r--r-- 1 elliot elliot 0    Oct 3   1998 file3
elliot@ubuntu-linux:~$ ls -l -u
total 8
drwxr-xr-x 6 elliot elliot 4096 Jan 25 22:13 Desktop
drwxr-xr-x 3 elliot elliot 4096 Jan 25 22:18 dir1
-rw-r--r-- 1 elliot elliot 0    Feb 29 2004  file1
-rw-r--r-- 1 elliot elliot 0    Apr 11 2010  file2
-rw-r--r-- 1 elliot elliot 0    Oct 3  1998  file3
```

As you can see, the last modification time of `file1` is changed to `Jan 25 23:08`, but the access time is left unchanged: `Feb 29 2004`. Now this time around, let's only change the access time of `file2`. To do this, we pass the `-a` option to the `touch` command:

```
elliot@ubuntu-linux:~$ touch -a file2
elliot@ubuntu-linux:~$ ls -l
total 8
drwxr-xr-x 6 elliot elliot 4096 Jan 25 22:13 Desktop
drwxr-xr-x 3 elliot elliot 4096 Jan 25 22:18 dir1
-rw-r--r-- 1 elliot elliot    0 Jan 25 23:08 file1
-rw-r--r-- 1 elliot elliot    0 Apr 11  2010 file2
-rw-r--r-- 1 elliot elliot    0 Oct  3  1998 file3
elliot@ubuntu-linux:~$ ls -l -u
total 8
drwxr-xr-x 6 elliot elliot 4096 Jan 25 22:13 Desktop
drwxr-xr-x 3 elliot elliot 4096 Jan 25 22:18 dir1
-rw-r--r-- 1 elliot elliot    0 Feb 29  2004 file1
-rw-r--r-- 1 elliot elliot    0 Jan 25 23:20 file2
-rw-r--r-- 1 elliot elliot    0 Oct  3  1998 file3
elliot@ubuntu-linux:~$
```

As you can see, the modification time of `file2` was left unchanged, but the access time is changed to the current time. Now to change both the modification and access times of `file3`, you can run the `touch` command with no options:

```
elliot@ubuntu-linux:~$ ls -l file3
-rw-r--r-- 1 elliot elliot 0 Oct 3 1998 file3
```

```
elliot@ubuntu-linux:~$ touch file3
elliot@ubuntu-linux:~$ ls -l file3
-rw-r--r-- 1 elliot elliot 0 Jan 25 23:27 file3
elliot@ubuntu-linux:~$ ls -l -u file3
-rw-r--r-- 1 elliot elliot 0 Jan 25 23:27 file3
```

Awesome! You can also pass the -t option to the ls command to list the files sorted by modification times, newest first:

```
elliot@ubuntu-linux:~$ ls -l -t
total 8
-rw-r--r-- 1 elliot elliot    0 Jan 25 23:27 file3
-rw-r--r-- 1 elliot elliot    0 Jan 25 23:08 file1
drwxr-xr-x 3 elliot elliot 4096 Jan 25 22:18 dir1
drwxr-xr-x 6 elliot elliot 4096 Jan 25 22:13 Desktop
-rw-r--r-- 1 elliot elliot    0 Apr 11  2010 file2
```

You can add the -u option to sort by access times instead:

```
elliot@ubuntu-linux:~$ ls -l -t -u
total 8
-rw-r--r-- 1 elliot elliot    0 Jan 25 23:27 file3
-rw-r--r-- 1 elliot elliot    0 Jan 25 23:20 file2
-rw-r--r-- 1 elliot elliot    0 Jan 25 23:20 file1
drwxr-xr-x 3 elliot elliot 4096 Jan 25 22:18 dir1
drwxr-xr-x 6 elliot elliot 4096 Jan 25 22:13 Desktop
```

You can also pass the -r option to reverse the sorting:

```
elliot@ubuntu-linux:~$ ls -l -t -r
total 8
-rw-r--r-- 1 elliot elliot    0 Apr 11  2010 file2
drwxr-xr-x 6 elliot elliot 4096 Jan 25 22:13 Desktop
drwxr-xr-x 3 elliot elliot 4096 Jan 25 22:18 dir1
-rw-r--r-- 1 elliot elliot    0 Jan 25 23:08 file1
-rw-r--r-- 1 elliot elliot    0 Jan 25 23:27 file3
```

Making directories

To create directories in Linux, we use the mkdir command, which is short for **make directory**.

In `elliot`'s desktop, let's create a directory named `games` by running the `mkdir games` command:

```
elliot@ubuntu-linux:~/Desktop$ mkdir games
elliot@ubuntu-linux:~/Desktop$ ls -l
total 8
drwxr-xr-x 2 elliot elliot 4096 Jan 20 20:20 games
-rw-r--r-- 1 elliot elliot 37 Jan 19 14:20 hello.txt
elliot@ubuntu-linux:~/Desktop$
```

Notice that my current working directory is /home/elliot/Destkop; that's why I was able to use a relative path.

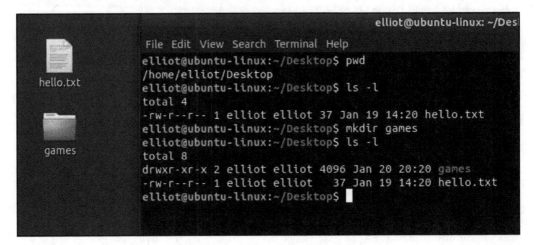

Figure 12: games Directory Created on the Desktop

You can also create multiple directories at the same time. For example, you can create three directories – `Music`, `Movies`, and `Books` – on your desktop by running the `mkdir Music Movies Books` command:

```
elliot@ubuntu-linux:~/Desktop$ mkdir Music Movies Books
elliot@ubuntu-linux:~/Desktop$ ls -l
total 20
drwxr-xr-x 2 elliot elliot 4096 Jan 21 01:54 Books
drwxr-xr-x 2 elliot elliot 4096 Jan 20 20:20 games
-rw-r--r-- 1 elliot elliot   37 Jan 19 14:20 hello.txt
drwxr-xr-x 2 elliot elliot 4096 Jan 21 01:54 Movies
drwxr-xr-x 2 elliot elliot 4096 Jan 21 01:54 Music
```

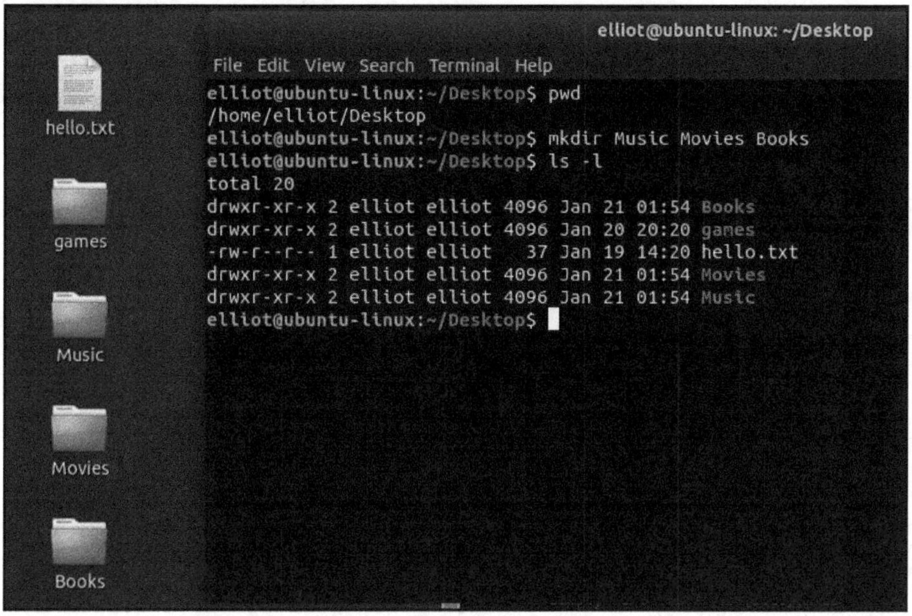

Figure 13: Directories Created on the Desktop

You can also use the -p option to create a whole path of directories. For example, you can create the path /home/elliot/dir1/dir2/dir3 by running the mkdir -p dir1/dir2/dir3 command:

```
elliot@ubuntu-linux:~$ pwd
/home/elliot
elliot@ubuntu-linux:~$ mkdir -p dir1/dir2/dir3
elliot@ubuntu-linux:~$ ls
blabla Desktop dir1
elliot@ubuntu-linux:~$ cd dir1
elliot@ubuntu-linux:~/dir1$ ls
dir2
elliot@ubuntu-linux:~/dir1$ cd dir2
elliot@ubuntu-linux:~/dir1/dir2$ ls
dir3
elliot@ubuntu-linux:~/dir1/dir2$ cd dir3
elliot@ubuntu-linux:~/dir1/dir2/dir3$ pwd
/home/elliot/dir1/dir2/dir3
elliot@ubuntu-linux:~/dir1/dir2/dir3$
```

It created dir1 in the /home/elliot directory, and then it created dir2 inside of dir1, and finally, it created dir3 inside of dir2.

You can use the recursive −R option to do a recursive listing on /home/elliot/dir1 and see all the files underneath /home/elliot/dir1 without the hassle of changing to each directory:

```
elliot@ubuntu-linux:~$ ls -R dir1
dir1:
dir2

dir1/dir2:
dir3

dir1/dir2/dir3:
elliot@ubuntu-linux:~$
```

As you can see, it listed all the files under /home/elliot/dir1. It even displayed the hierarchy.

You can also create a new directory with multiple subdirectories by including them inside a pair of curly brackets and each subdirectory separated by a comma like in the following:

```
elliot@ubuntu-linux:~/dir1/dir2/dir3$ mkdir -p dir4/{dir5,dir6,dir7}
elliot@ubuntu-linux:~/dir1/dir2/dir3$ ls -R dir4
dir4:
dir5 dir6 dir7

dir4/dir5:

dir4/dir6:

dir4/dir7:
```

As you can see, we created dir4, and inside it, we created three directories – dir5, dir6, and dir7.

Combining command options

You have learned a lot of different options that you can use with the ls command. Table 4 summarizes all the options we have used so far.

ls option	What it does
−l	Long and detailed listing of files.
−a	List the hidden files.
−d	List directories themselves, not their contents.

-t	Sort files by modification times.
-u	When used with −l, it shows access times instead of modification times. When used with −lt, it will sort by, and show, access times.
-r	Will reverse listing order.
-R	List subdirectories recursively.

Table 4: Popular ls Command Options

You will often be wanting to use two or more command options at a time. For example, ls -a -l is commonly used to do a long listing for all the files in a directory.

Also, ls -l -a -t -r is a very popular combination because sometimes you would want to see the listing of the files sorted by modification times (oldest first). For that reason, combining the command options is more efficient and so running the ls -latr command:

```
elliot@ubuntu-linux:~$ ls -latr
total 120
-rw-r--r--  1 elliot elliot        0     Apr 11   2010 file2
-rw-r--r--  1 elliot elliot      807     Dec 26 23:47 .profile
-rw-r--r--  1 elliot elliot     3771     Dec 26 23:47 .bashrc
drwxr-xr-x  9 root   root       4096     Jan 17 04:37 ..
-rw-r--r--  1 elliot elliot      220     Jan 20 17:23 .bash_logout
drwxr-xr-x  6 elliot elliot     4096     Jan 25 22:13 Desktop
-rw-r--r--  1 elliot elliot        0     Jan 25 23:08 file1
-rw-r--r--  1 elliot elliot        0     Jan 25 23:27 file3
drwxr-xr-x  3 elliot elliot     4096     Jan 25 23:52 dir1
-rw-------  1 elliot elliot     3152     Jan 26 00:01 .bash_history
drwxr-xr-x 17 elliot elliot     4096     Jan 30 23:32 .
```

Will yield the same result as running the ls -l -a -t -r command:

```
elliot@ubuntu-linux:~$ ls -l -a -t -r
total 120
-rw-r--r--  1 elliot elliot     0 Apr 11   2010 file2
-rw-r--r--  1 elliot elliot   807 Dec 26 23:47 .profile
-rw-r--r--  1 elliot elliot  3771 Dec 26 23:47 .bashrc
drwxr-xr-x  9 root   root    4096 Jan 17 04:37 ..
-rw-r--r--  1 elliot elliot   220 Jan 20 17:23 .bash_logout
drwxr-xr-x  6 elliot elliot  4096 Jan 25 22:13 Desktop
-rw-r--r--  1 elliot elliot     0 Jan 25 23:08 file1
-rw-r--r--  1 elliot elliot     0 Jan 25 23:27 file3
drwxr-xr-x  3 elliot elliot  4096 Jan 25 23:52 dir1
-rw-------  1 elliot elliot  3152 Jan 26 00:01 .bash_history
drwxr-xr-x 17 elliot elliot  4096 Jan 30 23:32 .
```

Before this chapter comes to an end, I want to show you a pretty cool tip. First, let's create a directory named `averylongdirectoryname`:

```
elliot@ubuntu-linux:~$ mkdir averylongdirectoryname
elliot@ubuntu-linux:~$ ls -ld averylongdirectoryname
drwxr-xr-x 2 elliot elliot 4096 Mar 2 12:57 averylongdirectoryname
```

Tab Completion is one of the most useful features in the Linux command line. You can use this to feature to let the shell automatically complete (suggest) command names and file paths. To demonstrate, type (don't run) the following text on your terminal:

```
elliot@ubuntu-linux:~$ cd ave
```

Now press the *Tab* key on your keyboard, and the shell will automatically complete the directory name for you:

```
elliot@ubuntu-linux:~$ cd averylongdirectoryname/
```

Pretty cool! Alright, this takes us to the end of this chapter, and it's time for you to do the lovely knowledge check.

Knowledge check

For the following exercises, open up your terminal and try to solve the following tasks:

1. Do a long listing for all the files in `/var/log`.
2. Display the contents of the file `/etc/hostname`.
3. Create three files – `file1`, `file2`, and `file3` – in `/home/elliot`.
4. List all the files (including hidden files) of `elliot`'s home directory.
5. Create a directory named `fsociety` in `/home/elliot`.

True or false

1. `/home/root` is the home directory of the root user.
2. `dir1/dir2/dir3` is an example of an absolute path.
3. `/home/elliot/Desktop` is an example of an absolute path.
4. `touch -m file1` will update `file1` access time.
5. `mkdir dir1 dir2 dir3` will create three directories – `dir1`, `dir2`, and `dir3`.

3
Meet the Editors

First of all, let me tell you something that may surprise you. Linux implements what is called "Everything is a file" philosophy. This means that on your Linux system, everything is represented by a file. For example, your hard disk is represented by a file. A running program (process) is represented by a file. Even your peripheral devices, such as your keyboard, mouse, and printer, are all represented by files.

With that being said, an immediate consequence of "Everything is a file" philosophy is that Linux administrators spend a substantial amount of their time editing and viewing files. And so you will often see Linux administrators very proficient at using text editors. And this chapter is dedicated to just that. I want you to be very comfortable using various text editors in Linux.

There are a lot, and I mean a whole lot, of text editors out there that you can use. However, in this chapter, I will cover the most popular Linux editors that will get the job done.

Graphical editors – gedit and kate

We start with the most basic and simple editors out there. These are the graphical editors! If you are using a **GNOME** version of any Linux distribution, then you will have the text editor gedit installed by default. On the other hand, if you are using a **KDE** version of Linux, then you will have the text editor kate installed by default.

DESKTOP ENVIRONMENT

GNOME and KDE are two examples of desktop environments. Each desktop environment implements a different graphical user interface, which is a very fancy way of saying that your desktop will look different!

Anyways, there is really not a lot to discuss on graphical editors. They are pretty intuitive and easy to use. For example, if you want to view a text file with `gedit`, then you run the `gedit` command followed by any filename:

    elliot@ubuntu-linux:~$ gedit /proc/cpuinfo

This will open the `gedit` graphical editor, and it displays your CPU information.

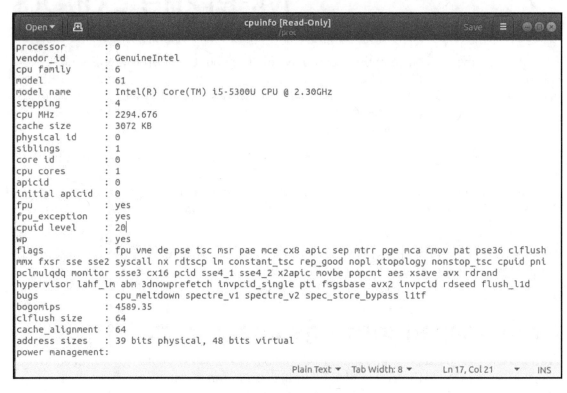

Figure 1: Opening /proc/cpuinfo with gedit

If you don't have `gedit` and have `kate` instead, then you can run:

    elliot@ubuntu-linux:~$ kate /proc/cpuinfo

```
                        cpuinfo — Kate
File  Edit  View  Projects  Bookmarks  Sessions  Tools  Settings  Help
            cpuinfo                    ✖
processor    : 0
vendor_id    : GenuineIntel
cpu family   : 6
model        : 61
model name   : Intel(R) Core(TM) i5-5300U CPU @ 2.30GHz
stepping     : 4
cpu MHz      : 2294.676
cache size   : 3072 KB
physical id  : 0
siblings     : 1
core id      : 0
cpu cores    : 1
apicid       : 0
initial apicid  : 0
fpu      : yes
fpu_exception    : yes
cpuid level : 20
wp       : yes
flags        : fpu vme de pse tsc msr pae mce cx8 apic sep mtrr pge mca cmov
pat pse36 clflush mmx fxsr sse sse2 syscall nx rdtscp lm constant_tsc
rep_good nopl xtopology nonstop_tsc cpuid pni pclmulqdq monitor ssse3 cx16
pcid sse4_1 sse4_2 x2apic movbe popcnt aes xsave avx rdrand hypervisor
lahf_lm abm 3dnowprefetch invpcid_single pti fsgsbase avx2 invpcid rdseed
flush_l1d
bugs         : cpu_meltdown spectre_v1 spectre_v2 spec_store_bypass l1tf
bogomips     : 4589.35
clflush size    : 64
cache_alignment : 64
address sizes   : 39 bits physical, 48 bits virtual
power management:

Line 5, Column 55          INSERT  Soft Tabs: 4 ▾   UTF-8  ▾  Normal ▾
Q Search and Replace
```

Figure 2: Opening /proc/cpuinfo with kate

You can also use the graphical editors to create new files on your system. For example, if you want to create a file named cats.txt in /home/elliot, then you can run the gedit /home/elliot/cats.txt command:

```
elliot@ubuntu-linux:~$ gedit /home/elliot/cats.txt
```

Figure 3: Creating cats.txt with gedit

Now insert the line "I love cats!" then save and close the file. The file `cats.txt` now exists in my home directory, and I can view it with the `cat` command:

```
elliot@ubuntu-linux:~$ pwd
/home/elliot
elliot@ubuntu-linux:~$ ls -l cats.txt
-rw-r--r-- 1 elliot elliot 13 Feb 2 14:54 cats.txt
elliot@ubuntu-linux:~$ cat cats.txt
I love cats!
```

Similarly, you can use any other graphical text editor to create files on your system.

OK! That's enough talk about graphical text editors. Let's move on to explore the serious world of non-graphical text editors.

The nano editor

The `nano` editor is a very popular and easy-to-use command-line editor. You can open the `nano` editor by running the `nano` command:

```
elliot@ubuntu-linux:~$ nano
```

This will open up your `nano` editor, and you should see a screen like that in the following screenshot:

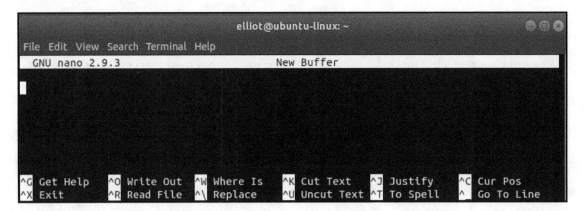

Figure 4: Inside nano

Now add the six lines that are shown in the following screenshot:

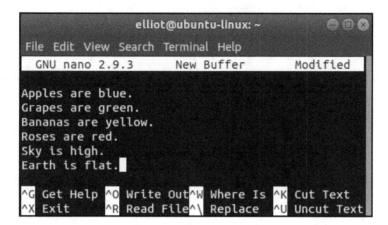

Figure 5: Add these six lines

Look at the bottom of the `nano` editor screen; you will see a lot of shortcuts:

Figure 6: nano shortcuts

I have included all the useful nano shortcuts in the following table:

nano shortcut	What it does
Ctrl+O	Saves the current file (write out).
Ctrl+K	Cuts the current line and stores it in the buffer.
Ctrl+U	Pastes the line stored in the buffer.
Ctrl+W	Searches for a string (word) in the file.
Ctrl+\	Replaces a string (word) in the file with another string.
Ctrl+R	Reads another file.
Ctrl+G	Views help information on how to use nano.
Ctrl+V	Moves to the next page.
Ctrl+Y	Moves to the previous page.
Ctrl+X	Exits the nano editor.

Table 5: nano shortcuts

Notice that the *Ctrl+O* shortcut is triggered by pressing *Ctrl* and then the letter *O*. You don't have to press the + key or the upper case letter *O*.

Now let's use the shortcut *Ctrl+O* to save the file; it will ask you for a filename, you can insert `facts.txt`:

Figure 7: Saving the file

Then press *Enter* to confirm. Now let's exit the `nano` editor (use the *Ctrl+X* shortcut) to verify that the file `facts.txt` is created:

```
elliot@ubuntu-linux:~$ ls -l facts.txt
-rw-r--r-- 1 elliot elliot 98 Apr 30 15:17 facts.txt
```

Now let's open `facts.txt` again to fix the false facts we have added there! To open the file `facts.txt` with the `nano` editor, you can run the `nano facts.txt` command:

```
elliot@ubuntu-linux:~$ nano facts.txt
```

The first line in the file `facts.txt` states that "Apples are blue." We certainly need to correct this false fact, so let's use the shortcut *Ctrl+* to replace the word `blue` with `red`.

When you press *Ctrl+*, it will ask you to enter the word that you want to replace; you can enter `blue`, as shown in the following screenshot:

Figure 8: The word to replace

Hit *Enter*, and then it will ask you to enter the substitute word. You can enter `red`, as shown in the following screenshot:

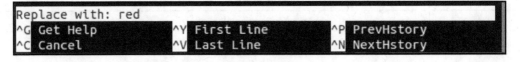

Figure 9: The substitute word

You can then hit *Enter*, and it will go through each instance of the word `blue` and ask you if you want to replace it. Luckily, we only have one occurrence of `blue`.

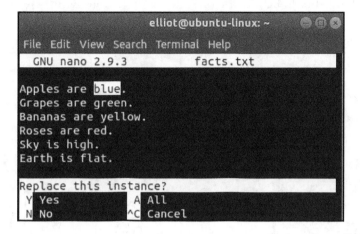

Figure 10: Replacing blue with red

Press *Y* and BOOM! The word `red` replaced `blue`.

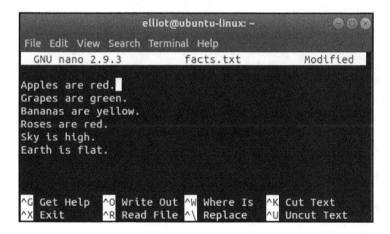

Figure 11: red replaced blue

There is one more word we need to change here. We can all agree that the Earth is not flat, right? I hope we all do! Now let's replace the word `flat` with `round` precisely as we did before, and the result should be like the one shown in the following screenshot:

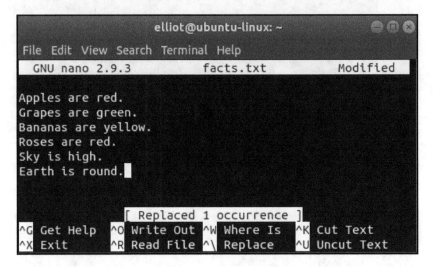

Figure 12: flat replaced with round

Now let's save and exit the file. So we use the *Ctrl+O* shortcut to save and then *Ctrl+X* to exit.

The `nano` editor is pretty simple to use. And practice makes perfect, so the more you use it, the easier it will become for you. You can practice all the shortcuts in `Table 5` as an exercise.

The vi editor

The `nano` editor is usually the editor of choice for beginners. It is a great editor, but let's just say that it's not the most efficient editor out there. The `vi` editor is a more advanced Linux editor with tons of features and is by far the most popular editor among advanced Linux users.

Let's open the `facts.txt` file with the `vi` editor; to do that, you run the `vi facts.txt` command:

```
elliot@ubuntu-linux:~$ vi facts.txt
```

This will open the `vi` editor, as shown in the following screenshot:

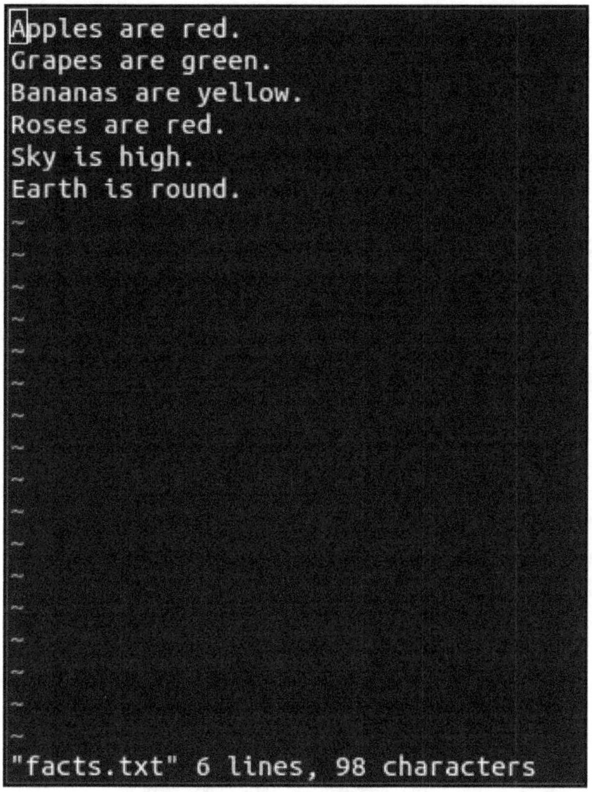

Figure 13: The facts.txt file opened in vi

Unlike the `nano` editor, the `vi` editor works in two different modes:

1. `insert` mode
2. `command` mode

The `insert` mode enables you to insert text into a file. On the other hand, the `command` mode allows you to do things like copying, pasting, and deleting text. The `command` mode also allows you to search and replace text along with many other things.

Insert mode

By default, you enter command mode when you first open the vi editor, and you can't insert text while you are in command mode. To insert text, you need to switch to insert mode. There are several ways you can use to change to insert mode; Table 6 lists all of them.

Key	What it does
i	Inserts text before the current cursor position.
I	Inserts text at the beginning of the current line.
a	Appends text after the current cursor position.
A	Appends text after the end of the current line.
o	Creates a new line below the current line.
O	Creates a new line above the current line.

Table 6: vi insert mode

You can navigate in the vi editor with your arrow keys, just like you would do in the nano editor. Now navigate to the last line in the file facts.txt and then press the letter o to switch into insert mode. You can now add the line "Linux is cool!"

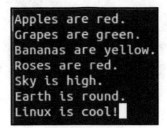

Figure 14: Adding a line in vi

With insert mode, you can add as much text as you want. To switch back to command mode, you need to press the *Esc* key.

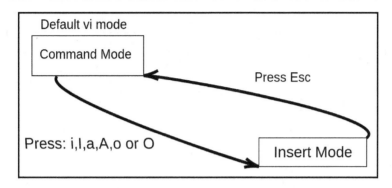

Figure 15: Switching between Insert Mode and Command Mode

The preceding screenshot illustrates how to switch back and forth between command mode and insert mode.

Command mode

Anything you want to do aside from adding text can be achieved from command mode. There are a whole lot of commands you can use with the vi editor. You may think I am joking, but there are books and courses out there that only discuss the vi editor. However, Table 7 will get you up and running with the vi editor as it lists the most popular commands you can use with vi.

vi command	What it does
yy	Copy (yank) the current line.
3yy	Copy (yank) three lines (starting with the current line).
yw	Copy (yank) one word starting at the cursor position.
2yw	Copy (yank) two words starting at the cursor position.
p	Paste after the current cursor position.
P	Paste before the current cursor position.
dd	Cut (delete) the current line.
4dd	Cut (delete) four lines (starting with the current line).
dw	Cut (delete) one word starting at the cursor position.
x	Delete the character at the cursor position.
u	Undo the last change.
U	Undo all changes to the line.
/red	Search for the word red in the file.

:%s/bad/good	Replace the word bad with good.
:set number	Show line numbers.
:set nonumber	Hide line numbers.
:7	Go to line number 7.
G	Jump to the end of the file.
gg	Jump to the beginning of the file.

Table 7: vi commands

As you can see, Table 7 has a lot of commands, so I will not go through all of them; that's left for you as an exercise. However, I will discuss some of the commands to help you get going with the vi editor.

Let's start by showing line numbers as it will make our life much easier! To do that, you run the :set number command, as shown in the following screenshot:

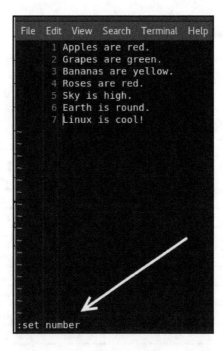

Figure 16: Show line numbers

Now let's copy line 4. You want to make sure the cursor is on line 4; you can do that by running the : 4 command, as shown in the following screenshot:

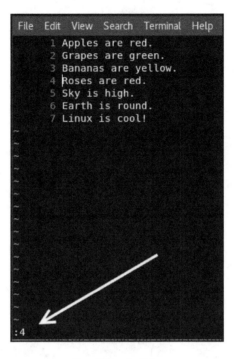

Figure 17: Go to the 4th line

Now press the sequence yy, and it will copy the entire line. Let's paste it three times at the end of the file. So navigate to the last line and then press *p* three times, it will paste the copied line three times, as shown in the following screenshot:

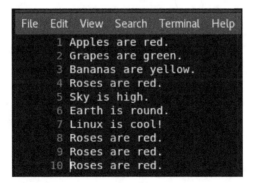

Figure 18: Copying and pasting in vi

Alright! Let's replace the word `cool` with `awesome` because we all know Linux is not just cool; it's awesome! To do that, you run the `:%s/cool/awesome` command, as shown in the following screenshot:

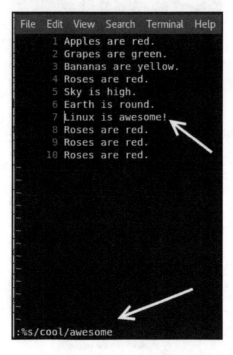

Figure 19: Replace cool with awesome

Let's also replace the word `Roses` with `Cherries` because we all know that not all roses are red. To do that, run the `:%s/Roses/Cherries` command, as shown in the following screenshot:

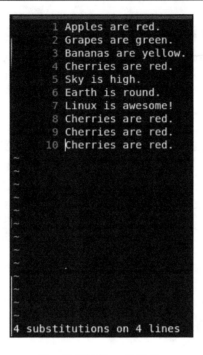

```
 1 Apples are red.
 2 Grapes are green.
 3 Bananas are yellow.
 4 Cherries are red.
 5 Sky is high.
 6 Earth is round.
 7 Linux is awesome!
 8 Cherries are red.
 9 Cherries are red.
10 Cherries are red.
~
~
~
~
~
~
~
~
4 substitutions on 4 lines
```

Figure 20: Replace Roses with Cherries

It will even tell you how many substitutions took place.

COOL TIP

You should know that `:%s/old/new` will only replace the first occurrence of the word `old` with `new` on all the lines. To replace all the occurrences of the word `old` with `new` on all the lines, you should use the global option `:%s/old/new/g`

To understand and make sense of the tip above, add the line "blue blue blue blue" to your `facts.txt` file and try to use the `:%s/blue/purple` command to replace the word `blue` with `purple`. You will see that it will only replace the first occurrence of `blue`. To make it replace all occurrences of `blue`, you have to use the global option `:%s/blue/purple/g`.

Saving and exiting vi

Eventually, when you are done viewing or editing a file in `vi`, you would want to exit the `vi` editor. There are multiple ways you can use to exit the `vi` editor, `Table 8` lists all of them.

vi command	What it does
`:w`	Save the file but do not quit `vi`.
`:wq`	Save the file and quit `vi`.
`ZZ`	Save the file and quit `vi` (same as `:wq`, just faster!).
`:x`	Save the file and quit `vi` (same as `:wq` or `ZZ`).
`:q`	Quit `vi` without saving.
`:q!`	Forcefully quit `vi` without saving.

Table 8: Saving and Exiting vi

So let's save our file and quit the `vi` editor. Of course, you can use any of the following commands:

1. `:wq`
2. `:x`
3. `ZZ`

They all achieve the same result, that is, saving and exiting `vi`.

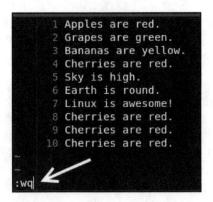

```
 1 Apples are red.
 2 Grapes are green.
 3 Bananas are yellow.
 4 Cherries are red.
 5 Sky is high.
 6 Earth is round.
 7 Linux is awesome!
 8 Cherries are red.
 9 Cherries are red.
10 Cherries are red.
~
~
:wq
```

Figure 21: Save and exit vi

If you have successfully exited the `vi` editor, I want to congratulate you because you are one of the elite. There are hundreds of memes and comics on the internet about how some people opened the `vi` editor, and were never able to exit!

File viewing commands

In some cases, you may just want to view a file without editing it. While you can still use text editors like `nano` or `vi` to view files, there are much faster ways to view a file in Linux.

The cat command

The `cat` command is one of the most popular and frequently used commands in Linux. The `cat` (short for **concatenate**) command concatenates and prints files to the standard output (terminal).

To view the `facts.txt` file that we created, you can run the `cat facts.txt` command:

```
elliot@ubuntu-linux:~$ cat facts.txt
Apples are red.
Grapes are green.
Bananas are yellow.
Cherries are red.
Sky is high.
Earth is round.
Linux is awesome!
Cherries are red.
Cherries are red.
Cherries are red.
```

You can now view the contents of the file `facts.txt` from the comfort of your terminal without having to open any text editor.

The `cat` command can do more than just viewing a file. It can also concatenate (put together) files. To demonstrate, create the following three files with your favorite text editor:

1. `file1.txt` (Insert the line "First File")
2. `file2.txt` (Insert the line "Second File")
3. `.file3.txt` (Insert the line "Third File")

Now let's view each of the three files using the `cat` command:

```
elliot@ubuntu-linux:~$ cat file1.txt
First File
elliot@ubuntu-linux:~$ cat file2.txt
Second File
elliot@ubuntu-linux:~$ cat file3.txt
Third File
```

Now let's concatenate both `file1.txt` and `file2.txt` together by running the `cat file1.txt file2.txt` command:

```
elliot@ubuntu-linux:~$ cat file1.txt file2.txt
First File
Second File
```

We can also concatenate all three files:

```
elliot@ubuntu-linux:~$ cat file1.txt file2.txt file3.txt
First File
Second File
Third File
```

Keep in mind that order matters; for example, running the `cat file2.txt file1.txt` command:

```
elliot@ubuntu-linux:~$ cat file2.txt file1.txt
Second File
First File
```

This will output the text in `file2.txt` first before `file1.txt`.

The tac command

The `tac` command is the twin brother of the `cat` command. It is basically `cat` written in reverse, and it does the same thing as the `cat` command but in a reversed fashion!

For example, if you want to view the `facts.txt` file in reverse order, you can run the `tac facts.txt` command:

```
elliot@ubuntu-linux:~$ tac facts.txt
Cherries are red.
Cherries are red.
Cherries are red.
Linux is awesome!
Earth is round.
```

```
Sky is high.
Cherries are red.
Bananas are yellow.
Grapes are green.
Apples are red.
```

The `tac` command also concatenates files, just like the `cat` command.

The more command

Viewing files with the `cat` command is a good choice when the file is small, and there aren't many lines of text to display. If you want to view a big file, it's better to use the `more` command. The `more` command displays the content of a file one page at a time; it is basically a paging program.

Let's view the contents of the file `/etc/services` with the `more` command:

```
elliot@ubuntu-linux:~$ more /etc/services
# Network services, Internet style
# Note that it is presently the policy of IANA to assign a single well-known
# port number for both TCP and UDP; hence, officially ports have two entries
# even if the protocol doesn't support UDP operations.

tcpmux 1/tcp # TCP port service multiplexer
systat 11/tcp users
netstat 15/tcp ftp 21/tcp
fsp 21/udp fspd
ssh 22/tcp # SSH Remote Login Protocol
telnet 23/tcp
smtp 25/tcp mail
whois 43/tcp nicname
tacacs 49/tcp # Login Host Protocol (TACACS)
tacacs 49/udp
--More--(7%)
```

It will show you the first page of the `/etc/services` files, and there is a percentage value at the bottom line that shows how far you have progressed through the file. You can use the following keys to navigate in `more`:

- *Enter* > to scroll down one line.
- Space Bar > to go to the next page.

- *b* > to go back one page.
- *q* > to quit.

The /etc/services file stores information on numerous services (applications) that can run on Linux.

The less command

The less command is an improved version of the more command. Yes, you read this correctly; less is better than more! In fact, the famous idiom *less is more* originated from the idea that less offers more than more.

The less command is another pager program, just like more; it allows you to view text files one page at a time. The advantage of less is that you can use the UP/DOWN arrow keys to navigate through the file. Also, less is faster than more.

You can view the /etc/services file with less by running the command:

```
elliot@ubuntu-linux:~$ less /etc/services
```

You can also use more navigation keys with less.

Heads or tails?

As its name suggests, the head command displays the first few lines of a file. By default, it shows the first ten lines of a file. For example, we know that facts.txt has ten lines in it, and so running the head facts.txt command will display all the file contents:

```
elliot@ubuntu-linux:~$ head facts.txt
Apples are red.
Grapes are green.
Bananas are yellow.
Cherries are red.
Sky is high.
Earth is round.
Linux is awesome!
Cherries are red.
Cherries are red.
Cherries are red.
```

You can also pass the −n option to specify the number of lines you wish to view. For example, to display the first three lines of `facts.txt`, you can run the `head −n 3 facts.txt` command:

```
elliot@ubuntu-linux:~$ head -n 3 facts.txt
Apples are red.
Grapes are green.
Bananas are yellow.
```

On the other hand, the `tail` command displays the last few lines of a file. By default, it shows the last ten lines. You can also use the −n option to specify the number of lines you wish to view. For example, to display the last two lines in `facts.txt`, you can run the `tail −n 2 facts.txt` command:

```
elliot@ubuntu-linux:~$ tail -n 2 facts.txt
Cherries are red.
Cherries are red.
```

Do you know what time it is? It's time for some knowledge check questions.

Knowledge check

For the following exercises, open up your Terminal and try to solve the following tasks:

1. Only view the first two lines of the file `facts.txt`.
2. Only view the last line of the file `facts.txt`.
3. Display the contents of the file `facts.txt` in a reversed order.
4. Open the file `facts.txt` using the `vi` editor.
5. Exit the `vi` editor and consider yourself one of the elites.

4

Copying, Moving, and Deleting Files

If you have ever owned a computer before, then you know how important it is to be able to copy and move files around. That's why I dedicated an entire chapter to talk just about that: copying, moving, and deleting files.

Copying one file

Sometimes you need to copy a single file. Luckily this is a simple operation on the command line. I have a file named `cats.txt` in my home directory:

```
elliot@ubuntu-linux:~$ cat cats.txt
I love cars!
I love cats!
I love penguins!
elliot@ubuntu-linux:~$
```

I can use the `cp` command to make a copy of `cats.txt` named `copycats.txt` as follows:

```
elliot@ubuntu-linux:~$ cp cats.txt copycats.txt
elliot@ubuntu-linux:~$ cat copycats.txt
I love cars!
I love cats!
I love penguins!
elliot@ubuntu-linux:~$
```

As you can see, the copied file `copycats.txt` has the same content as the original file `cats.txt`.

I can also copy the file `cats.txt` to another directory. For example, I can copy the file `cats.txt` to `/tmp` by running the `cp cats.txt /tmp` command:

```
elliot@ubuntu-linux:~$ cp cats.txt /tmp
elliot@ubuntu-linux:~$ cd /tmp
elliot@ubuntu-linux:/tmp$ ls
cats.txt
elliot@ubuntu-linux:/tmp$
```

Notice that the copied file has the same name as the original file. I can also make another copy in `/tmp` with a different name:

```
elliot@ubuntu-linux:~$ cp cats.txt /tmp/cats2.txt
elliot@ubuntu-linux:~$ cd /tmp
elliot@ubuntu-linux:/tmp$ ls
cats2.txt  cats.txt
elliot@ubuntu-linux:/tmp$
```

Copying multiple files

You may also want to copy multiple files at once. To demonstrate, let's begin by creating three files `apple.txt`, `banana.txt`, and `carrot.txt` in Elliot's home directory:

```
elliot@ubuntu-linux:~$ touch apple.txt banana.txt carrot.txt
elliot@ubuntu-linux:~$ ls
apple.txt carrot.txt copycats.txt dir1
banana.txt cats.txt Desktop
elliot@ubuntu-linux:~$
```

To copy the three newly created files to `/tmp`, you can run the `cp apple.txt banana.txt carrot.txt /tmp` command:

```
elliot@ubuntu-linux:~$ cp apple.txt banana.txt carrot.txt /tmp
elliot@ubuntu-linux:~$ cd /tmp
elliot@ubuntu-linux:/tmp$ ls
apple.txt banana.txt carrot.txt cats2.txt cats.txt
elliot@ubuntu-linux:/tmp$
```

Child's play! In general, the `cp` command follows the syntax:

```
cp source_file(s) destination
```

Copying one directory

You may also want to copy an entire directory; that's also easily accomplished. To demonstrate, create a directory named `cities` in your home directory, and inside `cities`, create three files `paris`, `tokyo`, and `london` as follows:

```
elliot@ubuntu-linux:~$ mkdir cities
elliot@ubuntu-linux:~$ cd cities/
elliot@ubuntu-linux:~/cities$ touch paris tokyo london
elliot@ubuntu-linux:~/cities$ ls
london paris tokyo
```

Now if you want to copy the `cities` directory to `/tmp`, you have to pass the recursive `-r` option to the `cp` command as follows:

```
elliot@ubuntu-linux:~/cities$ cd ..
elliot@ubuntu-linux:~$ cp -r cities /tmp
```

You will get an error message if you omitted the `-r` option:

```
elliot@ubuntu-linux:~$ cp cities /tmp
cp: -r not specified; omitting directory 'cities'
```

You can verify that the `cities` directory is copied to `/tmp` by listing the files in `/tmp`:

```
elliot@ubuntu-linux:~$ cd /tmp
elliot@ubuntu-linux:/tmp$ ls
apple.txt banana.txt carrot.txt cats2.txt cats.txt cities
elliot@ubuntu-linux:/tmp$ ls cities
london paris tokyo
```

Copying multiple directories

You can also copy multiple directories the same way you copy multiple files; the only difference is that you have to pass the recursive `-r` option to the `cp` command.

To demonstrate, create the three directories `d1`, `d2`, and `d3` in Elliot's home directory:

```
elliot@ubuntu-linux:~$ mkdir d1 d2 d3
```

Now you can copy all three directories to /tmp by running the `cp -r d1 d2 d3 /tmp` command:

```
elliot@ubuntu-linux:~$ cp -r d1 d2 d3 /tmp
elliot@ubuntu-linux:~$ cd /tmp
elliot@ubuntu-linux:/tmp$ ls
apple.txt banana.txt carrot.txt cats2.txt cats.txt cities d1 d2 d3
```

Moving one file

Sometimes, you may want to move a file (or a directory) to a different location instead of copying and wasting disk space.

To do this, you can use the `mv` command. For example, you can move the file `copycats.txt` from Elliot's home directory to /tmp by running the `mv copycats.txt /tmp` command:

```
elliot@ubuntu-linux:~$ mv copycats.txt /tmp
elliot@ubuntu-linux:~$ ls
apple.txt    carrot.txt cities d2  Desktop  Downloads
banana.txt  cats.txt    d1      d3  dir1      Pictures
elliot@ubuntu-linux:~$ cd /tmp
elliot@ubuntu-linux:/tmp$ ls
apple.txt   carrot.txt cats.txt copycats.txt d2
banana.txt cats2.txt   cities    d1            d3
```

Notice that `copycats.txt` is now gone from Elliot's home directory as it relocated to /tmp.

Moving multiple files

You can also move multiple files the same way you can copy multiple files. For example, you can move the three files `apple.txt`, `banana.txt`, and `carrot.txt` from /tmp to /home/elliot/d1 as follows:

```
elliot@ubuntu-linux:/tmp$ mv apple.txt banana.txt carrot.txt
/home/elliot/d1
elliot@ubuntu-linux:/tmp$ ls
cats2.txt cats.txt cities copycats.txt d1 d2 d3
elliot@ubuntu-linux:/tmp$ cd /home/elliot/d1
elliot@ubuntu-linux:~/d1$ ls
apple.txt banana.txt carrot.txt
elliot@ubuntu-linux:~/d1$
```

As you can see, the three files `apple.txt`, `banana.txt`, and `carrot.txt` are no longer located in `/tmp` as they all moved to `/home/elliot/d1`. In general, the `mv` command follows the syntax:

```
mv source_file(s) destination
```

Moving one directory

You can also use the `mv` command to move directories. For example, if you want to move the directory `d3` and put it inside `d2`, then you can run the `mv  d3  d2` command:

```
elliot@ubuntu-linux:~$ mv d3 d2
elliot@ubuntu-linux:~$ cd d2
elliot@ubuntu-linux:~/d2$ ls
d3
elliot@ubuntu-linux:~/d2$
```

Notice that you don't need to use the recursive `-r` option to move a directory.

Moving multiple directories

You can also move multiple directories at once. To demonstrate, create a directory named `big` in Elliot's home directory:

```
elliot@ubuntu-linux:~$ mkdir big
```

Now you can move the three directories `d1`, `d2`, and `cities` to the `big` directory as follows:

```
elliot@ubuntu-linux:~$ mv d1 d2 cities big
elliot@ubuntu-linux:~$ ls big
cities d1 d2
elliot@ubuntu-linux:~$
```

Renaming files

You can also use the `mv` command to rename files. For example, if you want to rename the file `cats.txt` to `dogs.txt`, you can run the `mv  cats.txt  dogs.txt` command:

```
elliot@ubuntu-linux:~$ mv cats.txt dogs.txt
elliot@ubuntu-linux:~$ cat dogs.txt
I love cars!
```

```
I love cats!
I love penguins!
elliot@ubuntu-linux:~$
```

If you want to rename the directory big to small, you can run the mv big small command:

```
elliot@ubuntu-linux:~$ mv big small
elliot@ubuntu-linux:~$ ls small
cities d1 d2
elliot@ubuntu-linux:~$
```

In summary, here is how the mv command works:

1. If the destination directory exists, the mv command will move the source file(s) to the destination directory.
2. If the destination directory doesn't exist, the mv command will rename the source file.

Keep in mind that you can only rename one file (or one directory) at a time.

Hiding files

You can hide any file by renaming it to a name that starts with a dot.

Let's try it; you can hide the file dogs.txt by renaming it to .dogs.txt as follows:

```
elliot@ubuntu-linux:~$ ls
apple.txt banana.txt carrot.txt dogs.txt Desktop dir1 small
elliot@ubuntu-linux:~$ mv dogs.txt .dogs.txt
elliot@ubuntu-linux:~$ ls
apple.txt banana.txt carrot.txt Desktop dir1 small
elliot@ubuntu-linux:~$
```

As you can see, the file dogs.txt is now hidden as it got renamed to .dogs.txt. You can unhide .dogs.txt by renaming it and removing the leading dot from the filename:

```
elliot@ubuntu-linux:~$ mv .dogs.txt dogs.txt
elliot@ubuntu-linux:~$ ls
apple.txt banana.txt carrot.txt dogs.txt Desktop dir1 small
elliot@ubuntu-linux:~$
```

Yes, Sir! You can also hide and unhide directories in the same manner. I will leave that for you to do as an exercise.

Removing files

You can use the rm command to remove (delete) files. For example, if you want to remove the file dogs.txt, you can run the rm dogs.txt command:

```
elliot@ubuntu-linux:~$ ls
apple.txt banana.txt carrot.txt dogs.txt Desktop dir1 small
elliot@ubuntu-linux:~$ rm dogs.txt
elliot@ubuntu-linux:~$ ls
apple.txt banana.txt carrot.txt Desktop dir1 small
```

You can also remove multiple files at once. For example, you can remove the three files apple.txt, banana.txt, and carrot.txt by running the rm apple.txt banana.txt carrot.txt command:

```
elliot@ubuntu-linux:~$ rm apple.txt banana.txt carrot.txt
elliot@ubuntu-linux:~$ ls
Desktop dir1 small
elliot@ubuntu-linux:~$
```

Removing directories

You can pass the recursive -r option to the rm command to remove directories. To demonstrate, let's first create a directory named garbage in Elliot's home directory:

```
elliot@ubuntu-linux:~$ mkdir garbage
elliot@ubuntu-linux:~$ ls
Desktop dir1 garbage small
```

Now let's try to remove the garbage directory:

```
elliot@ubuntu-linux:~$ rm garbage
rm: cannot remove 'garbage': Is a directory
elliot@ubuntu-linux:~$
```

Shoot! I got an error because I didn't pass the recursive -r option. I will pass the recursive option this time:

```
elliot@ubuntu-linux:~$ rm -r garbage
elliot@ubuntu-linux:~$ ls
Desktop dir1 small
```

Cool! We got rid of the garbage directory.

You can also use the rmdir command to remove only empty directories. To demonstrate, let's create a new directory named garbage2 and inside it, create a file named old:

```
elliot@ubuntu-linux:~$ mkdir garbage2
elliot@ubuntu-linux:~$ cd garbage2
elliot@ubuntu-linux:~/garbage2$ touch old
```

Now let's go back to Elliot's home directory and attempt to remove garbage2 with the rmdir command:

```
elliot@ubuntu-linux:~/garbage2$ cd ..
elliot@ubuntu-linux:~$ rmdir garbage2
rmdir: failed to remove 'garbage2': Directory not empty
```

As you can see, it wouldn't allow you to remove a nonempty directory. Therefore, let's delete the file old that's inside garbage2 and then reattempt to remove garbage2:

```
elliot@ubuntu-linux:~$ rm garbage2/old
elliot@ubuntu-linux:~$ rmdir garbage2
elliot@ubuntu-linux:~$ ls
Desktop dir1 small
elliot@ubuntu-linux:~$
```

Boom! The garbage2 directory is gone forever. One thing to remember here is that the rm -r command will remove any directory (both empty and nonempty). On the other hand, the rmdir command will only delete empty directories.

For the final example in this chapter, let's create a directory named garbage3, then create two files a1.txt and a2.txt inside it:

```
elliot@ubuntu-linux:~$ mkdir garbage3
elliot@ubuntu-linux:~$ cd garbage3/
elliot@ubuntu-linux:~/garbage3$ touch a1.txt a2.txt
elliot@ubuntu-linux:~/garbage3$ ls
a1.txt a2.txt
```

Now let's get back to Elliot's home directory and attempt to remove garbage3:

```
elliot@ubuntu-linux:~/garbage3$ cd ..
elliot@ubuntu-linux:~$ rmdir garbage3
rmdir: failed to remove 'garbage3': Directory not empty
elliot@ubuntu-linux:~$ rm -r garbage3
elliot@ubuntu-linux:~$ ls
Desktop dir1 Downloads Pictures small
elliot@ubuntu-linux:~$
```

As you can see, the `rmdir` command has failed to remove the nonempty directory `garbage3`, while the `rm -r` command has successfully removed it.

Nothing makes information stick in your head like a good knowledge-check exercise.

Knowledge check

For the following exercises, open up your Terminal and try to solve the following tasks:

1. Create three files `hacker1`, `hacker2`, and `hacker3` in your home directory.
2. Create three directories `Linux`, `Windows`, and `Mac` in your home directory.
3. Create a file named `cool` inside the `Linux` directory you created in task 2.
4. Create a file named `boring` inside the `Windows` directory you created in task 2.
5. Create a file named `expensive` in the `Mac` directory you created in task 2.
6. Copy the two files `hacker1` and `hacker2` to the `/tmp` directory.
7. Copy the two directories `Windows` and `Mac` to the `/tmp` directory.
8. Move the file `hacker3` to the `/tmp` directory.
9. Move the directory `Linux` to the `/tmp` directory.
10. Remove the file `expensive` from the `Mac` directory (in your home directory).
11. Remove the directory `Mac` from your home directory.
12. Remove the directory `Windows` from your home directory.
13. Remove the file `hacker2` from your home directory.
14. Rename the file `hacker1` to `hacker01`.

True or false

1. The `cp` command can copy directories without using the recursive option `-r`.
2. You have to use the recursive option `-r` when moving directories.
3. You can use the `mv` command to rename files or directories.
4. You can remove a non-empty directory with the `rmdir` command.
5. You can remove a non-empty directory with the `rm -r` command.

5
Read Your Manuals!

You may be telling yourself right now, "Linux is so hard! There are a lot of commands and even more command options! There is no way I can master all of these commands and commit them to memory." If this is what you think, believe me, you are smart. It's insane to remember all the Linux commands that exist, even the most experienced Linux administrator would never be able to remember all commands, not even Linus Torvalds himself!

So wait? If that's the case, what is the solution then? The answer lies in the beautiful world of Linux documentation. Linux is very well documented to the extent that it's hard to get lost in it. There are a variety of tools in Linux that help you in not just remembering the commands, but also in understanding how to use them.

Having met a lot of Linux professionals throughout my career, I noticed that the most skilled Linux administrators are not the ones who remember, but the ones who know how to make the most use of the Linux documentation. Ladies and gentlemen, I highly recommend you fasten your seatbelt and read this chapter carefully. I promise you that the fear in your heart will go away soon!

The four categories of linux commands

All Linux commands must fall into one of these following four categories:

1. **An executable program**: Which is usually written in the C programming language. The `cp` command is an example of an executable command.
2. **An alias**: Which is basically another name for a command (or a group of commands).
3. **A shell builtin**: The shell supports internal commands as well. The `exit` and `cd` commands are two examples of a shell builtin command.

4. **A shell function**: These are functions that help us achieve a specific task and are essential in writing shell scripts. We will cover this in more detail later, for now, just know they exist.

Determining a command's type

You can use the `type` command to determine the type (category) of a command. For example, if you want to know the type of the `pwd` command you can simply run the `type` `pwd` command:

```
elliot@ubuntu-linux:~$ type pwd
pwd is a shell builtin
```

So now you know that the `pwd` command is a shell builtin command. Now let's figure out the type of the `ls` command:

```
elliot@ubuntu-linux:~$ type ls
ls is aliased to `ls --color=auto'
```

As you can see, the `ls` command is aliased to `ls --color=auto`. Now you know why you see a colorful output every time you run the `ls` command. Let's see the type of the `date` command:

```
elliot@ubuntu-linux:~$ type date
date is /bin/date
```

Any command that lives in `/bin` or `/sbin` is an executable program. Therefore, we can conclude that the `date` command is an executable program as it resides in `/bin`.

Finally, let's determine the type of the `type` command itself:

```
elliot@ubuntu-linux:~$ type type
type is a shell builtin
```

It turns out the `type` command is a shell builtin command.

Finding a command's location

Every time you run an executable command, there a file somewhere on the system that gets executed. You can use the `which` command to determine the location of an executable command. For example, if you want to know the location of the `rm` command, you can run the `which rm` command:

```
elliot@ubuntu-linux:~$ which rm
/bin/rm
```

So now you know that `rm` lives in the `/bin` directory. Let's see the location of the `reboot` command:

```
elliot@ubuntu-linux:~$ which reboot
/sbin/reboot
```

As you can see, the `reboot` command lives in the `/sbin` directory.

What does the command do?

You can use the `whatis` command to get a brief description of what a command does. For example, if you want to know the purpose of the `free` command, you can run the `whatis free` command:

```
elliot@ubuntu-linux:~$ whatis free
free (1)                - Display amount of free and used memory in the system
```

As you can see, the `free` command, as we already know, displays the amount of free and used memory in the system. Cool! Now let's see what the `df` command does:

```
elliot@ubuntu-linux:~$ whatis df
df (1)                  - report file system disk space usage
```

Finally, let's see what the `which` command does:

```
elliot@ubuntu-linux:~$ whatis which
which (1)               - locate a command
```

As we already know, `which` displays a command's location.

The man page

The whatis command gives you a brief description of what a command does; however, it doesn't teach you how to use a command. For that, you can use the man pages.

The man page is a **manual** page that has proper documentation to help you understand how to use a command. The same as when you buy a new phone, you get a manual that shows you how to use your phone and how to update your software on your phone, etc.

In general, if you want to read the man page of a command, you can run:

```
man command_name
```

For example, if you want to view the man page of the touch command, you can run the man touch command:

```
elliot@ubuntu-linux:~$ man touch
```

```
TOUCH(1)                                              User Commands
        TOUCH(1)

NAME
        touch - change file timestamps

SYNOPSIS
        touch [OPTION]... FILE...

DESCRIPTION
        Update the access and modification times of each FILE to the current time.

        A FILE argument that does not exist is created empty, unless -c or -h is supplied.

        A FILE argument string of - is handled specially and causes touch to change the times of the file associated with standard output.

        Mandatory arguments to long options are mandatory for short options too.

        -a        change only the access time

        -c, --no-create
                  do not create any files

        -d, --date=STRING
                  parse STRING and use it instead of current time

        -f        (ignored)

        -h, --no-dereference
                  affect each symbolic link instead of any referenced file (useful only on systems that can change the timestamps of a symlink)

        -m        change only the modification time

        -r, --reference=FILE
                  use this file's times instead of current time
```

Figure 1: touch man page

As you can see in the preceding screenshot, the touch man page shows you how to use the command, and it also lists and explains all the command options.

`Table 9` shows you how to move around while browsing `man` pages.

man keys	What it does
Space	Scrolls forward one page.
Ctrl+F	Scrolls forward one page (same as space).
Ctrl+B	Scrolls backward one page.
`/word`	Will search for a word (pattern) in the `man` page. For example, `/access` will search for the word `access` in the `man` page
q	Will quit the `man` page.
n	After you search for a word, you can use *n* to look for the next occurrence of the word in the `man` page.
N	After you search for a word, you can use *N* to look for the previous occurrence of the word in the `man` page.

I can't stress enough the importance of `man` pages. They can be your best friend in the darkest moments, trust me!

You should also know that there is a man page for `man` itself:

```
elliot@ubuntu-linux:~$ man man
```

It describes how to use `man` pages.

Help for shell builtins

If you play around enough with `man` pages, you may notice that a lot of shell builtin commands do not have a `man` page. For instance, there is no `man` page for the `cd` or the `exit` commands:

```
elliot@ubuntu-linux:~$ type cd
cd is a shell builtin
elliot@ubuntu-linux:~$ man cd
No manual entry for cd
elliot@ubuntu-linux:~$ type exit
exit is a shell builtin
elliot@ubuntu-linux:~$ man exit
No manual entry for exit
```

That's because shell builtin commands do not have man pages, but do not freak out just yet! You can still find help on how to use shell builtins by using the `help` command. For example, to get help on how to use the `exit` command, you can run:

```
elliot@ubuntu-linux:~$ help exit
exit: exit [n]
    Exit the shell.

    Exits the shell with a status of N. If N is omitted, the exit status
    is that of the last command executed.
```

Similarly, to get help on how to use the `cd` command, you can run the `help cd` command:

```
elliot@ubuntu-linux:~$ help cd
cd: cd [-L|-P] [dir]
    Change the shell working directory.

    Change the current directory to DIR. The default DIR is the value of
    the HOME shell variable.

    The variable CDPATH defines the search path for the directory
containing DIR.
    Alternative directory names in CDPATH are separated by a colon (:).
    A null directory name is the same as the current directory.
    If DIR begins with a slash (/), then CDPATH is not used.

    If the directory is not found, and the shell option `cdable_vars' is
set,
    the word is assumed to be a variable name. If that variable has a
value,
    its value is used for DIR.

    Options:
        -L force symbolic links to be followed
        -P use the physical directory structure without following symbolic
links
    The default is to follow symbolic links, as if `-L' were specified.

    Exit Status:
    Returns 0 if the directory is changed; non-zero otherwise.
```

The info page

The GNU project launched the `info` pages as an alternative documentation to the `man` pages. The GNU project once claimed that `man` pages are outdated and needed replacement and so they came up with the `info` pages.

You can view the `info` page of any command by running:

```
info command_name
```

For example, to view the `info` page of the `ls` command, you can run the `info ls` command:

```
elliot@ubuntu-linux:~$ info ls

Next: dir invocation, Up: Directory listing

10.1 'ls': List directory contents
====================================

The 'ls' program lists information about files (of any type, including
directories). Options and file arguments can be intermixed arbitrarily, as
usual.

For non-option command-line arguments that are directories, by default 'ls'
lists the contents of directories, not recursively, and omitting files with
names beginning with '.'. For other non-option arguments, by default 'ls'
lists just the file name. If no non-option argument is specified, 'ls'
operates on the current directory, acting as if it had been invoked with a
single argument of '.'.

By default, the output is sorted alphabetically, according to the locale
settings in effect.(1) If standard output is a terminal, the output is in
columns (sorted vertically) and control characters are output as question
marks; otherwise, the output is listed one per line and control characters
are output as-is.

Because 'ls' is such a fundamental program, it has accumulated many options
over the years. They are described in the subsections below; within each
section, options are listed alphabetically (ignoring case). The division of
options into the subsections is not absolute, since some options affect
more than one aspect of 'ls''s operation.
```

The info pages sometimes offer more details compared to man pages. However, man pages remain the most popular go-to destination for help documentation on Linux.

The very helpful apropos command

The apropos command is one of the most helpful and yet underrated Linux commands. Let's see a brief description of what the apropos command does:

```
elliot@ubuntu-linux:~$ whatis apropos
apropos (1)            - search the manual page names and descriptions
```

WOW! The apropos command helps you in searching for the right command to use to achieve a specific task. For example, let's say you want to rename a file, but you are unsure which Linux command to use; in this case, you can run the apropos rename command:

```
elliot@ubuntu-linux:~$ apropos rename
file-rename (1p)    - renames multiple files
File::Rename (3pm)  - Perl extension for renaming multiple files
gvfs-rename (1)     - (unknown subject)
mmove (1)           - move or rename an MSDOS file or subdirectory
mren (1)            - rename an existing MSDOS file
mv (1)              - move (rename) files
prename (1p)        - renames multiple files
rename (1)          - renames multiple files
rename.ul (1)       - rename files
```

BOOM! It listed all the commands that have the word rename showing in the description of their man pages. I bet you can spot the mv command in the output.

Let's say you want to view the calendar but you're unsure which command to use; in this case, you can run:

```
elliot@ubuntu-linux:~$ apropos calendar
cal (1)             - displays a calendar and the date of Easter
calendar (1)        - reminder service
ncal (1)            - displays a calendar and the date of Easter
```

You can see that it displayed the cal command in the output.

For the last example, let's say you want to display your CPU information, but you don't know which command to use; in this case, you can run:

```
elliot@ubuntu-linux:~$ apropos cpu
chcpu (8)           - configure CPUs
cpuid (4)           - x86 CPUID access device
```

```
cpuset (7)             - confine processes to processor and memory node
subsets
lscpu (1)              - display information about the CPU architecture
msr (4)                - x86 CPU MSR access device
sched (7)              - overview of CPU scheduling
taskset (1)            - set or retrieve a process's CPU affinity
```

Here you go! You can see that it listed the lscpu command that we have used earlier. The apropos command is here to rescue you whenever you forget a command or you're unsure which command to use. You just have to supply a keyword (preferably a verb) that highlights what you want to accomplish to the apropos command:

```
apropos keyword
```

COOL TIP

The man -k command will display the same result as the apropos command.

```
elliot@ubuntu-linux:~$ man -k cpu
chcpu (8)              - configure CPUs
cpuid (4)              - x86 CPUID access device
cpuset (7)             - confine processes to processor and memory node
subsets
lscpu (1)              - display information about the CPU architecture
msr (4)                - x86 CPU MSR access device
sched (7)              - overview of CPU scheduling
taskset (1)            - set or retrieve a process's CPU affinity
```

The /usr/share/doc directory

The /usr/share/doc directory is another excellent place to look for help in Linux. This directory has very intensive documentation; it doesn't just show you how to use a command; sometimes, it will even show the name and contact information of the authors who developed the command. Moreover, it may also include a TODO file that contains a list of unfinished tasks/features; contributors usually check the TODO files to help fix bugs and develop new features.

To demonstrate, let's go to the nano documentation directory:

```
elliot@ubuntu-linux:~$ cd /usr/share/doc/nano
elliot@ubuntu-linux:/usr/share/doc/nano$ pwd
/usr/share/doc/nano
```

Now list the contents of the directory to see what's inside:

```
elliot@ubuntu-linux:/usr/share/doc/nano$ ls
AUTHORS                copyright faq.html        nano.html    README    TODO
changelog.Debian.gz    examples  IMPROVEMENTS.gz NEWS.gz      THANKS.gz
```

Cool! You can view the AUTHORS file to see the team of developers who contributed to the nano editor program. You can also view the TODO file if you are eager to know if there is anything left for you to do! You can also check the README file for a general description of the nano editor. There is even a link faq.html that contains frequently asked questions.

As you saw in this chapter, Linux has a variety of helpful tools available at your disposal; so make sure you utilize them!

Knowledge check

For the following exercises, open up your Terminal and try to solve the following tasks:

1. You need to know if the echo command is a shell builtin or an executable program, which command would you run?
2. Display the location of the uptime command executable file.
3. Show a brief description of the mkdir command.
4. You forgot how to use the mv command, what are you going to do?
5. You forgot which command is used to display the calendar, what are you going to do?
6. The history command is a shell builtin and so it doesn't have a man page. You want to clear your history but don't know how. What are you going to do?

True or false

1. The command whereis is used to locate commands.
2. You can use man -p and apropos interchangeably.
3. You can use the whatis command to get a brief description of a command.
4. You can use the type command to determine if a command is an alias, shell builtin, or an executable program.

6
Hard versus Soft Links

In this chapter, we further our knowledge on Linux files, and we discuss the differences between hard and soft links. If you have ever created a shortcut in Windows (or macOS) before, you will quickly grasp the concept of a soft link. But before we discuss hard and soft links, you first have to understand the concept of an inode.

File inodes

When you go to a grocery store, you will find that each product has a set of attributes like:

- Product type: Chocolate
- Product price: $2.50
- Product supplier: Kit Kat
- Amount left: 199

These attributes can be displayed on any product in the grocery store by scanning the product's barcode. And each barcode is unique, of course. Well, you can apply this analogy to Linux. Every file on Linux has a set of attributes like:

- File type
- File size
- File owner
- File permissions
- Number of hard links
- File timestamp

These attributes are stored in a data structure called the inode (index node), and each inode is identified by a number (inode number). So you can think of inode numbers like the barcodes in a grocery store. Every file in Linux has an inode number and every inode number points to a file data structure, that is, the inode. And here is a formal definition of an inode:

> **What is an Inode?**
>
> An inode is simply a file data structure that stores file information (attributes), and every inode is uniquely identified by a number (inode number).

Displaying file inode number

There are two commands you can use to view the inode number of a file:

1. `ls -i` file
2. `stat` file

For example, to view the inode number of `facts.txt`, you can run the command `ls -i facts.txt`:

```
elliot@ubuntu-linux:~$ ls -i facts.txt
924555 facts.txt
```

And it will spit out the inode number for you. You can also use the `stat` command:

```
elliot@ubuntu-linux:~$ stat facts.txt
File: facts.txt
Size: 173 Blocks: 8 IO Block: 4096 regular file
Device: 801h/2049d Inode: 924555 Links: 1
Access: (0644/-rw-r--r--) Uid: ( 1000/ tom) Gid: ( 1000/ tom)
Access: 2019-05-08 13:41:16.544000000 -0600
Modify: 2019-05-08 12:50:44.112000000 -0600
Change: 2019-05-08 12:50:44.112000000 -0600
Birth: -
```

The `stat` command doesn't just list the inode number of a file; it also lists all the file attributes as you can see from the command output.

Creating soft links

Now since you understand what a file inode is, you can easily understand the concept of hard and soft links. And let us start with soft links:

WHAT IS A SOFT LINK?

A soft link (also referred to as a symbolic link) is simply a file that points to another file.

A picture is worth a thousand words, so the following diagram will help you visualize soft links.

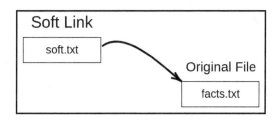

Figure 1: A soft link visualization

To create a soft link, we use the `ln` command with the `-s` option as follows:

```
ln -s original_file soft_link
```

So to create a soft link named `soft.txt` to the `facts.txt` file, you can run the command `ln -s facts.txt soft.txt`:

```
elliot@ubuntu-linux:~$ ln -s facts.txt soft.txt
```

Now let's do a long listing on the soft link file `soft.txt` that we just created:

```
elliot@ubuntu-linux:~$ ls -l soft.txt
lrwxrwxrwx 1 tom tom 9 May 8 21:48 soft.txt -> facts.txt
```

You will notice two things. First, the letter `l` in the first column of the output `lrwxrwxrwx`, which signals that the file is a link (soft link), and secondly you can see the right arrow `soft.txt → facts.txt`, which basically tells us that `soft.txt` is a soft link that points to the file `facts.txt`.

Now let's check the contents of the file `soft.txt`:

```
elliot@ubuntu-linux:~$ cat soft.txt
Apples are red.
Grapes are green.
Bananas are yellow.
Cherries are red.
Sky is high.
Earth is round.
Linux is awesome!
Cherries are red.
Cherries are red.
Cherries are red.
```

Of course, it contains the same data that the original file `facts.txt` has. In fact, if you edit the soft link, it will actually edit the original file as well.

To demonstrate, open the file `soft.txt` with any text editor and add the line "Grass is green." at the very end of the file, and then save and exit so the contents of `soft.txt` will be as follows:

```
elliot@ubuntu-linux:~$ cat soft.txt
Apples are red.
Grapes are green.
Bananas are yellow.
Cherries are red.
Sky is high.
Earth is round.
Linux is awesome!
Cherries are red.
Cherries are red.
Cherries are red.
Grass is green.
```

Now let's check the contents of the original file `facts.txt`:

```
elliot@ubuntu-linux:~$ cat facts.txt
Apples are red.
Grapes are green.
Bananas are yellow.
Cherries are red.
Sky is high.
Earth is round.
Linux is awesome!
Cherries are red.
Cherries are red.
Cherries are red.
Grass is green.
```

As you can see, the new line "Grass is green." is also there. That's because every time you edit a soft link, it actually edits the original file that it points to as well.

Now if you delete the soft link, nothing will happen to the original file, it remains intact:

```
elliot@ubuntu-linux:~$ rm soft.txt
elliot@ubuntu-linux:~$ cat facts.txt
Apples are red.
Grapes are green.
Bananas are yellow.
Cherries are red.
Sky is high.
Earth is round.
Linux is awesome!
Cherries are red.
Cherries are red.
Cherries are red.
Grass is green.
```

Now let's create the soft link `soft.txt` again:

```
elliot@ubuntu-linux:~$ ln -s facts.txt soft.txt
```

If you delete the original file `facts.txt`, the soft link `soft.txt` will become useless! But before we delete the `facts.txt` file, let's make a copy of it in `/tmp` because we will need it later on:

```
elliot@ubuntu-linux:~$ cp facts.txt /tmp
```

Now let's delete the file `facts.txt` from `elliot`'s home directory and see what happens to the soft link:

```
elliot@ubuntu-linux:~$ rm facts.txt
elliot@ubuntu-linux:~$ cat soft.txt
cat: soft.txt: No such file or directory
```

As you can see, the soft link `soft.txt` becomes useless as it's now pointing to nowhere. Keep in mind that the file `soft.txt` still exists, as shown in the following screenshot.

```
elliot@ubuntu-linux: ~
File  Edit  View  Search  Terminal  Help
elliot@ubuntu-linux:~$ cat soft.txt
cat: soft.txt: No such file or directory
elliot@ubuntu-linux:~$ ls -l soft.txt
lrwxrwxrwx 1 elliot elliot 9 Nov 28 18:33 soft.txt -> facts.txt
elliot@ubuntu-linux:~$
```

Figure 2: soft.txt becomes useless!

The following diagram shows you that the soft link `soft.txt` points to nowhere after the original file `facts.txt` has been deleted.

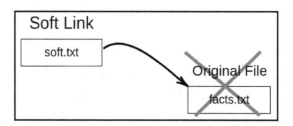

Figure 3: soft.txt points to nowhere

Now if we moved `facts.txt` back to `elliot`'s home directory:

```
elliot@ubuntu-linux:~$ mv /tmp/facts.txt /home/elliot
```

The soft link `soft.txt` will be useful again! You can say that we resurrected the soft link!

```
elliot@ubuntu-linux:~$ cat soft.txt
Apples are red.
Grapes are green.
Bananas are yellow.
Cherries are red.
Sky is high.
Earth is round.
Linux is awesome!
Cherries are red.
Cherries are red.
Cherries are red.
Grass is green.
```

Let's compare the inode numbers of the soft link `soft.txt` and the original file `facts.txt`:

```
elliot@ubuntu-linux:~$ ls -i soft.txt facts.txt
925155 facts.txt 924556 soft.txt
```

As you can see, the inode numbers of the two files are different. Finally, let's run the `stat` command on the soft link `soft.txt`:

```
elliot@ubuntu-linux:~$ stat soft.txt
File: soft.txt -> facts.txt
Size: 9 Blocks: 0 IO Block: 4096 symbolic link
Device: 801h/2049d Inode: 924556 Links: 1
Access: (0777/lrwxrwxrwx) Uid: ( 1000/ tom) Gid: ( 1000/ tom)
Access: 2019-05-08 22:04:58.636000000 -0600
Modify: 2019-05-08 22:02:18.356000000 -0600
Change: 2019-05-08 22:02:18.356000000 -0600
Birth: -
```

As you can see, it lists the file as a symbolic link, which is another name for a soft link.

So as you have seen so far, a soft link has the following properties:

- The inode of a soft link is different from the original file.
- A soft link becomes useless once the original file is deleted.
- Any change to the soft link is actually a change in the original file.
- You can create soft links to directories.

You can create soft links to directories the same way you can create soft links to files. To demonstrate, let's first create a directory named `sports` in `elliot`'s home directory. And inside `sports`, create three files – `swimming`, `soccer`, and `hockey` – as follows:

```
elliot@ubuntu-linux:~$ mkdir sports
elliot@ubuntu-linux:~$ touch sports/swimming sports/soccer sports/hockey
elliot@ubuntu-linux:~$ ls sports
hockey soccer swimming
```

Now let's create a soft link named `softdir1` to the `sports` directory:

```
elliot@ubuntu-linux:~$ ln -s sports softdir1
```

Now if you change to `softdir1`, you are actually changing to `sports`, and so you will see the same directory contents:

```
elliot@ubuntu-linux:~$ cd softdir1
elliot@ubuntu-linux:~/softdir1$ ls
hockey soccer swimming
```

Of course, the same thing holds for directories as well; that is, if you delete the original directory, the soft link will become useless!

Creating hard links

The story is a little bit different when it comes to hard links. That's because a hard link is a replica of the original file. And here is a definition of a hard link:

WHAT IS A HARD LINK?

A hard link is simply an additional name for an existing file. It has the same inode of the original file, and hence, it's indistinguishable from the original file.

You can think of it as a nickname. When somebody calls you by your nickname, they are still referring to you.

A hard link has the following properties:

- A hard link has (shares) the same inode of the original file.
- A hard link remains intact if the original file gets deleted.
- Any change in the hard link is reflected in the original file.
- You can't create hard links to directories.

The following diagram helps you visualize hard links:

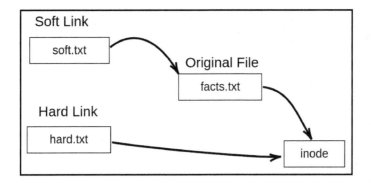

Figure 4: A hard link visualization

We use the same `ln` command to create hard links, but this time we omit the `-s` option:

```
ln original_file hard_link
```

So to create a hard link named `hard.txt` to the file `facts.txt`, you can simply run the command `ln facts.txt hard.txt`:

```
elliot@ubuntu-linux:~$ ln facts.txt hard.txt
```

Now let's do a long listing on the hard link `hard.txt` and the original file `facts.txt`:

```
elliot@ubuntu-linux:~$ ls -l hard.txt
-rw-rw-r-- 2 tom tom 210 May 9 00:07 hard.txt
elliot@ubuntu-linux:~$ ls -l facts.txt
-rw-rw-r-- 2 tom tom 210 May 9 00:07 facts.txt
```

They are identical! The hard link also has the same contents just like the original file:

```
elliot@ubuntu-linux:~$ cat hard.txt
Apples are red.
Grapes are green.
Bananas are yellow.
Cherries are red.
Sky is high.
Earth is round.
Linux is awesome!
Cherries are red.
Cherries are red.
Cherries are red.
Grass is green.
```

Now add the line "Swimming is a sport." to the very end of the hard link `hard.txt` with the text editor of your choice:

```
elliot@ubuntu-linux:~$ cat hard.txt
Apples are red.
Grapes are green.
Bananas are yellow.
Cherries are red.
Sky is high.
Earth is round.
Linux is awesome!
Cherries are red.
Cherries are red.
Cherries are red.
Grass is green.
Swimming is a sport.
```

Now just like in the case with soft links, the content of the original file has also changed:

```
elliot@ubuntu-linux:~$ cat facts.txt
Apples are red.
Grapes are green.
Bananas are yellow.
Cherries are red.
Sky is high.
Earth is round.
Linux is awesome!
Cherries are red.
Cherries are red.
Cherries are red.
Grass is green.
Swimming is a sport.
```

Now let's check the inode numbers of both files:

```
elliot@ubuntu-linux:~ ls -i hard.txt facts.txt
925155 facts.txt 925155 hard.txt
```

Notice that both files have the same inode number. Now let's run the `stat` command on both files:

```
elliot@ubuntu-linux:~$ stat hard.txt facts.txt
File: hard.txt
Size: 210  Blocks: 8  IO Block: 4096  regular file
Device: 801h/2049d  Inode: 925155  Links: 2
Access: (0664/-rw-rw-r--)  Uid: ( 1000/ elliot)  Gid: ( 1000/ elliot)
Access: 2019-05-09 00:07:36.884000000 -0600
Modify: 2019-05-09 00:07:25.708000000 -0600
```

```
Change: 2019-05-09 00:07:25.720000000 -0600
Birth: -
File: facts.txt
Size: 210 Blocks: 8 IO Block: 4096 regular file
Device: 801h/2049d Inode: 925155 Links: 2
Access: (0664/-rw-rw-r--) Uid: ( 1000/ elliot) Gid: ( 1000/ elliot)
Access: 2019-05-09 00:07:36.884000000 -0600
Modify: 2019-05-09 00:07:25.708000000 -0600
Change: 2019-05-09 00:07:25.720000000 -0600
Birth: -
```

The output of the stat command is identical for both files. And also, the number of Links: 2 here means that there are two hard links to the file. Hmmm! We have only created one hard link to the file facts.txt, then how come it listed two hard links? Well, the original file is a hard link to itself, and so any file has a minimum of one hard link (itself).

Now unlike the case with soft links, if you delete the original file facts.txt:

```
elliot@ubuntu-linux:~$ rm facts.txt
```

The hard link remains intact:

```
elliot@ubuntu-linux:~$ cat hard.txt
Apples are red.
Grapes are green.
Bananas are yellow.
Cherries are red.
Sky is high.
Earth is round.
Linux is awesome!
Cherries are red.
Cherries are red.
Cherries are red.
Grass is green.
Swimming is a sport.
```

The following diagram shows you why the hard link remains intact.

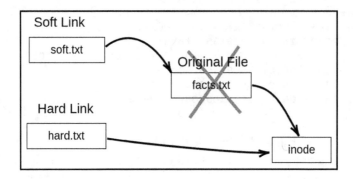

Figure 5: hard.txt remains intact

Now notice that after the removal of the file `facts.txt`, the number of hard links count of the file `hard.txt` will decrease to one:

```
elliot@ubuntu-linux:~$ stat hard.txt
File: hard.txt
Size: 210 Blocks: 8 IO Block: 4096 regular file
Device: 801h/2049d Inode: 925155 Links: 1
Access: (0664/-rw-rw-r--) Uid: ( 1000/ elliot) Gid: ( 1000/ elliot)
Access: 2019-05-09 00:17:21.176000000 -0600
Modify: 2019-05-09 00:07:25.708000000 -0600
Change: 2019-05-09 00:17:18.696000000 -0600
Birth: -
```

You can't create a hard link to a directory. If you don't believe me, then try creating a hard link named `variables` to the `/var` directory:

```
elliot@ubuntu-linux:~$ ln /var variables
ln: /var: hard link not allowed for directory
```

I told you hard links are not allowed for directories! Why do you doubt me?

MIND-BLOWING FACT

There is NO WAY to differentiate between an original file and a hard link. For example, if you are given two files, and one of them happens to be a hard link for the other file, there is NO WAY to tell which file is the original! It is like the chicken and egg dilemma; no one knows which one came first!

Knowledge check

For the following exercises, open up your Terminal and try to solve the following tasks:

1. Display the inode number of the `/var/log` directory.
2. Display the number of hard links for the `/boot` directory.
3. Create a new directory named `coins` in your home directory.
4. Create a soft link to `coins` named `currency`.
5. Inside the `coins` directory, create two files – `silver` and `gold`.
6. Create a new file `bronze` inside `currency`.
7. List the contents of both directories – `coins` and `currency`.
8. Create a new file `beverages` with the line "coffee is awesome" in your home directory and create a hard link named `drinks` to `beverages`.
9. Add the line "lemon is refreshing" to the `drinks` file and then remove the `beverages` file.
10. Display the contents of your `drinks` file.

True or false

1. The **File Name** is a part of the inode data structure.
2. The **File Size** is a part of the inode data structure.
3. You can create soft links to directories.
4. You can create hard links to directories.
5. The minimum number of hard links for a directory is 2.
6. Soft links have the same inode number as the original file.
7. Hard links have the same inode number as the original file.

7
Who Is Root?

So far, user `elliot` has been able to do quite a few things on the system. However, there are a whole lot of things that user `elliot` can't do! To demonstrate, let's try to create a file named `happy` in the `/var` directory:

```
elliot@ubuntu-linux:~$ touch /var/happy
touch: cannot touch '/var/happy': Permission denied
```

Oops! We got a `Permission denied` error.

Now let's try to create a new directory named `games` in `/etc`:

```
elliot@ubuntu-linux:/$ mkdir /etc/games
mkdir: cannot create directory '/etc/games': Permission denied
```

Again! We are getting the same error, `Permission denied`!

So what's going on here? Well, the user `elliot` doesn't have permission to do whatever he wants on the system! So who then? Who has permission to do anything on the system? It's the root user.

WHO IS ROOT?

`root` is a Linux user that has permission to do anything on the system. `root` is also known as the superuser.

Accessing the root user

You can run the `sudo -i` command to access the `root` user for the first time on your system:

```
elliot@ubuntu-linux:~$ sudo -i
[sudo] password for elliot:
root@ubuntu-linux:~#
```

You will be prompted to enter your password, and then, all of a sudden, you have got superpowers!

Notice how the command prompt changed instead of a dollar sign ($), it now shows a # to greet the root user.

Let's run the `whoami` command to make sure that we are now logged in as the root user:

```
root@ubuntu-linux:~# whoami
root
```

Awesome! Now let's display the current working directory:

```
root@ubuntu-linux:~# pwd
/root
```

Remember earlier that I told you that the home directory for the `root` user is `/root` and not under `/home`.

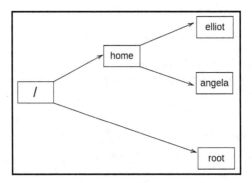

Figure 1: /root is the home directory for the root user

Now let's rerun both commands that we got permission denied for, but this time, we run both commands as the `root` user.

```
root@ubuntu-linux:~# touch /var/happy
root@ubuntu-linux:~# ls -l /var/happy
-rw-r--r-- 1 root root 0 Apr 15 10:53 /var/happy
```

As you can see, nothing can stop the `root` user from doing anything! Now let's create the directory `games` in `/etc`:

```
root@ubuntu-linux:~# mkdir /etc/games
root@ubuntu-linux:~# ls -ld /etc/games
drwxr-xr-x 2 root root 4096 Apr 15 10:55 /etc/games
```

We got no error, and that's because you have the power to do whatever you want as the root user. But ALWAYS remember, with great power comes great responsibility.

Setting the root password

You can also use the su command to switch to the root user but first, you need to set the root's password:

```
root@ubuntu-linux:~# passwd
Enter new UNIX password:
Retype new UNIX password:
passwd: password updated successfully
```

Amazing, now exit the root user:

```
root@ubuntu-linux:~# exit
logout
elliot@ubuntu-linux:~$ whoami
elliot
```

Now you can use the su root command to switch to the root user:

```
elliot@ubuntu-linux:~$ su root
Password:
root@ubuntu-linux:/home/elliot# whoami
root
```

The dash difference

Notice that my current working directory is now /home/elliot and not /root. If I want to change that, I can exit back to user elliot and rerun the su command but this time, I will add a dash (hyphen) before root as follows:

```
root@ubuntu-linux:/home/elliot# exit
exit
elliot@ubuntu-linux:~$ su - root
Password:
root@ubuntu-linux:~# pwd
/root
```

So what is the difference?

Here's the deal. When you don't add the dash before the username, the shell preserves the current user shell environment settings, which includes the current working directory. On the other hand, when you add the dash, the shell acquires the environment settings of the new user (the user you switched to).

So let's do some practice. If you want to switch to user elliot but preserve root's shell environment settings, then you don't need the dash:

```
root@ubuntu-linux:~# pwd
/root
root@ubuntu-linux:~# su elliot
elliot@ubuntu-linux:/root$ pwd
/root
elliot@ubuntu-linux:/root$
```

Notice how the current working directory didn't change when I switched to user elliot. Now, let's exit and switch back again to user elliot, but this time, we will put a dash before the username:

```
elliot@ubuntu-linux:/root$ exit
exit
root@ubuntu-linux:~# pwd
/root
root@ubuntu-linux:~# su - elliot
elliot@ubuntu-linux:~$ pwd
/home/elliot
```

Now notice how the current working directory changed from /root to /home/elliot. So here, the shell acquired the environment settings of user elliot.

A COOL TIP

If you run su with no username, then su will switch to the root user. So if you want to save yourself some typing, you can omit the username every time you want to switch to the root user.

Let's try out our cool tip! As user elliot, run the su command without specifying a username:

```
elliot@ubuntu-linux:~$ su
Password:
root@ubuntu-linux:/home/elliot#
```

You can then enter the `root` password to log in as `root`.

You can also use the dash to acquire `root`'s shell environment settings:

```
elliot@ubuntu-linux:~$ su -
Password:
root@ubuntu-linux:~# pwd
/root
```

This time I landed in `/root` because I used the dash.

Well, this was a short chapter, but the `root` user certainly deserves a whole section by itself. Also, remember that you have got superpowers when you are the `root` user as you have the permission to do anything on your system. And so if you are not very careful, you can damage your system, and that's why there is a very famous Linux meme that says, "Don't drink and root!."

Knowledge check

For the following exercises, open up your Terminal and try to solve the following tasks:

1. Switch to the `root` user.
2. Change the password for the `root` user.
3. Switch to user `elliot` and land in `/home/elliot`.
4. Now switch to user root but preserve the current working directory `/home-/elliot`.

True or false

1. The `root` user is the most powerful user in Linux.
2. Using the `su` command without specifying a username will switch you to the root user.
3. We use the `passroot` command to change the password for the `root` user.

8

Controlling the Population

Linux is a multiuser operating system, which means that many users are allowed to access the system at the same time. In real life, you barely find a Linux server with just one user. On the contrary, you see a lot of users on one server. So let's get real and populate our system with various users and groups. In this chapter, you will learn how to add users and groups to your Linux system. You will also learn how to manage user and group accounts in all sorts of ways. Furthermore, you will also learn how to manage Linux file permissions.

The /etc/passwd file

In Linux, user information is stored in the /etc/passwd file. Every line in /etc/passwd corresponds to exactly one user. When you first open /etc/passwd, you will see a lot of users, and you will wonder, *where are all these users coming from?* The answer is simple: most of these users are service users, and they are used by your system to start up various applications and services. However, our main focus of this chapter will be system users; those are real people like you and me!

Every line in /etc/passwd consists of 7 fields, each separated by a colon, and each field represents a user attribute. For example, the entry for user elliot will look something like this:

```
  1   2   3    4      5               6            7
elliot:x:1000:1000:Elliot Alderson:/home/elliot:/bin/bash
```

Figure 1: The 7 fields in /etc/passwd

The following table breaks down those seven fields in `/etc/passwd` and explains each one of them:

Field	What does it store?
1	This field stores the username.
2	This field usually has an X in it, which means the user's password is encrypted and stored in the file `/etc/shadow`.
3	This field stores the **UID (User ID)** number.
4	This field stores the primary **GID (Group ID)** of the user.
5	This field stores a comment on the user, which is usually the user's first and last name.
6	This field stores the path of the user's home directory.
7	This field stores the user's default shell.

Table 10: Understanding /etc/passwd

Adding users

Before you can add a user on your system, you have to become `root`:

```
elliot@ubuntu-linux:~$ su -
Password:
root@ubuntu-linux:~#
```

Now, we are ready to add users. We all love Tom & Jerry, so let's begin by adding user `tom`. To do that, you need to run the command `useradd -m tom`:

```
root@ubuntu-linux:~# useradd -m tom
```

And just like that, the user `tom` is now added to our system. You will also see a new line added to the end of the `/etc/passwd` file for the new user `tom`; let's view it with the lovely `tail` command:

```
root@ubuntu-linux:~# tail -n 1 /etc/passwd
tom:x:1007:1007::/home/tom:/bin/sh
```

We used the −m option with the `useradd` command to ensure that a new home directory will be created for user `tom`. So let's try to change to the `/home/tom` directory to make sure it's indeed created:

```
root@ubuntu-linux:~# cd /home/tom
root@ubuntu-linux:/home/tom# pwd
/home/tom
```

Awesome! We verified that `/home/tom` is created.

The first thing you may want to do after creating a new user is to set the user's password. You can set `tom`'s password by running the command `passwd tom`:

```
root@ubuntu-linux:~# passwd tom
Enter new UNIX password:
Retype new UNIX password:
passwd: password updated successfully
```

Now, let's create user `jerry`. But this time, we will choose the following attributes for user `jerry`:

UID	777
Comment	Jerry the Mouse
Shell	/bin/bash

This is easy to do with the `useradd` command:

```
root@ubuntu-linux:~# useradd −m −u 777 −c "Jerry the Mouse" −s /bin/bash
jerry
```

The −u option is used to set the UID for `jerry`. We also used the −c option to add a comment for user `jerry`, and finally we used the −s option to set the default shell for `jerry`.

Now, let's view the last two lines of the `/etc/passwd` file to make some comparisons:

```
root@ubuntu-linux:~# tail −n 2 /etc/passwd
tom:x:1007:1007::/home/tom:/bin/sh
jerry:x:777:1008:Jerry the Mouse:/home/jerry:/bin/bash
```

Notice how the comment field for user `tom` is empty as we didn't add any comments while creating user `tom`, and notice how the UID for user `tom` was chosen by the system, but we have chosen `777` for user `jerry`. Also, notice that the default shell for user `tom` is chosen by the system to be `/bin/sh`, which is an older version of `/bin/bash`. However, we chose the newer shell `/bin/bash` for user `jerry`.

Now, let's set the password for user `jerry`:

```
root@ubuntu-linux:~# passwd jerry
Enter new UNIX password:
Retype new UNIX password:
passwd: password updated successfully
```

Amazing! We have now created two users: `tom` and `jerry`. Now, let's switch to user `tom`:

```
root@ubuntu-linux:~# su - tom
$ whoami tom
$ pwd
/home/tom
$
```

We were able to switch to user `tom`, but as you can see, the shell looks so much different as the command prompt doesn't display the username or the hostname. That's because the default shell for user `tom` is `/bin/sh`. You can use the `echo $SHELL` command to display the user's default shell:

```
$ echo $SHELL
/bin/sh
```

As you can see, it displayed `/bin/sh`. Now, let's exit and switch to user `jerry`:

```
$ exit
root@ubuntu-linux:~# su - jerry
jerry@ubuntu-linux:~$ whoami
jerry
jerry@ubuntu-linux:~$ echo $SHELL
/bin/bash
```

Everything looks better with user `jerry` as we did set his default shell to be `/bin/bash`. Alright, now let's switch back to the `root` user:

```
jerry@ubuntu-linux:~$ exit
logout
root@ubuntu-linux:~#
```

Modifying user attributes

So we are not happy that the default shell for user `tom` is /bin/sh, and we want to change it to /bin/bash. We can use the `usermod` command to modify user attributes.

For example, to change the default shell for user `tom` to be /bin/bash, you can run the command `usermod -s /bin/bash tom`:

```
root@ubuntu-linux:~# usermod -s /bin/bash tom
```

Notice that you can also use the full name for the command option; so you can use --shell instead of -s. Anyways, let's see if we successfully changed the default shell for user `tom`:

```
root@ubuntu-linux:~# su - tom
tom@ubuntu-linux:~$ whoami
tom
tom@ubuntu-linux:~$ echo $SHELL
/bin/bash
```

Great! We successfully did it. You can also change the UID of `tom` to 444 by running the command `usermod -u 444 tom`:

```
root@ubuntu-linux:~# usermod -u 444 tom
```

And we can indeed check that the UID of `tom` has changed by taking a peek at the /etc/passwd file:

```
root@ubuntu-linux:~# tail -n 2 /etc/passwd
tom:x:444:1007::/home/tom:/bin/bash
jerry:x:777:1008:Jerry the Mouse:/home/jerry:/bin/bash
```

We can even modify the comment field of user `tom`. Right now, it's empty, but you can set the comment field of user `tom` to "Tom the Cat" by running the command:

```
root@ubuntu-linux:~# usermod --comment "Tom the Cat" tom
```

And again, we can verify that the comment is changed by looking at the /etc/passwd file:

```
root@ubuntu-linux:~# tail -n 2 /etc/passwd
tom:x:444:1007:Tom the Cat:/home/tom:/bin/bash
jerry:x:777:1008:Jerry the Mouse:/home/jerry:/bin/bash
```

Defining the skeleton

If you list the contents of /home/jerry and /home/tom, you will see that they are empty:

```
root@ubuntu-linux:~# ls -l /home/tom
total 0
root@ubuntu-linux:~# ls -l /home/jerry
total 0
```

The reason that both /home/jerry and /home/tom are empty is that the skeleton file /etc/skel is also empty:

```
root@ubuntu-linux:~# ls -l /etc/skel
total 0
```

 WHAT IS /etc/skel?

This is the skeleton file. Any file or directory you create in /etc/skel will be copied to the home directory of any new user created.

Now, with your favorite text editor, create the file welcome.txt in /etc/skel and insert the line "Hello Friend!" in it:

```
root@ubuntu-linux:/etc/skel# ls
welcome.txt
root@ubuntu-linux:/etc/skel# cat welcome.txt
Hello Friend!
```

Alright, so now you have created the file welcome.txt in /etc/skel, which means that any new user created will now have the file welcome.txt in their home directory. To demonstrate, let's create a new user named edward and then we will take a peek at his home directory:

```
root@ubuntu-linux:~# useradd -m -c "Edward Snowden" -s /bin/bash edward
```

Now, let's set the password for user edward:

```
root@ubuntu-linux:~# passwd edward
Enter new UNIX password:
Retype new UNIX password:
passwd: password updated successfully
```

Now, the moment of truth comes! Let's switch to user edward and list the contents of his home directory:

```
root@ubuntu-linux:~# su - edward
edward@ubuntu-linux:~$ ls
welcome.txt
edward@ubuntu-linux:~$ cat welcome.txt
Hello Friend!
```

You can see that the file welcome.txt is copied to edward's home directory. Every new user created on the system will now have a cool greeting message! Notice that old users like tom and jerry will not have the file welcome.txt in their home directory as they were created before we added the file welcome.txt in /etc/skel.

Changing the defaults

We are too tired of specifying the default shell every time we create a new user. But luckily, there is a file where you can specify the default shell for any new user created. This amazing file is /etc/default/useradd.

Open up the file /etc/default/useradd and look for the following line:

```
SHELL=/bin/sh
```

Change it to:

```
SHELL=/bin/bash
```

Awesome! Now, any new user created will have /bin/bash as the default shell. Let's test it by creating a new user named spy:

```
root@ubuntu-linux:~# useradd -m spy
```

Now, set the password for user spy:

```
root@ubuntu-linux:~# passwd spy
Enter new UNIX password:
Retype new UNIX password:
passwd: password updated successfully
```

Finally, let's switch to user spy and check the default shell:

```
root@ubuntu-linux:~# su - spy
spy@ubuntu-linux:~$ echo $SHELL
/bin/bash
```

```
spy@ubuntu-linux:~$ exit
logout
root@ubuntu-linux:~#
```

Hooray! We can see that bash is the default shell for user spy.

Keep in mind that /bin/sh and /bin/bash are not the only two valid shells on your system; there are more! Check out the file /etc/shells to see a complete list of all the valid shells on your system:

```
root@ubuntu-linux:~# cat /etc/shells
# /etc/shells: valid login shells
/bin/sh
/bin/bash
/bin/rbash
/bin/dash
```

You can change other user defaults in /etc/default/useradd, including:

- The default home directory (HOME=/home)
- The default skel directory (SKEL=/etc/skel)

I will leave that for you to do as an exercise.

Removing users

Sometimes a user is no longer needed to be on the system, for example, an employee leaving the company or a user that only needed temporary access to a server. In any case, you need to know how to delete users.

The last user we created was spy, right? Well, we don't need any spies on our system, so let's delete the user spy; you can delete user spy by running the command userdel spy:

```
root@ubuntu-linux:~# userdel spy
```

And just like that, user spy is deleted. However, the home directory of spy still exists:

```
root@ubuntu-linux:~# ls -ld /home/spy
drwxr-xr-x 2 1008 1010 4096 Apr 17 10:24 /home/spy
```

We would have to manually delete it:

```
root@ubuntu-linux:~# rm -r /home/spy
```

But this is inconvenient. Imagine after every user you delete, you then have to go and manually remove their home directory. Luckily, there is a better solution; you can use the – r option to automatically remove the user's home directory.

Let's give it a try with user edward:

```
root@ubuntu-linux:~# userdel -r edward
```

Now, let's check to see if the home directory for user edward still exists:

```
root@ubuntu-linux:~# ls -ld /home/edward
ls: cannot access '/home/edward': No such file or directory
```

And as you can see, edward's home directory is removed.

The /etc/group file

In schools, kids are usually grouped into different groups. For example, kids who like dancing will be part of the dance group. The geeky kids will form the science group. In case you are wondering, I used to be part of the sports group because I was pretty damn fast!

We have the same concept in Linux as users who share similar characteristics are placed in the same group.

WHAT IS A GROUP?

A group is a collection of users who share the same role or purpose.

All groups have their information stored in the file /etc/group. And just like with the /etc/passwd file, every line in /etc/group corresponds to exactly one group, and each line consists of 4 fields. For example, one of the most famous groups in Linux is the sudo group:

```
1   2  3    4
sudo:x:27:elliot
```

Figure 2: The 4 fields in /etc/group

The following table breaks down those four fields in /etc/group and explains each one of them:

Field	What does it store?
1	This field stores the group name.
2	This field usually has an X in it, which means the group password is encrypted and stored in the file /etc/gshadow.
3	This field stores the **GID** (**Group ID**) number.
4	This field stores the usernames of the group members.

Table 11: Understanding /etc/group

Adding groups

Let's create a group named cartoon. To do that, you need to run the command groupadd cartoon:

```
root@ubuntu-linux:~# groupadd cartoon
```

Notice that a new line with the group information will be added to the end of the file /etc/group:

```
root@ubuntu-linux:~# tail -n 1 /etc/group
cartoon:x:1009:
```

Notice that the group cartoon currently has no members, and that's why the fourth field is currently empty.

Let's create another group named developers, but this time, we will specify a GID of 888:

```
root@ubuntu-linux:~# groupadd --gid 888 developers
```

Let's check the developers group entry in /etc/group:

```
root@ubuntu-linux:~# tail -n 1 /etc/group
developers:x:888:
```

And it looks just like we expect it to be. Cool!

Adding group members

Users `tom` and `jerry` are both cartoon characters, so it makes sense to add them both to the `cartoon` group.

To add `tom` to the `cartoon` group, you simply run the command `usermod -aG cartoon tom`:

```
root@ubuntu-linux:~# usermod -aG cartoon tom
```

Likewise, you can add `jerry` to the `cartoon` group:

```
root@ubuntu-linux:~# usermod -aG cartoon jerry
```

Now, let's have a peek at the `/etc/group` file:

```
root@ubuntu-linux:~# tail -n 2 /etc/group
cartoon:x:1009:tom,jerry
developers:x:888:
```

As you can see, both `tom` and `jerry` are now listed as members of the `cartoon` group.

You can use the `id` command to view the group memberships of any user on the system. For example, if you want to check which groups `tom` belongs to, you can run the command `id tom`:

```
root@ubuntu-linux:~# id tom
uid=444(tom) gid=1007(tom) groups=1007(tom),1009(cartoon)
```

Let's do some more practice by creating three new users – `sara`, `peter`, and `rachel`:

```
root@ubuntu-linux:~# useradd -m sara
root@ubuntu-linux:~# useradd -m peter
root@ubuntu-linux:~# useradd -m rachel
```

And remember to set the password for each user:

```
root@ubuntu-linux:~# passwd sara
Enter new UNIX password:
Retype new UNIX password:
passwd: password updated successfully
root@ubuntu-linux:~# passwd peter
Enter new UNIX password:
Retype new UNIX password:
passwd: password updated successfully
root@ubuntu-linux:~# passwd rachel
Enter new UNIX password:
```

```
Retype new UNIX password:
passwd: password updated successfully
root@ubuntu-linux:~#
```

Now imagine if all the three new users are software developers; this means that they have the same role, and so they should be members of the same group. So let's add all three users to the `developers` group:

```
root@ubuntu-linux:~# usermod -aG developers sara
root@ubuntu-linux:~# usermod -aG developers peter
root@ubuntu-linux:~# usermod -aG developers rachel
```

Now, let's have a peek at the `/etc/group` file:

```
root@ubuntu-linux:~# tail -n 5 /etc/group
cartoon:x:1009:tom,jerry
developers:x:888:sara,peter,rachel
sara:x:1001:
peter:x:1002:
rachel:x:1003:
```

We can see that the group `developers` now has the three members – `sara`, `peter`, and `rachel`. But there is something strange! It seems like when we have created the users `sara`, `peter`, and `rachel`, it also created them as groups! But why did this happen? Well, let me explain it to you in the next section.

Primary versus secondary groups

Every user in Linux must be a member of a primary group. Primary groups are also referred to as login groups. By default, whenever a new user is created, a group is also created with the same name as the user, and this group becomes the primary group of the new user.

On the other hand, a user may or may not be a member of a secondary group. Secondary groups are also sometimes referred to as supplementary groups. You can think of a secondary group as any group that a user is a member of aside from the user's primary group.

Do not worry if you don't understand the concept of primary and secondary groups just yet; it will become crystal clear by the end of this chapter.

Let's create a new user named `dummy`:

```
root@ubuntu-linux:~# useradd -m dummy
```

Now, if you look at the last line of the /etc/group file, you will see that a group named dummy is also created:

```
root@ubuntu-linux:~# tail -n 1 /etc/group
dummy:x:1004:
```

This dummy group is the primary group of user dummy; and if you run the id command on user dummy:

```
root@ubuntu-linux:~# id dummy
uid=1004(dummy) gid=1004(dummy) groups=1004(dummy)
```

You will see that user dummy is indeed a member of the dummy group. Now, let's add user dummy to the cartoon group:

```
root@ubuntu-linux:~# usermod -aG cartoon dummy
```

Let's run the id command on user dummy again:

```
root@ubuntu-linux:~# id dummy
uid=1004(dummy) gid=1004(dummy) groups=1004(dummy),1009(cartoon)
```

You can see that user dummy is a member of two groups: dummy and cartoon. However, dummy is the primary group and cartoon is the secondary group.

The primary group is always preceded by gid= in the output of the id command:

```
root@ubuntu-linux:~# id dummy
uid=1004(dummy) gid=1004(dummy) groups=1004(dummy),1009(cartoon)
                     Primary                           Secondary
```

Figure 3: Primary versus secondary group

Now let's add user dummy to the developers group:

```
root@ubuntu-linux:~# usermod -aG developers dummy
```

Next, run the id command on user dummy again:

```
root@ubuntu-linux:~# id dummy
uid=1004(dummy) gid=1004(dummy)
groups=1004(dummy),1009(cartoon),888(developers)
```

As you can see, user dummy is a member of two secondary groups: cartoon and developers.

Alright! Enough with all this dummy stuff. Let's remove the user dummy:

```
root@ubuntu-linux:~# userdel -r dummy
```

Every user must be a member of only one primary group; however, there are no restrictions on the choice of the primary group!

To demonstrate, let's create a user named smurf with cartoon being the primary group of user smurf. This can easily be done by using the --gid option with the useradd command:

```
root@ubuntu-linux:~# useradd -m --gid cartoon smurf
```

Now, take a peek at the /etc/group file:

```
root@ubuntu-linux:~# tail -n 1 /etc/group
rachel:x:1003:
```

You will see that there is no group created with the name smurf. Amazing! That's because we already specified another primary group for user smurf.

Now let's check user smurf's group memberships:

```
root@ubuntu-linux:~# id smurf
uid=1004(smurf) gid=1009(cartoon) groups=1009(cartoon)
```

As you can see, smurf is only a member of the group cartoon, which is also his primary group, of course.

You can also change the primary group of existing users. For example, you can set the developers group to be the primary group of user smurf as follows:

```
root@ubuntu-linux:~# usermod -g developers smurf
root@ubuntu-linux:~# id smurf
uid=1004(smurf) gid=888(developers) groups=888(developers)
```

Removing groups

You can remove a group if it is no longer needed. To demonstrate, let's create a group named temp:

```
root@ubuntu-linux:~# groupadd temp
```

Now, you can use the `groupdel` command to remove the `temp` group:

```
root@ubuntu-linux:~# groupdel temp
```

Now, let's try removing the group `sara`:

```
root@ubuntu-linux:~# groupdel sara
groupdel: cannot remove the primary group of user 'sara'
```

We get an error message as we are not allowed to remove primary groups of existing users.

File ownership and permissions

Every file in Linux is owned by a specific user and a specific group. To demonstrate, let's switch to user `smurf`, and create a file named `mysmurf` in `smurf`'s home directory:

```
root@ubuntu-linux:~# su - smurf
smurf@ubuntu-linux:~$ touch mysmurf
```

Now do a long listing on the file `mysmurf`:

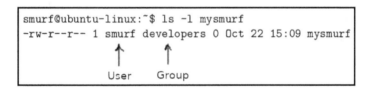

Figure 4: User and group owners

You will see the name of the user (the user owner) who owns the file in the third column of the output, which is, by default, the user who created the file.

On the fourth column of the output, you will see the name of the group (the group owner) of the file, which is, by default, the primary group of the user owner.

The `developers` group is the primary group of user `smurf`, and hence `developers` became the group owner of the file `mysmurf`.

If you do a long listing on the `sports` directory that's inside `elliot`'s home directory:

```
smurf@ubuntu-linux:~$ ls -ld /home/elliot/sports
drwxr-xr-x 2 elliot elliot 4096 Oct 22 12:56 /home/elliot/sports
```

You will see that user `elliot` is the user owner, and the group `elliot` is the group owner; that's because the group `elliot` is the primary group of user `elliot`.

Changing file ownership

You can use the `chown` command to change a file's ownership. In general, the syntax of the `chown` command is as follows:

```
chown   user:group file
```

For example, you can change the ownership of the file `mysmurf`, so that user `elliot` is the owner, and group `cartoon` is the group owner, as follows:

```
smurf@ubuntu-linux:~$
smurf@ubuntu-linux:~$ chown elliot:cartoon mysmurf
chown: changing ownership of 'mysmurf': Operation not permitted
```

Oh! Only the `root` user can do it; let's switch to the `root` user and try again:

```
smurf@ubuntu-linux:~$ su -
Password:
root@ubuntu-linux:~# cd /home/smurf
root@ubuntu-linux:/home/smurf# chown elliot:cartoon mysmurf
```

Success! Now let's view the ownership of the file `mysmurf`:

```
root@ubuntu-linux:/home/smurf# ls -l mysmurf
-rw-r--r-- 1 elliot cartoon 0 Oct 22 15:09 mysmurf
```

As you can see, we have successfully changed the ownership of `mysmurf`. Also, you can change the user owner without changing the group owner. For example, if you want the user `root` to be the owner of `mysmurf`, you can run the following command:

```
root@ubuntu-linux:/home/smurf# chown root mysmurf
root@ubuntu-linux:/home/smurf# ls -l mysmurf
-rw-r--r-- 1 root cartoon 0 Oct 22 15:09 mysmurf
```

As you can see, only the user owner is changed to `root`, but `cartoon` remains the group owner.

You can also change the group owner without changing the user owner. For example, if you want the group `developers` to be the group owner of `mysmurf`, then you can run:

```
root@ubuntu-linux:/home/smurf# chown :developers mysmurf
root@ubuntu-linux:/home/smurf# ls -l mysmurf
-rw-r--r-- 1 root developers 0 Oct 22 15:09 mysmurf
```

FOR YOUR INFORMATION

`chgrp` can also be used to change the group owner of a file. I will leave that for you to do as an exercise!

Understanding file permissions

In Linux, every file is assigned access permissions for three different entities; these entities are:

- The user owner of the file
- The group owner of the file
- Everyone else (also referred to as others/world)

We are already familiar with the user owner and the group owner; everyone else refers to any user on the system who is not the user owner and not the group owner.

You can think of these three entities like you, your friends, and everyone else. There are some things that you don't like to share with anyone, other things you like to share with your friends, and things you may like to share with everyone.

Each file has three types of access permissions:

- Read
- Write
- Execute

The meaning of each of these access permissions is not the same for files and directories. The following diagram explains the differences between access permissions for files versus directories:

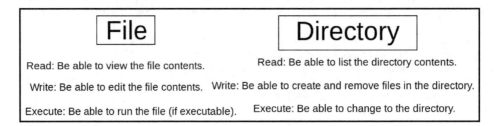

Figure 5: File versus directory permissions

You can view the permissions of a file by doing a long listing. For example, to see the current permissions set on the mysmurf file, you can run:

```
root@ubuntu-linux:~# ls -l /home/smurf/mysmurf
-rw-r--r-- 1 root developers 0 Oct 22 15:09 /home/smurf/mysmurf
```

Now pay attention to the first column of the output, which is -rw-r--r--. Notice that it consists of ten slots; the first slot determines the type of the file. The remaining nine slots are divided into three sets, each with three slots, just like in the following diagram:

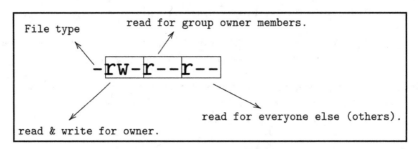

Figure 6: Understanding permissions

Notice the first slot determines the file type; it can be:

- – for regular files
- d for directories
- l for soft links
- b for block devices
- c for character devices

The next three slots determine the permissions granted for the owner of the file. The first of these slots determines the read permission; it can either be:

- r for read access
- – for no read access

The second of these slots determines the write permission; it can either be:

- w for write access
- – for no write access

The third slot determines the execute permission; it can either be:

- x for execute access
- – for no execute access

The same logic is applied to the next three slots, which determine the permissions for the group owner, and lastly, the final three slots, which determine the permissions for everyone else.

Now let's get our hands dirty and do some examples to reinforce our understanding of file permissions. Let's first edit the mysmurf file and add the following line Smurfs are blue! so it looks like this:

```
root@ubuntu-linux:~# cat /home/smurf/mysmurf
Smurfs are blue!
```

Now switch to user smurf and try reading the contents of the file mysmurf:

```
root@ubuntu-linux:~# su - smurf
smurf@ubuntu-linux:~$ cat mysmurf
Smurfs are blue!
```

Cool! User smurf can read the contents of the file mysmurf. Keep in mind that user smurf is not the owner of the file, but he is a member of the group developers:

```
smurf@ubuntu-linux:~$ id smurf
uid=1004(smurf) gid=888(developers) groups=888(developers)
```

So smurf can read the file because the group permission of mysmurf is r--. But can he edit the file? Let's see what will happen if user smurf tried to add the line I am smurf! to the file mysmurf:

```
smurf@ubuntu-linux:~$ echo "I am smurf!" >> mysmurf
bash: mysmurf: Permission denied
```

Permission denied! Yup, that's because there is no write permission for the group owner (or others). Only the user owner has read and write permissions to the file mysmurf, and the owner happens to be root in this case. Now, if we changed the file ownership and made smurf the owner of the file mysmurf, then he will be able to edit the file; so let's change the file ownership first:

```
smurf@ubuntu-linux:~$ su -
Password:
root@ubuntu-linux:~# chown smurf /home/smurf/mysmurf
root@ubuntu-linux:~# ls -l /home/smurf/mysmurf
-rw-r--r-- 1 smurf developers 17 Oct 23 11:06 /home/smurf/mysmurf
```

Now let's switch back to user smurf and reattempt to edit the file mysmurf:

```
root@ubuntu-linux:~# su - smurf
smurf@ubuntu-linux:~$ echo "I am smurf!" >> mysmurf
smurf@ubuntu-linux:~$ cat mysmurf
Smurfs are blue!
I am smurf!
```

Cool! So user smurf has successfully edited the file. Now let's switch to user elliot and attempt to add the line I am not smurf! to the mysmurf file:

```
smurf@ubuntu-linux:~$ su - elliot
Password:
elliot@ubuntu-linux:~$ cd /home/smurf/
elliot@ubuntu-linux:/home/smurf$ echo "I am not smurf!" >> mysmurf
bash: mysmurf: Permission denied
```

Permission denied! Notice that elliot is not the user owner and is not even a member of the developers group, so he is regarded as everyone else (others). However, he can read the file because others have read permission r--:

```
elliot@ubuntu-linux:/home/smurf$ cat mysmurf
Smurfs are blue!
I am smurf!
```

Changing file permissions

Now, what if we want to give elliot permission to edit the file mysmurf without changing file ownership as we did before? Well! This is very simple; you can use the chmod command to change file permissions.

Let's first switch to the `root` user:

```
elliot@ubuntu-linux:/home/smurf$ su -
Password:
root@ubuntu-linux:~# cd /home/smurf
root@ubuntu-linux:/home/smurf#
```

Now you can add the write permission for others (everyone else) by running the command:

```
root@ubuntu-linux:/home/smurf# chmod o+w mysmurf
```

Here `o+w` means **others+write**, which means adding the write permission to others. Now do a long listing on `mysmurf`:

```
root@ubuntu-linux:/home/smurf# ls -l mysmurf
-rw-r--rw- 1 smurf developers 29 Oct 23 11:34 mysmurf
```

As you can see, others can now read and write `rw-` to the `mysmurf` file. Now, switch back to user `elliot` and try to add the line `I am not smurf!` again:

```
root@ubuntu-linux:/home/smurf# su elliot
elliot@ubuntu-linux:/home/smurf$ echo "I am not smurf!" >> mysmurf
elliot@ubuntu-linux:/home/smurf$ cat mysmurf
Smurfs are blue!
I am smurf!
I am not smurf!
```

Success! User `elliot` can edit the file `mysmurf`. Now it's time to discuss the execute permission; let's go to `elliot`'s home directory, and create a file named `mydate.sh`:

```
elliot@ubuntu-linux:/home/smurf$ cd /home/elliot
elliot@ubuntu-linux:~$ touch mydate.sh
```

Now add the following two lines to the file `mydate.sh`:

```
#!/bin/bash
date
```

You can add both lines by running the following two `echo` commands:

```
elliot@ubuntu-linux:~$ echo '#!/bin/bash' >> mydate.sh
elliot@ubuntu-linux:~$ echo date >> mydate.sh
```

Do not worry about the meaning of the line '`#/bin/bash`' now; I will explain it in a later chapter. Anyways, let's view the content of the file `mydate.sh`:

```
elliot@ubuntu-linux:~$ cat mydate.sh
#!/bin/bash
date
```

Now do a long listing on the file `mydate.sh`:

```
elliot@ubuntu-linux:~$ ls -l mydate.sh
-rw-rw-r-- 1 elliot elliot 17 Oct 23 12:28 mydate.sh
```

Notice the absence of the execute permission here for everyone (the user owner, group owner, and others). Let's add the execute permission to everyone; you can do that by running the following command:

```
elliot@ubuntu-linux:~$ chmod a+x mydate.sh
elliot@ubuntu-linux:~$ ls -l mydate.sh
-rwxrwxr-x 1 elliot elliot 17 Oct 23 12:28 mydate.sh
```

Here `a+x` means **all+execute**, which means add the execute permission to everyone. Also, notice that we were able to run the `chmod` command as user `elliot` only because he is the owner of the file `mydate.sh`.

Finally, just enter the full path of `mydate.sh` and hit *Enter*:

```
elliot@ubuntu-linux:~$ /home/elliot/mydate.sh
Wed Oct 23 12:38:51 CST 2019
```

Wow! The current date is displayed! You have created your first Bash script and have run it! Bash scripting will be covered in detail in a later chapter. But now at least you know what it means for a file to be executable. Now remove the execute permission by running the command:

```
elliot@ubuntu-linux:~$ chmod a-x mydate.sh
elliot@ubuntu-linux:~$ ls -l mydate.sh
-rw-rw-r-- 1 elliot elliot 17 Oct 23 12:28 mydate.sh
```

Here `a-x` means **all-execute**, which means remove the execute permission from everyone. Now try to run the script again:

```
elliot@ubuntu-linux:~$ /home/elliot/mydate.sh
bash: /home/elliot/mydate.sh: Permission denied
```

We get a permission denied error! This is because the file `mydate.sh` is no longer executable. Most Linux commands are executable files. For example, take a look at the `date` command. First, we run the `which` command to get the location of the `date` command:

```
elliot@ubuntu-linux:~$ which date
/bin/date
```

Now do a long listing on `/bin/date`:

```
elliot@ubuntu-linux:~$ ls -l /bin/date
-rwxr-xr-x 1 root root 100568 Jan 18 2018 /bin/date
```

As you can see, it has execute permissions for everyone. Now watch what happens when you remove the execute permission:

```
elliot@ubuntu-linux:~$ su -
Password:
root@ubuntu-linux:~# chmod a-x /bin/date
```

Now try running the `date` command:

```
root@ubuntu-linux:~# date
-su: /bin/date: Permission denied
```

The `date` command is no longer working! Please let's fix that by adding the execute permission back:

```
root@ubuntu-linux:~# chmod a+x /bin/date
root@ubuntu-linux:~# date
Wed Oct 23 12:56:15 CST 2019
```

Now let's remove the user owner read permission on the file `mysmurf`:

```
root@ubuntu-linux:~# cd /home/smurf/
root@ubuntu-linux:/home/smurf# chmod u-r mysmurf
root@ubuntu-linux:/home/smurf# ls -l mysmurf
--w-r--rw- 1 smurf developers 45 Oct 23 12:02 mysmurf
```

Here `u-r` means **user-read**, which means remove the read permission from the user owner. Now let's switch to user `smurf` and try to read the file `mysmurf`:

```
root@ubuntu-linux:/home/smurf# su - smurf
smurf@ubuntu-linux:~$ cat mysmurf
cat: mysmurf: Permission denied
```

Poor `smurf`. He can't even read his own file. But since he is the file owner; he can get the read permission back:

```
smurf@ubuntu-linux:~$ chmod u+r mysmurf
smurf@ubuntu-linux:~$ cat mysmurf Smurfs are blue!
I am smurf!
I am not smurf!
```

You have seen how to add (+) and remove (–) permissions with the `chmod` command. You can also use the equal sign = to set permissions. For example, if you want the group owner (`developers`) of the file `mysmurf` to only have write permission, you can run the command:

```
smurf@ubuntu-linux:~$ chmod g=w mysmurf
smurf@ubuntu-linux:~$ ls -l mysmurf
-rw--w-rw- 1 smurf developers 45 Oct 23 12:02 mysmurf
```

So now, the `developers` group members only has write permission –w– to the file `mysmurf`. Here are more examples:

- `chmod ug=rwx mysmurf`: This will give the user owner and group owner full permissions.
- `chmod o-rw mysmurf`: This will remove read and write permissions from others.
- `chmod a= mysmurf`: This will give zero (no) permissions to everyone.
- `chmod go= mysmurf`: This will give zero permissions to the group owner and others.
- `chmod u+rx mysmurf`: This will add read and execute permissions to the user owner.

Let's give zero permissions to everyone:

```
smurf@ubuntu-linux:~$ chmod a= mysmurf
smurf@ubuntu-linux:~$ ls -l mysmurf
---------- 1 smurf developers 45 Oct 23 12:02 mysmurf
```

So now user `smurf` can't read, write, or execute the file:

```
smurf@ubuntu-linux:~$ cat mysmurf
cat: mysmurf: Permission denied
smurf@ubuntu-linux:~$ echo "Hello" >> mysmurf
-su: mysmurf: Permission denied
```

How about the `root` user? Well let's switch to `root` to find out:

```
smurf@ubuntu-linux:~$ su -
Password:
root@ubuntu-linux:~# cd /home/smurf/
root@ubuntu-linux:/home/smurf# cat mysmurf
Smurfs are blue!
I am smurf!
I am not smurf!
root@ubuntu-linux:/home/smurf# echo "I got super powers" >> mysmurf
root@ubuntu-linux:/home/smurf# cat mysmurf
Smurfs are blue!
I am smurf!
I am not smurf!
I got super powers
root@ubuntu-linux:/home/smurf# ls -l mysmurf
---------- 1 smurf developers 64 Oct 23 13:38 mysmurf
```

As you can see, the `root` user can do anything! That's because `root` can bypass file permissions! In other words, file permissions don't apply to the `root` user.

Directory permissions

Now let's see how read, write, and execute permissions work on a directory. The easiest example will be the `root`'s home directory `/root`. Let's do a long listing on `/root`:

```
root@ubuntu-linux:~# ls -ld /root
drwx------ 5 root root 4096 Oct 22 14:28 /root
```

As you can see, full permissions are given to the owner `root` and zero permissions for everyone else. Let's create a file inside `/root` named `gold`:

```
root@ubuntu-linux:~# touch /root/gold
```

Now let's switch to user `smurf` and try to list the contents of the `/root` directory:

```
root@ubuntu-linux:~# su - smurf
smurf@ubuntu-linux:~$ ls /root
ls: cannot open directory '/root': Permission denied
```

User `smurf` gets a permission denied error as he's got no read permissions on the directory `/root`. Now, can `smurf` create a file inside `/root`?

```
smurf@ubuntu-linux:~$ touch /root/silver
touch: cannot touch '/root/silver': Permission denied
```

He cannot since he has no write permissions on /root. Can he delete a file inside /root?

```
smurf@ubuntu-linux:~$ rm /root/gold
rm: cannot remove '/root/gold': Permission denied
```

Again, no write permissions, so he can't delete a file in /root. Finally, can user smurf change to the /root directory?

```
smurf@ubuntu-linux:~$ cd /root
-su: cd: /root: Permission denied
```

He cannot because smurf needs the execute permission to be able to change to the /root directory. Now, let's switch back to the root user and start adding some permissions:

```
smurf@ubuntu-linux:~$ exit
logout
root@ubuntu-linux:~# chmod o+rx /root
```

Here, we added the read and execute permissions to others, so user smurf can now list the contents of the /root directory:

```
root@ubuntu-linux:~# su - smurf
smurf@ubuntu-linux:~$ ls /root
gold
```

He can even change to the /root directory as we have added the execute permission as well:

```
smurf@ubuntu-linux:~$ cd /root
smurf@ubuntu-linux:/root$
```

But he still has no write permissions, so he can't create or delete files in /root:

```
smurf@ubuntu-linux:/root$ rm gold
rm: remove write-protected regular empty file 'gold'? y
rm: cannot remove 'gold': Permission denied
smurf@ubuntu-linux:/root$ touch silver
touch: cannot touch 'silver': Permission denied
```

Let's add the write permission to others:

```
smurf@ubuntu-linux:/root$ su -
Password:
root@ubuntu-linux:~# chmod o+w /root
```

Finally, switch to user `smurf` and try to create or remove a file in `/root`:

```
smurf@ubuntu-linux:~$ cd /root
smurf@ubuntu-linux:/root$ rm gold
rm: remove write-protected regular empty file 'gold'? y
smurf@ubuntu-linux:/root$ touch silver
smurf@ubuntu-linux:/root$ ls
silver
```

So `smurf` can now create and delete files in `/root` as he has the write permission.

Using octal notation

Instead of the letters `r`, `w`, and `x`, you can use the numbers 4, 2, and 1 to set file permissions. Take a look at the following image:

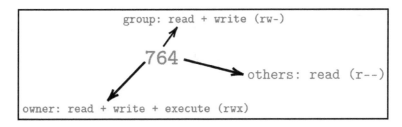

Figure 7: Understanding octal notation

Notice that the first number, 7, is basically the addition of the three numbers: 4 (r) + 2 (w) + 1 (x), which sets full permissions to the file owner. The second number, 6, is the addition of the two numbers: 4 (r) + 2 (w), which sets the read and write permissions to the group owner. Finally, the third number, 4, which sets the read permission to others.

I know what you are thinking: "Why would I want to do math when I can just use the literal notation `rwx`?" And trust me, I feel you. A lot of people prefer the literal notation over the numeric notation, but some people just love numbers way too much!

Let's do some practice with the octal notation. There are currently zero permissions on the file `mysmurf`:

```
smurf@ubuntu-linux:~$ ls -l mysmurf
---------- 1 smurf developers 64 Oct 23 13:38 mysmurf
```

We can use `777` to give full permissions to everyone:

```
smurf@ubuntu-linux:~$ chmod 777 mysmurf
smurf@ubuntu-linux:~$ ls -l mysmurf
-rwxrwxrwx 1 smurf developers 64 Oct 23 13:38 mysmurf
```

Cool! Now you can use the triplet `421` to give read permission for the owner, write permission for the group owner, and execute permission for others:

```
smurf@ubuntu-linux:~$ chmod 421 mysmurf
smurf@ubuntu-linux:~$ ls -l mysmurf
-r---w---x 1 smurf developers 64 Oct 23 13:38 mysmurf
```

Let's do one more example. What if you want to give full permissions to the owner, read permission for the group owner, and zero permissions for others? That's easy; the correct triplet will be `740`:

```
smurf@ubuntu-linux:~$ chmod 740 mysmurf
smurf@ubuntu-linux:~$ ls -l mysmurf
-rwxr----- 1 smurf developers 64 Oct 23 13:38 mysmurf
```

Numbers are easy to work with once you get the hang of it. Just remember that:

- `4`: Read
- `2`: Write
- `1`: Execute
- `0`: Zero permissions

The following table summarizes all the possible permissions combinations:

Number	Meaning	Literal Equivalence
0	Zero/No Permissions	---
1	Execute	--x
2	Write	-w-
3	Write + Execute	-wx
4	Read	r--
5	Read + Execute	r-x
6	Read + Write	rw-
7	Read + Write + Execute	rwx

Table 12: Octal notation versus literal notation

This chapter was a bit lengthy. Go take a break and then come back and attack the knowledge check exercises!

Knowledge check

For the following exercises, open up your Terminal and try to solve the following tasks:

1. Create a new user `abraham` with a user ID of `333`.
2. Create a new group `admins`.
3. Add user `abraham` to the `admins` group.
4. Make `admins` the group owner of the directory `/home/abraham`.
5. Members of the `admins` group can only list the contents of the directory `/home/abraham`.

True or false

1. `chmod a=rxw facts.txt` will have the same result as `chmod 777 facts.txt`.
2. `chmod a=rw facts.txt` will have the same result as `chmod 665 facts.txt`.
3. User `elliot` can have more than one primary group.

Piping and I/O Redirection 9

One of the main principles in Linux is that *Each program does one thing well* and thus, every Linux command is designed to accomplish a single task efficiently. In this chapter, you will learn how to use Linux pipes to unleash the real power of Linux commands by combining their functionality to carry out more complex tasks. You will also learn about I/O (input/output) redirection, which will enable you to read user input and save command output to a file.

Linux pipes

In Linux, you can use a pipe to send the output of one command to be the input (argument) of another command:

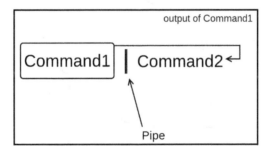

Figure 1 – A Linux pipe

A pipe is represented by the vertical bar character on your keyboard. Linux pipes are very useful as they allow you to accomplish a relatively complex task in an easy way, and throughout the book, you will see that they come in handy very often.

Before we do an example, let's first rename the `hard.txt` file to `facts.txt`, as we removed the `facts.txt` file back in Chapter 6, *Hard vs. Soft Links*:

```
elliot@ubuntu-linux:~$ mv hard.txt facts.txt
```

Now let's use the `head` command to view the first five lines of `facts.txt`:

```
elliot@ubuntu-linux:~$ head -n 5 facts.txt
Apples are red.
Grapes are green.
Bananas are yellow.
Cherries are red.
Sky is high.
```

Now I want to display only the fifth line `Sky is high.` of the file `facts.txt`; how can I do that?

That's where the power of Linux pipes comes into play. If you pipe the output of the previous command to the `tail -n 1` command, you will get the fifth line:

```
elliot@ubuntu-linux:~$ head -n 5 facts.txt | tail -n 1
Sky is high.
```

So by using a pipe, I was able to send the output of the command `head -n 5 facts.txt` to the input (argument) of the command `tail -n 1`.

Let's do another example. If you want to display the seventh line of the file `facts.txt`, then you will show the first seven lines using the `head` command, then use a pipe to `tail` the last line:

```
elliot@ubuntu-linux:~$ head -n 7 facts.txt | tail -n 1
Linux is awesome
```

You can also use more than one pipe at a time as demonstrated in the following diagram:

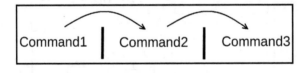

Figure 2: Two pipes

For example, you already know that the `lscpu` command displays your processor information. The fourth line of the `lscpu` command output shows how many CPUs your machine has. You can display the fourth line of the `lscpu` command by using two pipes:

```
elliot@ubuntu-linux:~$ lscpu | head -n 4 | tail -n 1
CPU(s):        1
```

So let's break down what happened here. The first pipe we used was to show the first four lines of the `lscpu` command:

```
elliot@ubuntu-linux:~$ lscpu | head -n 4
Architecture:      x86_64
CPU op-mode(s):    32-bit, 64-bit
Byte Order:        Little Endian
CPU(s):            1
```

We then used the second pipe to `tail` the last line, which gets us the fourth line in this case:

```
elliot@ubuntu-linux:~$ lscpu | head -n 4 | tail -n 1
CPU(s):            1
```

You can similarly display the second line of `lscpu`, which shows your CPU operation modes, but I will leave that for you to do as an exercise.

Input and output redirection

In this section, you will get to learn one of the coolest Linux features, which is I/O (input/output) redirection. Most Linux commands work with three different streams of data:

- Standard input (also referred to as `stdin`)
- Standard output (also referred to as `stdout`)
- Standard error (also referred to as `stderr`)

Most of the commands we have discussed so far produce some output. This output is sent to a special file called standard output (also referred to as `stdout`). By default, the standard output file is linked to the terminal, and that's why every time you run a command, you see the output on your terminal. Also, sometimes commands will produce error messages. These error messages are sent to another special file called standard error (also referred to as `stderr`), and it's also linked to the terminal by default.

Redirecting standard output

You know that running the `date` command will display the current date on your terminal:

```
elliot@ubuntu-linux:~$ date
Sat May 11 06:02:44 CST 2019
```

Now by using the greater than sign >, you can redirect the output of the `date` command to a file instead of your terminal! Have a look:

```
elliot@ubuntu-linux:~$ date > mydate.txt
```

As you can see, there is no output displayed on your screen! That's because the output got redirected to the file `mydate.txt`:

```
elliot@ubuntu-linux:~$ cat mydate.txt
Sat May 11 06:04:49 CST 2019
```

Cool! Let's try some more examples. You can print a line on your terminal with the `echo` command:

```
elliot@ubuntu-linux:~$ echo "Mars is a planet."
Mars is a planet.
```

If you want to redirect the output to a file named `planets.txt`, you can run the command:

```
elliot@ubuntu-linux:~$ echo "Mars is a planet." > planets.txt
elliot@ubuntu-linux:~$ cat planets.txt
Mars is a planet
```

Awesome! Notice that the file `planets.txt` was also created in the process. Now let's add more planets to the file `planets.txt`:

```
elliot@ubuntu-linux:~$ echo "Saturn is a planet." > planets.txt
elliot@ubuntu-linux:~$ cat planets.txt
Saturn is a planet.
```

Hmmm. We added the line "Saturn is a planet." but the line "Mars is a planet." is now removed! That's because redirecting standard output with > overwrites the file. What we need in this case is to append to the file and this can be done by using a double greater than sign >>. So now let's append the line "Mars is a planet." back to the file `planets.txt`:

```
elliot@ubuntu-linux:~$ echo "Mars is a planet." >> planets.txt
elliot@ubuntu-linux:~$ cat planets.txt
Saturn is a planet.
Mars is a planet.
```

Great! As you can see, it added the line "Mars is a planet." to the end of the file. Let's append one more planet:

```
elliot@ubuntu-linux:~$ echo "Venus is a planet." >> planets.txt
elliot@ubuntu-linux:~$ cat planets.txt
Saturn is a planet.
Mars is a planet.
Venus is a planet.
```

Awesome! One more thing you need to know here is that the standard output (stdout) is linked to file descriptor 1.

WHAT IS A FILE DESCRIPTOR?

A file descriptor is a number that uniquely identifies an open file in a computer's operating system.

And so running the command:

```
elliot@ubuntu-linux:~$ date > mydate.txt
```

Is the same as running the command:

```
elliot@ubuntu-linux:~$ date 1> mydate.txt
```

Notice that the 1 in 1> references file descriptor 1 (stdout).

Redirecting standard error

You will get an error message if you try to display the contents of a file that doesn't exist:

```
elliot@ubuntu-linux:~$ cat blabla
cat: blabla: No such file or directory
```

Now, this error message comes from standard error (stderr). If you try to redirect errors the same way we did with the standard output, it will not work:

```
elliot@ubuntu-linux:~$ cat blabla > error.txt
cat: blabla: No such file or directory
```

As you can see, it still displays the error message on your terminal. That's because stderr is linked to file descriptor 2. And thus, to redirect errors, you have to use 2>:

```
elliot@ubuntu-linux:~$ cat blabla 2> error.txt
```

Now if you displayed the contents of the file error.txt, you would see the error message:

```
elliot@ubuntu-linux:~$ cat error.txt
cat: blabla: No such file or directory
```

Let's try to remove a file that doesn't exist:

```
elliot@ubuntu-linux:~$ rm brrrr
rm: cannot remove 'brrrr': No such file or directory
```

This also produces an error message. We can append this error message to the file error.txt using 2>>:

```
elliot@ubuntu-linux:~$ rm brrrr 2>> error.txt
```

Now if you display the contents of the file error.txt:

```
elliot@ubuntu-linux:~$ cat error.txt
cat: blabla: No such file or directory
rm: cannot remove 'brrrr': No such file or directory
```

You will see both error messages.

Redirecting all output to the same file

There are some situations where you can get both standard output and an error message at the same time. For example, if you run the following command:

```
elliot@ubuntu-linux:~$ cat planets.txt blabla
Saturn is a planet.
Mars is a planet.
Venus is a planet.
cat: blabla: No such file or directory
```

You will see that it displayed the contents of the file planets.txt, but it also displayed an error message at the very last line (because there is no file blabla to concatenate).

You can choose to redirect the error to another file:

```
elliot@ubuntu-linux:~$ cat planets.txt blabla 2> err.txt
Saturn is a planet.
Mars is a planet.
Venus is a planet.
```

This way, you only see the standard output on the screen. Or you may choose to redirect the standard output:

```
elliot@ubuntu-linux:~$ cat planets.txt blabla 1> output.txt
cat: blabla: No such file or directory
```

This way, you only see the error on the screen. Now, what if you want to redirect both the standard output and the error to the same file? In this case, you have to run:

```
elliot@ubuntu-linux:~$ cat planets.txt blabla > all.txt 2>&1
```

&1 is referencing the standard output while 2> is referencing the standard error. So what we are basically saying here is: "Redirect the stderr to the same place we are redirecting the stdout."

Now if you displayed the contents of the file all.txt:

```
elliot@ubuntu-linux:~$ cat all.txt
Saturn is a planet.
Mars is a planet.
Venus is a planet.
cat: blabla: No such file or directory
```

You can see it includes both the stdout and stderr.

Discarding output

Sometimes you don't need to redirect output to anywhere; you just want to throw it away and get rid of it. In this case, you can redirect the output to /dev/null. This is often used with error messages. For example:

```
elliot@ubuntu-linux:~$ cat planets.txt blabla 2> /dev/null
Saturn is a planet.
Mars is a planet.
Venus is a planet.
```

This will redirect the error message to /dev/null. You can think of /dev/null as a garbage collector.

Redirecting standard input

Some Linux commands interact with the user input through the standard input (which is your keyboard by default). For example, the `read` command reads input from the user and stores it in a variable. For example, you can run the command `read weather`:

```
elliot@ubuntu-linux:~$ read weather
It is raining.
```

It will then wait for you to enter a line of text. I entered the line `It is raining.` and so it stored the line in the `weather` variable. You can use the `echo` command to display the contents of a variable:

```
elliot@ubuntu-linux:~$ echo $weather
It is raining.
```

Notice that you have to precede the variable name with a dollar sign. The `read` command is particularly useful in shell scripts, which we will cover later on. Now notice I wrote the line `It is raining.` using my keyboard. However, I can redirect standard input to come from a file instead using the less-than sign <, for example:

```
elliot@ubuntu-linux:~$ read message < mydate.txt
```

This will read the contents of the file `mydate.txt` and store it in the `message` variable:

```
elliot@ubuntu-linux:~$ echo $message
Sat May 11 06:34:52 CST 2019
```

As you can see, the variable `message` now has the same contents as the file `my- date.txt`.

Knowledge check

For the following exercises, open up your terminal and try to solve the following tasks:

1. Display only the *5th* line of the file `facts.txt`.
2. Save the output of the `free` command into a file named `system.txt`.
3. Append the output of the `lscpu` command to the file `system.txt`.
4. Run the command `rmdir /var` and redirect the error message to the file `error.txt`.

10

Analyzing and Manipulating Files

In this chapter, you will learn various Linux commands that will help you analyze and manipulate files. You will learn how to compare two files and get the file size. You will also learn how to reveal the type of a file and display the number of characters, words, and lines in a file. Furthermore, you will learn how to sort files, remove duplicate lines, and much more!

Spot the difference

You can use the `diff` command to compare the contents of two files and highlight the differences between them.

To demonstrate, let's first make a copy of the file `facts.txt` named `facts2.txt`:

```
elliot@ubuntu-linux:~$ cp facts.txt facts2.txt
```

Now let's append the line "`Brazil is a country.`" to the file `facts2.txt`:

```
elliot@ubuntu-linux:~$ echo "Brazil is a country." >> facts2.txt
```

Now, run the `diff` command on both files:

```
elliot@ubuntu-linux:~$ diff facts.txt facts2.txt
12a13
> Brazil is a country.
```

Cool! It outputs the difference between the two files, which in this case, is the line `Brazil is a country.`

Viewing file size

You can use the du command to view file size. **du** stands for **disk usage**. If you want to see how many bytes are in a file, you can run the du command with the -b option:

```
elliot@ubuntu-linux:~$ du -b facts.txt
210 facts.txt
```

The facts.txt file has 210 bytes. One character is equal to one byte in size, so now you know that the facts.txt file has exactly 210 characters.

You can also use the -h option, which will print the file size in a human-readable format. For example, to view the size of the dir1 directory and its contents, you can run:

```
elliot@ubuntu-linux:~$ du -h dir1
4.0K      dir1/cities
16K       dir1/directory2
24K       dir1
```

Counting characters, words, and lines

The word count wc command is yet another very handy command. It counts the number of lines, words, and characters in a file. For example, to display the number of lines in the file facts.txt, you can use the -l option:

```
elliot@ubuntu-linux:~$ wc -l facts.txt
12 facts.txt
```

There are a total of 12 lines in the file facts.txt. To display the number of words, you can use the -w option:

```
elliot@ubuntu-linux:~$ wc -w facts.txt
37 facts.txt
```

So there is a total of 37 words in the file facts.txt. To display the number of characters (bytes), you can use the -c option:

```
elliot@ubuntu-linux:~$ wc -c facts.txt
210 facts.txt
```

There is a total of 210 characters in the file `facts.txt`. Without any options, the `wc` command will display the number of lines, words, and characters side by side:

```
elliot@ubuntu-linux:~$ wc facts.txt
12 37 210 facts.txt
```

Viewing the file type

You can determine a file's type by using the `file` command. For example, if you want to determine the type of the file `/var`, you can run:

```
elliot@ubuntu-linux:~$ file /var
/var: directory
```

And as you would expect, the output shows that `/var` is a directory. If you want to show the type of the `facts.txt` file, you can run:

```
elliot@ubuntu-linux:~$ file facts.txt
facts.txt: ASCII text
```

The output shows that `facts.txt` is an ASCII text file.

WHAT IS ASCII?

ASCII, which is short for **American Standard Code for Information Interchange**, is a code for representing 128 English characters as numbers, with each letter assigned a number from 0 to 127.

Your computer doesn't understand human language (letters), just numbers! And so each character in the English language is translated to a number. Your computer sees any text file as just a bunch of numbers piled together!

Now let's create a soft link named `soft.txt` to the `facts.txt` file:

```
elliot@ubuntu-linux:~$ ln -s soft.txt facts.txt
```

And run the `file` command on `soft.txt`:

```
elliot@ubuntu-linux:~$ file soft.txt
soft.txt: symbolic link to facts.txt
```

As you can see, it shows that `soft.txt` is a symbolic (soft) link to `facts.txt`.

Sorting files

You can use the `sort` command to sort text files. For example, you can view the `facts.txt` file in sorted alphabetical order by running the command:

```
elliot@ubuntu-linux:~$ sort facts.txt
Apples are red.
Bananas are yellow.
Cherries are red.
Cherries are red.
Cherries are red.
Cherries are red.
Earth is round.
Grapes are green.
Grass is green.
Linux is awesome!
Sky is high.
Swimming is a sport.
```

You can also use the `-r` option to sort in reverse order:

```
elliot@ubuntu-linux:~$ sort -r facts.txt
Swimming is a sport.
Sky is high.
Linux is awesome!
Grass is green.
Grapes are green.
Earth is round.
Cherries are red.
Cherries are red.
Cherries are red.
Cherries are red.
Bananas are yellow.
Apples are red.
```

You can also use the `-n` option to sort by numerical values rather than literal values.

Showing unique lines

You can use the `uniq` command to omit repeated lines in a file. For example, notice that the line `Cherries are red.` is included four times in the file `facts.txt`:

To view `facts.txt` without repeated lines, you can run:

```
elliot@ubuntu-linux:~$ uniq facts.txt
Apples are red.
Grapes are green.
Bananas are yellow.
Cherries are red.
Sky is high.
Earth is round.
Linux is awesome!
Cherries are red.
Grass is green.
Swimming is a sport.
```

Notice that `Cherries are red.` is still shown twice in the output. That's because the `uniq` command only omits repeated lines but not duplicates! If you want to omit duplicates, you have to `sort` the file first and then use a pipe to apply the `uniq` command on the sorted output:

```
elliot@ubuntu-linux:~$ sort facts.txt | uniq
Apples are red.
Bananas are yellow.
Cherries are red.
Earth is round.
Grapes are green.
Grass is green.
Linux is awesome!
Sky is high.
Swimming is a sport.
```

Boom! We have successfully omitted repeated and duplicate lines.

Searching for patterns

The `grep` command is one of the most popular and useful commands in Linux. You can use `grep` to print the lines of text that match a specific pattern. For example, if you want to only display the lines that contain the word `green` in `facts.txt`, you can run:

```
elliot@ubuntu-linux:~$ grep green facts.txt
Grapes are green.
Grass is green.
```

As you can see, it only printed the two lines that contain the word `green`.

The `grep` command can also be very useful when used with pipes. For example, to only list the `txt` files in your home directory, you can run the command:

```
elliot@ubuntu-linux:~$ ls | grep txt
all.txt
error.txt
facts2.txt
facts.txt
Mars.txt
mydate.txt
output.txt
planets.txt
soft.txt
```

You can use the `-i` option to make your search case-insensitive. For example, if you want to print the lines that contain the word `Earth` in `facts.txt`, then use the command:

```
elliot@ubuntu-linux:~$ grep earth facts.txt
elliot@ubuntu-linux:~$
```

This will show no result because `grep` is case-sensitive by default. However, if you pass the `-i` option:

```
elliot@ubuntu-linux:~$ grep -i earth facts.txt
Earth is round.
```

It will make the search case-insensitive, and hence it will display the line `Earth is round.`

The stream editor

You can use the stream editor command `sed` to filter and transform text. For example, to substitute the word `Sky` with the word `Cloud` in `facts.txt`, you can run the command:

```
elliot@ubuntu-linux:~$ sed 's/Sky/Cloud/' facts.txt
Apples are red.
Grapes are green.
Bananas are yellow.
Cherries are red.
Cloud is high.
Earth is round.
Linux is awesome!
Cherries are red.
Cherries are red.
Cherries are red.
```

```
Grass is green.
Swimming is a sport.
```

As you can see in the output, the word `Sky` is replaced with `Cloud`. However, the file `facts.txt` is not edited. To overwrite (edit) the file, you can use the `-i` option:

```
elliot@ubuntu-linux:~$ sed -i 's/Sky/Cloud/' facts.txt
elliot@ubuntu-linux:~$ cat facts.txt
Apples are red.
Grapes are green.
Bananas are yellow.
Cherries are red.
Cloud is high.
Earth is round.
Linux is awesome!
Cherries are red.
Cherries are red.
Cherries are red.
Grass is green.
Swimming is a sport.
```

As you can see, the change is reflected in the file.

Translating characters

You can use the `tr` command to translate characters. I am not talking about translating to different languages here; instead, I am using the second meaning of the word translate, that is, to change from one form to another.

If you read the `man` page of the `tr` command, you will see in the description that it: **Translate[s], squeeze[s], and/or delete[s] characters from standard input, writing to standard output.** And so the `tr` command doesn't accept any arguments.

One popular use of the `tr` command is to change lower case letters to upper case (or vice versa). For example, if you want to display all the words in `facts.txt` in upper case, you can run:

```
elliot@ubuntu-linux:~$ cat facts.txt | tr [:lower:] [:upper:]
APPLES ARE RED.
GRAPES ARE GREEN.
BANANAS ARE YELLOW.
CHERRIES ARE RED.
CLOUD IS HIGH.
EARTH IS ROUND.
LINUX IS AWESOME!
```

```
CHERRIES ARE RED.
CHERRIES ARE RED.
CHERRIES ARE RED.
GRASS IS GREEN.
SWIMMING IS A SPORT.
```

You can also display all the words in lower case:

```
elliot@ubuntu-linux:~$ cat facts.txt | tr [:upper:] [:lower:]
apples are red.
grapes are green.
bananas are yellow.
cherries are red.
cloud is high.
earth is round.
linux is awesome!
cherries are red.
cherries are red.
cherries are red.
grass is green.
swimming is a sport.
```

You can also use the -d option to delete characters. For example, to remove all spaces in facts.txt, you can run:

```
elliot@ubuntu-linux:~$ cat facts.txt | tr -d ' '
Applesarered.
Grapesaregreen.
Bananasareyellow.
Cherriesarered.
Cloudishigh.
Earthisround.
Linuxisawesome!
Cherriesarered.
Cherriesarered.
Cherriesarered.
Grassisgreen.
Swimmingisasport.
```

A COOL TIP

The tr command doesn't change (edit) the contents of the file. It just writes the changes to the standard output. However, you can use output redirection to store the output into another file.

For example, running the command:

```
elliot@ubuntu-linux:~$ cat facts.txt | tr [:lower:] [:upper:] > upper.txt
```

will store the output of the command:

```
cat facts.txt | tr [:lower:] [:upper:]
```

into the file upper.txt.

Cutting text

If you want to view only a part (or a section) of a file, then the cut command can prove very helpful. For instance, you can see that each line in the facts.txt file consists of several words that are separated by a single space. If you only want to view the first word in each line (first column/field), then you can run the following command:

```
elliot@ubuntu-linux:~$ cut -d ' ' -f1 facts.txt
Apples
Grapes
Bananas
Cherries
Cloud
Earth
Linux
Cherries
Cherries
Cherries
Grass
Swimming
```

The -d option is the delimiter, and it has to be a single character. In this case, I chose the delimiter to be the space character ' '. I also used the -f1 option to view only the first field (column).

If you want to view the third word of each line (third field), then you can use -f3 instead of -f1 as follows:

```
elliot@ubuntu-linux:~$ cut -d ' ' -f3 facts.txt
red.
green.
yellow.
red.
high.
round.
```

```
awesome!
red.
red.
red.
green.
a
```

You can also select more than one field at a time. For example, to view the first and the third word of each line, you can use -f1,3:

```
elliot@ubuntu-linux:~$ cut -d ' ' -f1,3 facts.txt
Apples red.
Grapes green.
Bananas yellow.
Cherries red.
Cloud high.
Earth round.
Linux awesome!
Cherries red.
Cherries red.
Cherries red.
Grass green.
Swimming a
```

Text processing with awk

awk is a very powerful tool you can use in Linux to analyze and process text. In fact, awk is not like any command you have learned so far, and that's because awk is actually a programming language. You will find books that are solely written to explain and discuss the use of awk. However, I am only going to show you the very basics of awk here, and you can dig further on your own.

You can use awk to achieve the same functionality as the cut command. For example, to view the first word of each line in the file facts.txt, you can run:

```
elliot@ubuntu-linux:~$ awk '{print $1}' facts.txt
Apples
Grapes
Bananas
Cherries
Cloud
Earth
Linux
Cherries
Cherries
```

```
Cherries
Grass
Swimming
```

Notice we didn't need to specify the space character ' ' as a delimiter as we did with the `cut` command and that's because `awk` is smart enough to figure it out on its own. You can also view more than one field at a time; for example, to view the first and the second word of each line, you can run:

```
elliot@ubuntu-linux:~$ awk '{print $1,$2}' facts.txt
Apples are
Grapes are
Bananas are
Cherries are
Cloud is
Earth is
Linux is
Cherries are
Cherries are
Cherries are
Grass is
Swimming is
```

One advantage `awk` has over `cut` is that `awk` is smart enough to separate the file into different fields even if there is more than one character separating each field. The `cut` command only works if the file has a single delimiter like a single space, a colon, a comma, and so on.

To demonstrate, create a file named `animals.txt` and insert these four lines:

```
fox         is smart
whale is    big
cheetah  is             fast
penguin     is cute
```

Do not edit the format; keep the spaces messed up:

```
elliot@ubuntu-linux:~$ cat animals.txt
fox         is smart
whale is    big
cheetah  is             fast
penguin     is cute
```

Now, if you try to use the `cut` command to only show the third word in each line, it will fail because there is more than one space separating each word.

However, `awk` is smart enough to figure it out:

```
elliot@ubuntu-linux:~$ awk '{print $3}' animals.txt
smart
big
fast
cute
```

As you can see, the third word in each line is displayed. You can also use `awk` to search for patterns, just like the `grep` command. For example, to print the lines that contain the word `red` in `facts.txt`, you can run the command:

```
elliot@ubuntu-linux:~$ awk '/red/{print}' facts.txt
Apples are red.
Cherries are red.
Cherries are red.
Cherries are red.
Cherries are red.
```

Wildcard characters

The wildcard characters are special characters in Linux, and they are used to specify a group (class) of characters. `Table 13` lists all the Linux wildcards:

Wildcard	What it does
`*`	Matches any character(s).
`?`	Matches any single character.
`[characters]`	Matches the characters that are members of the set characters. For example, `[abc]` will match the characters a, b, or c.
`[!characters]`	Matches any character that is not a member of the set characters. It is basically the negation of `[characters]`. For example, `[!abc]` will match any character that is not a, b, or c.
`[[:class:]]`	Matches any character that is a member of the character class.

Table 13: Linux wildcards

You have already seen character classes before when we were discussing the `tr` command. Remember `[:lower:]` and `[:upper:]` represent lower and upper case letters, these are two examples of character classes. `Table 14` lists the most common character classes:

Character Class	What it represents
`[:alnum:]`	Represents all the alphanumeric letters, that is, any letter or number.
`[:alpha:]`	Represents all alphabetic letters, that is, any letter.
`[:digit:]`	Represents all digits, that is, any number.
`[:lower:]`	Represents any lower case letter.
`[:upper:]`	Represents any upper case letter.

Table 14: Character classes

Ok, enough with all that theory! Let's look at some examples. You can use the `*` wildcard to list all the `txt` files in your home directory:

```
elliot@ubuntu-linux:~$ ls -l *.txt
-rw-rw-r-- 1 elliot elliot  96 May 11 07:01 all.txt
-rw-rw-r-- 1 elliot elliot  91 May 12 06:10 animals.txt
-rw-rw-r-- 1 elliot elliot  92 May 11 06:48 error.txt
-rw-rw-r-- 1 elliot elliot 231 May 11 08:28 facts2.txt
-rw-rw-r-- 1 elliot elliot 212 May 11 18:37 facts.txt
-rw-rw-r-- 1 elliot elliot  18 May 11 06:12 Mars.txt
-rw-rw-r-- 1 elliot elliot  29 May 11 06:34 mydate.txt
-rw-rw-r-- 1 elliot elliot  57 May 11 07:00 output.txt
-rw-rw-r-- 1 elliot elliot  57 May 11 06:20 planets.txt
lrwxrwxrwx 1 elliot elliot   9 May  8 22:02 soft.txt -> facts.txt
-rw-rw-r-- 1 elliot elliot 212 May 12 05:09 upper.txt
```

If you want to list only the filenames that begin with the letter `f`, you can use `f*`:

```
elliot@ubuntu-linux:~$ ls -l f*
-rw-rw-r-- 1 elliot elliot 231 May 11 08:28 facts2.txt
-rw-rw-r-- 1 elliot elliot 212 May 11 18:37 facts.txt
```

If you want to list the filenames that contain three letters followed by a `.txt` extension, then you can use the `?` wildcard:

```
elliot@ubuntu-linux:~$ ls -l ???.txt
-rw-rw-r-- 1 elliot elliot 96 May 11 07:01 all.txt
```

You can also use more than one wildcard at the same time. For example, if you want to list only the filenames that begin with the letter a or f, you can use the `[af]` wildcard followed by the `*` wildcard:

```
elliot@ubuntu-linux:~$ ls -l [af]*
-rw-rw-r-- 1 elliot elliot 96 May 11 07:01 all.txt
-rw-rw-r-- 1 elliot elliot 91 May 12 06:10 animals.txt
-rw-rw-r-- 1 elliot elliot 231 May 11 08:28 facts2.txt
-rw-rw-r-- 1 elliot elliot 212 May 11 18:37 facts.txt
```

You can also use set negations, for example, to list all the `.txt` filenames that begin with any letter other than f, you can run use `[!f]*`:

```
elliot@ubuntu-linux:~$ ls -l [!f]*.txt
-rw-rw-r-- 1 elliot elliot 96 May 11 07:01 all.txt
-rw-rw-r-- 1 elliot elliot 91 May 12 06:10 animals.txt
-rw-rw-r-- 1 elliot elliot 92 May 11 06:48 error.txt
-rw-rw-r-- 1 elliot elliot 18 May 11 06:12 Mars.txt
-rw-rw-r-- 1 elliot elliot 29 May 11 06:34 mydate.txt
-rw-rw-r-- 1 elliot elliot 57 May 11 07:00 output.txt
-rw-rw-r-- 1 elliot elliot 57 May 11 06:20 planets.txt
lrwxrwxrwx 1 elliot elliot 9 May 8 22:02 soft.txt -> facts.txt
-rw-rw-r-- 1 elliot elliot 212 May 12 05:09 upper.txt
```

Now, before we do some examples of character classes, let's create the following four files:

```
elliot@ubuntu-linux:~$ touch One TWO 7wonders GTA1
```

Now, if you want to list the filenames that end with an upper case letter, you can use the character class `[:upper:]` as follows:

```
elliot@ubuntu-linux:~$ ls -l *[[:upper:]]
-rw-rw-r-- 1 elliot elliot 0 May 12 18:14 TWO
```

Notice that the character class itself is also surrounded by brackets.

If you want to list the filenames that begin with a digit (number), you can use the character class `[:digit:]` as follows:

```
elliot@ubuntu-linux:~$ ls -l [[:digit:]]*
-rw-rw-r-- 1 elliot elliot 0 May 12 18:14 7wonders
```

And the only match was the file 7wonders.

Regular expressions

Up until now, we have been using wildcards with filenames. **Regular expressions (Regex** for short) is another Linux feature that will allow you to search for a specific pattern in text files. Regex is also often used with the `grep` command.

`Table 15` lists the most common regular expressions and their uses:

Regex	What it does
*	Matches zero or more of the preceding characters or expressions.
+	Matches one or more of the preceding characters or expressions.
.	Matches any single character. Same as the ? wildcard.
^	Matches the following expression at the beginning of the line. For example, ^dog will match all lines that begin with the word dog.
$	Matches the preceding expression at the end of the line. For example, bird$ will match all lines that end with the word bird.
\	Used as an escape character to match a special character following the backslash. For example, * matches a star (asterisk).
[characters]	Matches the characters that are members of the set characters. For example, [abc] will match the characters a,b, or c.
[^characters]	Matches any character that is not a member of the set characters. It is basically the negation of [characters]. For example, [!abc] will match any character that is not a,b, or c.
{x,y}	Matches x to y occurrences of the preceding expression.
{x}	Matches exactly x occurrences of the preceding expression.
{x,}	Matches x or more occurrences of the preceding expression.
{,x}	Matches no more than x occurrences of the preceding expression.

Table 15: Regular expressions

Well, that's a long list of regular expressions. Let's do some practice with them. Create a file named `practice.txt` that contains the following text:

```
111222333
my cell number is 123-456-789.
you are a smart man
man is a linux command.
man ... oh man.
dog is a cute pet.
g
dg
ddg
```

```
dddg
Two stars **
tan
tantan
tantantan
```

To use regular expressions with the `grep` command, you can either use the `-E` option or the `egrep` command. The `egrep` command is simply an alias to `grep` `-E`.

Now, notice that the `*` regex is different from the `*` wildcard. To realize the difference, run the command:

elliot@ubuntu-linux:~$ egrep d*g practice.txt

This will give the following output:

```
elliot@ubuntu-linux:~$ egrep d*g practice.txt
dog is a cute pet.
g
dg
ddg
dddg
elliot@ubuntu-linux:~$
```

Figure 1: The * regex

Notice that `d*g` didn't match the word `dog`; instead, it matched with:

- g (zero occurrences of d)
- dg (one occurrence of d)
- ddg (two occurrences of d)
- dddg (three occurrences of d)

That's because the `*` `regex` matches zero or more of the preceding characters or expressions, unlike the `*` `wildcard`, which matches any character.

Now, to match one or more occurrences of d followed by g, you can use the regex d+g:

elliot@ubuntu-linux:~$ egrep d+g practice.txt
dg
ddg
dddg

To match the special character ∗, you can use the backslash between single or double quotes as follows:

```
elliot@ubuntu-linux:~$ egrep "\*" practice.txt
Two stars **
```

To match any pattern that contains the letter m followed by any single character, then the letter n, you can run:

```
elliot@ubuntu-linux:~$ egrep m.n practice.txt
you are a smart man
man is a linux command.
man ... oh man.
```

To match the lines that begin with the word man, you can run:

```
elliot@ubuntu-linux:~$ egrep ^man practice.txt
man is a linux command.
man ... oh man.
```

To match the lines that end with the word man, you can run:

```
elliot@ubuntu-linux:~$ egrep man$ practice.txt
you are a smart man
```

You can use character classes as well. For example, to search for all the lines that contain at least one digit, you can run:

```
elliot@ubuntu-linux:~$ egrep "[[:digit:]]{1,}" practice.txt
111222333
my cell number is 123-456-789.
```

You can also search for a specific pattern like telephone numbers:

```
elliot@ubuntu-linux:~$ egrep "[[:digit:]]{3}-[[:digit:]]{3}-[[:digit:]]{3}"
practice.txt
my cell number is 123-456-789.
```

This will search for the lines that contain three digits followed by a dash, then three digits followed by another dash, then another three digits.

I know you think `regex` is complicated, and it's hard to remember all of that, you are right! That's why there is a man page that has all the regular expressions we discussed:

```
elliot@ubuntu-linux:~$ man regex
```

Also, the `grep` man page includes explanations for all the regular expressions discussed in this chapter.

Knowledge check

For the following exercises, open up your Terminal and try to solve the following tasks:

1. Display the size (in bytes) of the file /etc/hostname.
2. Display only the group names in the file /etc/group.
3. Display the total number of lines in the file /etc/services.
4. Display only the lines that contain the word "bash" in the file /etc/passwd.
5. Display the output of the uptime command in all uppercase letters.

11
Let's Play Find and Seek

We all forget where we put our stuff sometimes; I always forget where I keep my wallet and where I save my files. I am pretty sure that you also forget where you keep your files, and so in this chapter, you will learn two different ways you can use to search and locate files.

The locate command

If you know the name of your file but you are unsure of the file's location, you can use the `locate` command to get the file's path.

The `locate` command searches for a file location in a prebuilt file database, and thus it's crucial to update the file database before using the `locate` command. If you don't update the database, the `locate` command may fail to retrieve the location of newly created files.

Updating the file database

To update the file database, you have to run the `updatedb` command as the root user:

```
root@ubuntu-linux:~# updatedb
```

The `updatedb` command will not display any output.

Now, let's say we forgot the location of the file `facts.txt`, and we don't remember where it is; in this case, you can run the `locate` command followed by the filename:

```
root@ubuntu-linux:~# locate facts.txt
/home/elliot/facts.txt
/var/facts.txt
```

BOOM! It displayed the location of the file `facts.txt`.

Now I will show you what will happen if you search for a newly created file without updating the file database.

Create an empty file named `ghost.txt` in the `/home` directory:

```
root@ubuntu-linux:/# touch /home/ghost.txt
```

Now try searching for the file `ghost.txt`:

```
root@ubuntu-linux:/# locate ghost.txt
root@ubuntu-linux:/#
```

The `locate` command couldn't find it! Why is that?........ That's because you created a new file, and the file database doesn't know about it yet. You have to run the `updatedb` command first to update the file database:

```
root@ubuntu-linux:/# updatedb
root@ubuntu-linux:/# locate ghost.txt
/home/ghost.txt
```

YES! After you update the file database, the `locate` command can now get the location of the file `ghost.txt`.

You can also use wildcards with the `locate` command. For example, `locate *.log` will search for all the log files in your system. You can also use the `-r` option to enable `regex` in your search.

The find command

The `find` command is a much more powerful command you can use to search for files in Linux. Unlike the `locate` command, the `find` command runs in real time, so you don't need to update any file database. The general syntax of the `find` command is as follows:

```
find [starting-point(s)] [options] [expression]
```

The `find` command will search under each starting-point (directory) you specify.

For example, to search for all the `.txt` files under your `/home` directory, you can run:

```
root@ubuntu-linux:~# find /home -name "*.txt"
/home/elliot/facts2.txt
/home/elliot/dir1/directory2/file1.txt
/home/elliot/dir1/directory2/file3.txt
/home/elliot/dir1/directory2/file2.txt
```

```
/home/elliot/soft.txt
/home/elliot/facts.txt
/home/elliot/practise.txt
/home/elliot/upper.txt
/home/elliot/mydate.txt
/home/elliot/all.txt
/home/elliot/Mars.txt
/home/elliot/output.txt
/home/elliot/planets.txt
/home/elliot/error.txt
/home/elliot/animals.txt
/home/ghost.txt
```

The -name option searches for filename; there are many other options you can use with the find command.

The -type option searches for file type; for example, to search for all the directories in /home/elliot/dir1, you can run:

```
root@ubuntu-linux:~# find /home/elliot/dir1 -type d
/home/elliot/dir1
/home/elliot/dir1/cities
/home/elliot/dir1/directory2
```

Notice it only listed the directories in /home/elliot/dir1. To list regular files instead, you can run:

```
root@ubuntu-linux:~# find /home/elliot/dir1 -type f
/home/elliot/dir1/cities/paris
/home/elliot/dir1/cities/london
/home/elliot/dir1/cities/berlin
/home/elliot/dir1/directory2/file1.txt
/home/elliot/dir1/directory2/file3.txt
/home/elliot/dir1/directory2/file2.txt
```

To search for both regular files and directories, you can use a comma:

```
root@ubuntu-linux:~# find /home/elliot/dir1 -type d,f
/home/elliot/dir1
/home/elliot/dir1/cities
/home/elliot/dir1/cities/paris
/home/elliot/dir1/cities/london
/home/elliot/dir1/cities/berlin
/home/elliot/dir1/directory2
/home/elliot/dir1/directory2/file1.txt
/home/elliot/dir1/directory2/file3.txt
/home/elliot/dir1/directory2/file2.txt
```

Now as the root user create the two files `large.txt` and `LARGE.TXT` in `/root`:

```
root@ubuntu-linux:~# touch large.txt LARGE.TXT
```

Let's say you forgot where these two files are located; in this case, you can use / as your starting-point:

```
root@ubuntu-linux:~# find / -name large.txt
/root/large.txt
```

Notice it only listed the location of `large.txt`. What if you wanted the other file `LARGE.TXT` as well? In this case, You can use the `-iname` option, which makes the search case insensitive:

```
root@ubuntu-linux:~# find / -iname large.txt
/root/LARGE.TXT
/root/large.txt
```

Let's append the line "12345" to the file `large.txt`:

```
root@ubuntu-linux:~# echo 12345 >> large.txt
```

Notice the size of the files `large.txt` and `LARGE.txt`:

```
root@ubuntu-linux:~# du -b large.txt LARGE.TXT
6 large.txt
0 LARGE.TXT
```

The file `LARGE.TXT` is zero bytes in size because it's empty. You can use the `-size` option to search for files based on their size.

For example, to search for empty files under the `/root` directory, you can run the command:

```
root@ubuntu-linux:~# find /root -size 0c
/root/LARGE.TXT
```

As you can see, it listed `LARGE.TXT` as it has zero characters; 0c means zero characters (or bytes). Now, if you want to search for files of size 6 bytes under `/root`, you can run:

```
root@ubuntu-linux:~# find /root -size 6c
/root/large.txt
```

As you can see, it listed the file `large.txt`.

You can even use size ranges in your search; Table 16 shows you some examples of using size ranges with the find command.

Command	What it does
find / -size +100M	Will search for all the files that are bigger than 100 MB.
find / -size -5c	Will search for all the files that are smaller than 5 bytes.
find / -size +50M -size -100M	Will search for all the files that are bigger than 50 MB, but smaller than 100 MB.
find / -size +1G	Will search for all the files that are bigger than 1 GB.

Table 16: Using size range

The -mtime and -atime options search for files based on modification and access times. The -exec is also a useful command option that allows you to run another command on the find results.

For example, you can do a long-listing on all the empty files in /root by running the command:

```
root@ubuntu-linux:~# find /root -size 0c -exec ls -l {} +
-rw-r--r-- 1 root root 0 May 16 14:31 /root/LARGE.TXT
```

A lot of people forget to include {} + when using the -exec option; {} + references all the files that are found in the find results.

You can use any command you want with the -exec option. For example, instead of long-listing, you may want to remove the files you get from the find results. In this case, you can run:

```
root@ubuntu-linux:~# find /root -size 0c -exec rm {} +
```

Now the file LARGE.TXT is removed:

```
root@ubuntu-linux:~# ls -l LARGE.TXT
ls: cannot access 'LARGE.TXT': No such file or directory
```

I highly recommend that you read the find man pages to explore the numerous other options that can be used.

Knowledge check

For the following exercises, open up your Terminal and try to solve the following tasks:

1. Use the `locate` command to find the path of the file `boot.log`.
2. Find all the files that are bigger than 50 MB in size.
3. Find all the files that are between 70 MB and 100 MB in size.
4. Find all the files that are owned by the user `smurf`.
5. Find all the files that are owned by the group `developers`.

12
You Got a Package

In this chapter, you will learn how to manage software applications on your Linux system. You will learn how to use the Debian package manager to download, install, remove, search, and update software packages.

What is a package?

In Linux, a package is a compressed archive file that contains all the necessary files for a particular software application to run. For example, a web browser like Firefox comes in a package that has all the files needed for Firefox to run.

The role of a package manager

Package managers are programs that we use in Linux to manage packages; that is, to download, install, remove, search, and update packages. Keep in mind that different Linux distributions have different package managers. For example, `dpkg`, which stands for Debian package manager, is the package manager for Ubuntu and other Debian-based Linux distributions. On the other hand, RedHat-based Linux distributions like Fedora and CentOS use `rpm`, which stands for RedHat Package Manager. Other Linux distributions like SUSE use `zypper` as the package manager and so on.

Where do packages come from?

Very rarely will you find experienced Linux users going to a website to download a software package as Windows or macOS users do. Instead, each Linux distribution has its list of sources from where it gets the majority of its software packages. These sources are also referred to as **repositories**. The following figure illustrates the process of downloading packages on your Linux system:

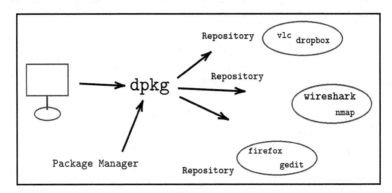

Figure 1: Packages live in repositories. Notice that the packages are stored across multiple repositories

How to download packages

On Ubuntu and other Debian Linux distributions, you can use the command-line utility apt-get to manage packages. Behind the scenes, apt-get makes use of the package manager dpkg. To download a package, you can run the command apt-get download followed by the package name:

```
apt-get download package_name
```

As the root user, change to the /tmp directory:

```
root@ubuntu-linux:~# cd /tmp
```

To download the cmatrix package, you can run the command:

```
root@ubuntu-linux:/tmp# apt-get download cmatrix
Get:1 http://ca.archive.ubuntu.com/ubuntu bionic/universe amd64 cmatrix
amd64
1.2a-5build3 [16.1 kB]
Fetched 16.1 kB in 1s (32.1 kB/s)
```

The `cmatrix` package will be downloaded in `/tmp`:

```
root@ubuntu-linux:/tmp# ls
cmatrix_1.2a-5build3_amd64.deb
```

Notice the `.deb` extension in the package name, which signals that it's a Debian package. On RedHat distributions, package names end with the `.rpm` extension. You can list the files inside the `cmatrix` package by running the command `dpkg -c` as follows:

```
root@ubuntu-linux:/tmp# dpkg -c cmatrix_1.2a-5build3_amd64.deb
drwxr-xr-x root/root      0 2018-04-03 06:17 ./
drwxr-xr-x root/root      0 2018-04-03 06:17 ./usr/
drwxr-xr-x root/root      0 2018-04-03 06:17 ./usr/bin/
-rwxr-xr-x root/root  18424 2018-04-03 06:17 ./usr/bin/cmatrix
drwxr-xr-x root/root      0 2018-04-03 06:17 ./usr/share/
drwxr-xr-x root/root      0 2018-04-03 06:17 ./usr/share/consolefonts/
-rw-r--r-- root/root   4096 1999-05-13 08:55
./usr/share/consolefonts/matrix.fnt
drwxr-xr-x root/root      0 2018-04-03 06:17 ./usr/share/doc/
drwxr-xr-x root/root      0 2018-04-03 06:17 ./usr/share/doc/cmatrix/
-rw-r--r-- root/root   2066 2000-04-03 19:29 ./usr/share/doc/cmatrix/README
-rw-r--r-- root/root    258 1999-05-13 09:12 ./usr/share/doc/cmatrix/TODO
-rw-r--r-- root/root   1128 2018-04-03 06:17
./usr/share/doc/cmatrix/copyright
drwxr-xr-x root/root      0 2018-04-03 06:17 ./usr/share/man/
drwxr-xr-x root/root      0 2018-04-03 06:17 ./usr/share/man/man1/
-rw-r--r-- root/root    932 2018-04-03 06:17
./usr/share/man/man1/cmatrix.1.gz
drwxr-xr-x root/root      0 2018-04-03 06:17 ./usr/share/menu/
-rw-r--r-- root/root    392 2018-04-03 06:17 ./usr/share/menu/cmatrix
```

Notice that we only downloaded the package, but we didn't install it yet. Nothing will happen if you run the `cmatrix` command:

```
root@ubuntu-linux:/tmp# cmatrix
bash: /usr/bin/cmatrix: No such file or directory
```

How to install packages

You can use the `-i` option with the `dpkg` command to install a downloaded package:

```
root@ubuntu-linux:/tmp# dpkg -i cmatrix_1.2a-5build3_amd64.deb
Selecting previously unselected package cmatrix.
(Reading database ... 178209 files and directories currently installed.)
Preparing to unpack cmatrix_1.2a-5build3_amd64.deb ...
```

```
Unpacking cmatrix (1.2a-5build3) ...
Setting up cmatrix (1.2a-5build3) ...
Processing triggers for man-db (2.8.3-2ubuntu0.1) ...
root@ubuntu-linux:/tmp#
```

And that's it! Now run the `cmatrix` command:

```
root@ubuntu-linux:/tmp# cmatrix
```

You will see the matrix running on your terminal like in the following image:

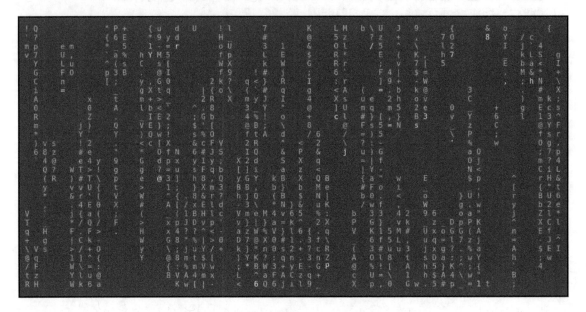

Figure 2: cmatrix

We have taken the long way to install the `cmatrix` package. We first downloaded the package, and then we installed it. You can install a package right away (without downloading it) by running the command `apt-get install` followed by the package name:

```
apt-get install package_name
```

For example, you can install the **GNOME Chess** game by running the command:

```
root@ubuntu-linux:/tmp# apt-get install gnome-chess
Reading package lists... Done
Building dependency tree
Reading state information... Done
Suggested packages:
```

```
   bbchess crafty fairymax fruit glaurung gnuchess phalanx sjeng stockfish
toga2
The following NEW packages will be installed:
   gnome-chess
0 upgraded, 1 newly installed, 0 to remove and 357 not upgraded.
Need to get 0 B/1,514 kB of archives.
After this operation, 4,407 kB of additional disk space will be used.
Selecting previously unselected package gnome-chess.
(Reading database ... 178235 files and directories currently installed.)
Preparing to unpack .../gnome-chess_1%3a3.28.1-1_amd64.deb ...
Unpacking gnome-chess (1:3.28.1-1) ...
Processing triggers for mime-support (3.60ubuntu1) ...
Processing triggers for desktop-file-utils (0.23-1ubuntu3.18.04.2) ...
Processing triggers for libglib2.0-0:amd64 (2.56.3-0ubuntu0.18.04.1) ...
Setting up gnome-chess (1:3.28.1-1) ...
Processing triggers for man-db (2.8.3-2ubuntu0.1) ...
Processing triggers for gnome-menus (3.13.3-11ubuntu1.1) ...
Processing triggers for hicolor-icon-theme (0.17-2) ...
```

Now you can start the game by running the gnome-chess command:

```
root@ubuntu-linux:/tmp# gnome-chess
```

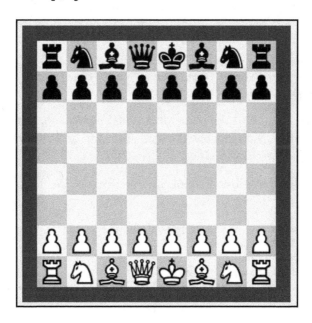

Figure 3: GNOME Chess

How to remove packages

You can easily remove a package by running the command `apt-get remove` followed by the package name:

```
apt-get remove package_name
```

For example, if you are tired of the matrix lifestyle and have decided to remove the `cmatrix` package, you can run:

```
root@ubuntu-linux:/tmp# apt-get remove cmatrix
Reading package lists... Done
Building dependency tree
Reading state information... Done
The following packages will be REMOVED:
    cmatrix
0 upgraded, 0 newly installed, 1 to remove and 357 not upgraded.
After this operation, 49.2 kB disk space will be freed.
Do you want to continue? [Y/n] y
(Reading database ... 178525 files and directories currently installed.)
Removing cmatrix (1.2a-5build3) ...
Processing triggers for man-db (2.8.3-2ubuntu0.1) ...
```

Now, if you run the `cmatrix` command, you will get an error:

```
root@ubuntu-linux:/tmp# cmatrix
Command 'cmatrix' not found, but can be installed with:
apt install cmatrix
```

The `apt-get remove` command removes (uninstalls) a package, but it doesn't remove the package configuration files. You can use the `apt-get purge` command to remove a package along with its configuration files.

For example, if you want to remove the `gnome-chess` package along with its configuration files, you can run:

```
root@ubuntu-linux:/tmp# apt-get purge gnome-chess
Reading package lists... Done
Building dependency tree
Reading state information... Done
The following package was automatically installed and is no longer
required:
  hoichess
Use 'apt autoremove' to remove it.
The following packages will be REMOVED:
  gnome-chess*
0 upgraded, 0 newly installed, 1 to remove and 357 not upgraded.
```

```
After this operation, 4,407 kB disk space will be freed.
Do you want to continue? [Y/n] y
(Reading database ... 178515 files and directories currently installed.)
Removing gnome-chess (1:3.28.1-1) ...
Processing triggers for mime-support (3.60ubuntu1) ...
Processing triggers for desktop-file-utils (0.23-1ubuntu3.18.04.2) ...
Processing triggers for libglib2.0-0:amd64 (2.56.3-0ubuntu0.18.04.1) ...
Processing triggers for man-db (2.8.3-2ubuntu0.1) ...
Processing triggers for gnome-menus (3.13.3-11ubuntu1.1) ...
Processing triggers for hicolor-icon-theme (0.17-2) ...
(Reading database ... 178225 files and directories currently installed.)
Purging configuration files for gnome-chess (1:3.28.1-1) ...
```

You can even see in the last line in the output it says `Purging configuration files for gnome-chess (1:3.28.1-1) ...`, which means that the configuration files for `gnome-chess` are being removed as well.

How to search for packages

Sometimes you are unsure of a package name. Then, in this case, you can't install it until you look it up. You can search for a package by using the command `apt-cache search` followed by your search term or keyword:

```
apt-cache search keyword
```

For example, let's say that you want to install the `wireshark` package, but you can only remember that the package name has the word `shark` in it. In this case, you can run the command:

```
root@ubuntu-linux:/tmp# apt-cache search shark
dopewars - drug-dealing game set in streets of New York City
dopewars-data - drug-dealing game set in streets of New York City - data
files forensics-extra - Forensics Environment - extra console components
(metapackage) kernelshark - Utilities for graphically analyzing function
tracing in the kernel libcrypto++-dev - General purpose cryptographic
library - C++ development libshark-dev - development files for Shark
libshark0 - Shark machine learning library
libwireshark-data - network packet dissection library -- data files
libwireshark-dev - network packet dissection library -- development files
libwireshark10 - network packet dissection library -- shared library
libwiretap-dev - network packet capture library -- development files
libwsutil-dev - network packet dissection utilities library -- development
files libwsutil8 - network packet dissection utilities library -- shared
library netmate - netdude clone that shows pcap dump lines in network
header style plowshare-modules - plowshare drivers for various file sharing
```

```
websites
shark-doc - documentation for Shark
tcpxtract - extract files from network traffic based on file signatures
tshark - network traffic analyzer - console version
wifite - Python script to automate wireless auditing using aircrack-ng
tools wireshark - network traffic analyzer - meta-package
wireshark-common - network traffic analyzer - common files
wireshark-dev - network traffic analyzer - development tools
wireshark-doc - network traffic analyzer - documentation
wireshark-gtk - network traffic analyzer - GTK+ version
wireshark-qt - network traffic analyzer - Qt version
zeitgeist-explorer - GUI application for monitoring and debugging zeitgeist
forensics-extra-gui - Forensics Environment - extra GUI components
(metapackage) horst - Highly Optimized Radio Scanning Tool
libvirt-wireshark - Wireshark dissector for the libvirt protocol
libwiretap7 - network packet capture library -- shared library
libwscodecs1 - network packet dissection codecs library -- shared library
minetest-mod-animals - Minetest mod providing animals
nsntrace - perform network trace of a single process by using network
namespaces libwireshark11 - network packet dissection library -- shared
library
libwiretap8 - network packet capture library -- shared library
libwscodecs2 - network packet dissection codecs library -- shared library
libwsutil9 - network packet dissection utilities library -- shared library
```

And you are bombarded with a massive output that lists all the package names that have the word `shark` in their package description. I bet you can spot the package `wireshark` in the middle of the output. We can get a much shorter and a refined output by using the `-n` option:

```
root@ubuntu-linux:/tmp# apt-cache -n search shark
kernelshark - Utilities for graphically analyzing function tracing in the
kernel libshark-dev - development files for Shark
libshark0 - Shark machine learning library
libwireshark-data - network packet dissection library -- data files
libwireshark-dev - network packet dissection library -- development files
libwireshark10 - network packet dissection library -- shared library
shark-doc - documentation for Shark
tshark - network traffic analyzer - console version
wireshark - network traffic analyzer - meta-package
wireshark-common - network traffic analyzer - common files
wireshark-dev - network traffic analyzer - development tools
wireshark-doc - network traffic analyzer - documentation
wireshark-gtk - network traffic analyzer - GTK+ version
wireshark-qt - network traffic analyzer - Qt version
libndpi-wireshark - extensible deep packet inspection library - wireshark
dissector
```

```
libvirt-wireshark - Wireshark dissector for the libvirt protocol
libwireshark11 - network packet dissection library -- shared library
```

This will only list the packages that have the word `shark` in their package names. Now, you can install `wireshark` by running the command:

```
root@ubuntu-linux:/tmp# apt-get install wireshark
```

How to show package information

To view package information, you can use the command `apt-cache show` followed by the package name:

```
apt-cache show package_name
```

For example, to display the `cmatrix` package information, you can run:

```
root@ubuntu-linux:~# apt-cache show cmatrix
Package: cmatrix
Architecture: amd64
Version: 1.2a-5build3
Priority: optional
Section: universe/misc
Origin: Ubuntu
Maintainer: Ubuntu Developers <ubuntu-devel-discuss@lists.ubuntu.com>
Original-Maintainer: Diego Fernández Durán <diego@goedi.net>
Bugs: https://bugs.launchpad.net/ubuntu/+filebug
Installed-Size: 48
Depends: libc6 (>= 2.4), libncurses5 (>= 6), libtinfo5 (>= 6)
Recommends: kbd
Suggests: cmatrix-xfont
Filename: pool/universe/c/cmatrix/cmatrix_1.2a-5build3_amd64.deb
Size: 16084
MD5sum: 8dad2a99d74b63cce6eeff0046f0ac91
SHA1: 3da3a0ec97807e6f53de7653e4e9f47fd96521c2
SHA256: cd50212101bfd71479af41e7afc47ea822c075ddb1ceed83895f8eaa1b79ce5d
Homepage: http://www.asty.org/cmatrix/
Description-en_CA: simulates the display from "The Matrix"
Screen saver for the terminal based in the movie "The Matrix".
 * Support terminal resize.
 * Screen saver mode: any key closes it.
 * Selectable color.
 * Change text scroll rate.
Description-md5: 9af1f58e4b6301a6583f036c780c6ae6
```

You can see a lot of useful information in the output, including the package description and the contact information of the maintainer of the package, which is useful if you find a bug and want to report it. You will also find out if the package depends on (requires) other packages.

Package dependency can turn into a nightmare, and so I highly recommend that you use the `apt-get install` command to install a package whenever possible as it checks and resolves package dependency while installing a package. On the other hand, the `dpkg -i` command doesn't check for package dependency. Keep that in mind!

You can use the `apt-cache depends` command to list package dependencies:

```
apt-cache depends package_name
```

For example, to view the list of packages that are needed to be installed for `cmatrix` to work properly, you can run the command:

```
root@ubuntu-linux:~# apt-cache depends cmatrix
cmatrix
  Depends: libc6
  Depends: libncurses5
  Depends: libtinfo5
  Recommends: kbd
  Suggests: cmatrix-xfont
```

As you can see, the `cmatrix` package depends on three packages:

- `libc6`
- `libncurses5`
- `libtinfo5`

Those three packages have to be installed on the system in order for `cmatrix` to run properly.

Listing all packages

You can use the `dpkg -l` command to list all the packages that are installed on your system:

```
root@ubuntu-linux:~# dpkg -l
```

You can also use the `apt-cache pkgnames` command to list all the packages that are available for you to install:

```
root@ubuntu-linux:~# apt-cache pkgnames
libdatrie-doc
libfstrcmp0-dbg
libghc-monadplus-doc
librime-data-sampheng
python-pyao-dbg
fonts-georgewilliams
python3-aptdaemon.test
libcollada2gltfconvert-dev
python3-doc8
r-bioc-hypergraph
.
.
.
.
.
```

You can pipe the output to the `wc -l` command to get the total number of available packages:

```
root@ubuntu-linux:~# apt-cache pkgnames | wc -l 64142
```

Wow! That's a massive number; over 64,000 available packages on my system.

You may also be interested to know which repositories (sources) your system used to obtain all these packages. These repositories are included in the file /etc/apt/sources.list and in any file with the suffix .list under the directory /etc/apt/sources.list.d/. You can check the man page:

```
root@ubuntu-linux:~# man sources.list
```

To learn how you can add a repository to your system.

You can also use the `apt-cache policy` command to list all the enabled repositories on your system:

```
root@ubuntu-linux:~# apt-cache policy
Package files:
100 /var/lib/dpkg/status
    release a=now
500 http://dl.google.com/linux/chrome/deb stable/main amd64
    Packages release v=1.0,o=Google LLC,a=stable,n=stable,l=Google,c=main,
    b=amd64 origin dl.google.com
100 http://ca.archive.ubuntu.com/ubuntu bionic-backports/main i386
```

```
        Packages release v=18.04,o=Ubuntu,a=bionic-backports,n=bionic,l=Ubuntu,
        c=main,b=i386 origin ca.archive.ubuntu.com
100 http://ca.archive.ubuntu.com/ubuntu bionic-backports/main amd64
        Packages release v=18.04,o=Ubuntu,a=bionic-backports,n=bionic,l=Ubuntu,
        c=main,b=amd64 origin ca.archive.ubuntu.com
500 http://ca.archive.ubuntu.com/ubuntu bionic/multiverse i386
        Packages release v=18.04,o=Ubuntu,a=bionic,n=bionic,
        l=Ubuntu,c=multiverse,b=i386 origin ca.archive.ubuntu.com
500 http://ca.archive.ubuntu.com/ubuntu bionic/multiverse amd64
        Packages release v=18.04,o=Ubuntu,a=bionic,n=bionic,l=Ubuntu,
        c=multiverse,b=amd64 origin ca.archive.ubuntu.com
500 http://ca.archive.ubuntu.com/ubuntu bionic/universe i386
        Packages release v=18.04,o=Ubuntu,a=bionic,n=bionic,l=Ubuntu,
        c=universe,b=i386 origin ca.archive.ubuntu.com
500 http://ca.archive.ubuntu.com/ubuntu bionic/universe amd64
        Packages release v=18.04,o=Ubuntu,a=bionic,n=bionic,l=Ubuntu,
        c=universe,b=amd64 origin ca.archive.ubuntu.com
500 http://ca.archive.ubuntu.com/ubuntu bionic/restricted i386
        Packages release v=18.04,o=Ubuntu,a=bionic,n=bionic,l=Ubuntu,
        c=restricted,b=i386 origin ca.archive.ubuntu.com
500 http://ca.archive.ubuntu.com/ubuntu bionic/restricted amd64
        Packages release v=18.04,o=Ubuntu,a=bionic,n=bionic,l=Ubuntu,
        c=restricted,b=amd64 origin ca.archive.ubuntu.com
500 http://ca.archive.ubuntu.com/ubuntu bionic/main i386
        Packages release v=18.04,o=Ubuntu,a=bionic,
        n=bionic,l=Ubuntu,c=main,b=i386 origin ca.archive.ubuntu.com
500 http://ca.archive.ubuntu.com/ubuntu bionic/main amd64
        Packages release v=18.04,o=Ubuntu,a=bionic,n=bionic,
        l=Ubuntu,c=main,b=amd64 origin ca.archive.ubuntu.com
Pinned packages:
```

If you are eager to know which repository provides a specific package, you can use the `apt-cache policy` command followed by the package name:

```
apt-cache policy package_name
```

For example, to know which repository provides the `cmatrix` package, you can run:

```
root@ubuntu-linux:~# apt-cache policy cmatrix
cmatrix:
  Installed: 1.2a-5build3
  Candidate: 1.2a-5build3
  Version table:
*** 1.2a-5build3 500
    500 http://ca.archive.ubuntu.com/ubuntu bionic/universe amd64 Packages
    100 /var/lib/dpkg/status
```

From the output, you can see that the `cmatrix` package comes from the bionic/universe repository at `http://ca.archive.ubuntu.com/ubuntu`.

Patching your system

If a newer release for a package is available, then you can upgrade it using the `apt-get install --only-upgrade` command followed by the package name:

```
apt-get install --only-upgrade package_name
```

For example, you can upgrade the `nano` package by running the command:

```
root@ubuntu-linux:~# apt-get install --only-upgrade nano
Reading package lists... Done
Building dependency tree
Reading state information... Done
nano is already the newest version (2.9.3-2).
The following package was automatically installed and is no longer
required:
  hoichess
Use 'apt autoremove' to remove it.
0 upgraded, 0 newly installed, 0 to remove and 357 not upgraded.
```

You can also upgrade all the installed packages on your system by running the commands:

1. `apt-get update`
2. `apt-get upgrade`

The first command `apt-get update` will update the list of available packages and their versions, but it doesn't do any installation or upgrade:

```
root@ubuntu-linux:~# apt-get update
Ign:1 http://dl.google.com/linux/chrome/deb stable InRelease
Hit:2 http://ca.archive.ubuntu.com/ubuntu bionic InRelease
Hit:3 http://ppa.launchpad.net/linuxuprising/java/ubuntu bionic InRelease
Hit:4 http://dl.google.com/linux/chrome/deb stable Release
Hit:5 http://security.ubuntu.com/ubuntu bionic-security InRelease
Hit:6 http://ca.archive.ubuntu.com/ubuntu bionic-updates InRelease
Hit:8 http://ca.archive.ubuntu.com/ubuntu bionic-backports InRelease
Reading package lists... Done
```

The second command `apt-get upgrade` will upgrade all the installed packages on your system:

```
root@ubuntu-linux:~# apt-get upgrade
Reading package lists... Done
Building dependency tree
Reading state information... Done
Calculating upgrade... Done
The following package was automatically installed and is no longer
required:
  hoichess
Use 'apt autoremove' to remove it.
The following packages have been kept back:
  gstreamer1.0-gl libcogl20 libgail-3-0 libgl1-mesa-dri libgstreamer-
gl1.0-0
  libreoffice-calc libreoffice-core libreoffice-draw libreoffice-gnome
    libreoffice-gtk3
  libwayland-egl1-mesa libxatracker2 linux-generic linux-headers-generic
  software-properties-common software-properties-gtk ubuntu-desktop
The following packages will be upgraded:
  apt apt-utils aptdaemon aptdaemon-data aspell base-files bash bind9-host
bluez
  python2.7-minimal python3-apt python3-aptdaemon python3-
aptdaemon.gtk3widgets
  python3-problem-report python3-update-manager python3-urllib3 python3.6
342 upgraded, 0 newly installed, 0 to remove and 30 not upgraded.
Need to get 460 MB of archives.
After this operation, 74.3 MB of additional disk space will be used.
Do you want to continue? [Y/n]
```

Remember that order matters; that is, you need to run the `apt-get update` command before you run the `apt-get upgrade` command.

In Linux lingo, the process of upgrading all the installed packages on your system is called **patching the system**.

Knowledge check

For the following exercises, open up your Terminal and try to solve the following tasks:

1. Install the `tmux` package on your system.
2. List all the dependencies of the `vim` package.
3. Install the `cowsay` package on your system.
4. Remove the `cowsay` package along with all its configuration files.
5. Upgrade all the packages on your system (patch your system).

13
Kill the Process

Any program that is running on your system is a process. In this chapter, you will learn all about Linux processes. You will learn how to view process information. You will also learn how to send different signals to a process. Furthermore, you will understand the differences between foreground and background processes.

What is a process?

A process is simply an instance of a running program. So any program running on your system is a process. All of the following are examples of processes:

- Firefox or any web browser running on your system is a process.
- Your Terminal that you are running right now is a process.
- Any game you may play on your system is a process.
- Copying files is a process.

And just like the case with files, every process is owned by a specific user. The owner of a process is simply the user who started that process.

To list all the processes that are owned by a specific user, you can run the command `ps -u` followed by the username:

```
ps -u username
```

For example, to list all the processes that are owned by `elliot`, you can run:

```
root@ubuntu-linux:~# ps -u elliot
  PID TTY          TIME CMD
 1365 ?        00:00:00 systemd
 1366 ?        00:00:00 (sd-pam)
 1379 ?        00:00:00 gnome-keyring-d
 1383 tty2     00:00:00 gdm-x-session
 1385 tty2     00:00:18 Xorg
```

```
1389 ?       00:00:00 dbus-daemon
1393 tty2    00:00:00 gnome-session-b
1725 ?       00:00:00 ssh-agent
1797 ?       00:00:00 gvfsd
  .
  .
  .
  .
```

The first column in the output lists the **process identifiers** (**PIDs**). The PID is a number that uniquely identifies a process, just like with file `inodes`. The last column of the output lists the process names.

You can use the `ps -e` command to list all the processes that are running on your system:

```
root@ubuntu-linux:~# ps -e
PID TTY       TIME    CMD
1   ?       00:00:01 systemd
2   ?       00:00:00 kthreadd
4   ?       00:00:00 kworker/0:0H
6   ?       00:00:00 mm_percpu_wq
7   ?       00:00:00 ksoftirqd/0
8   ?       00:00:00 rcu_sched
9   ?       00:00:00 rcu_bh
10  ?       00:00:00 migration/0
11  ?       00:00:00 watchdog/0
12  ?       00:00:00 cpuhp/0
13  ?       00:00:00 kdevtmpfs
  .
  .
  .
  .
```

You can also use the `-f` option to get more information:

```
root@ubuntu-linux:~# ps -ef
UID      PID  PPID C STIME TTY      TIME    CMD
root       1     0 0 11:23    ? 00:00:01 /sbin/init splash
root       2     0 0 11:23    ? 00:00:00 [kthreadd]
root       4     2 0 11:23    ? 00:00:00 [kworker/0:0H]
root       6     2 0 11:23    ? 00:00:00 [mm_percpu_wq]
root       7     2 0 11:23    ? 00:00:00 [ksoftirqd/0]
root       8     2 0 11:23    ? 00:00:01 [rcu_sched]
root       9     2 0 11:23    ? 00:00:00 [rcu_bh]
root      10     2 0 11:23    ? 00:00:00 [migration/0]
elliot   1835  1393 1 11:25 tty2 00:00:58 /usr/bin/gnome-shell
elliot   1853  1835 0 11:25 tty2 00:00:00 ibus-daemon --xim --panel disable
elliot   1857  1365 0 11:25    ? 00:00:00 /usr/lib/gnome-shell/gnome-shell
```

```
elliot 1865 1853 0 11:25 tty2 00:00:00 /usr/lib/ibus/ibus-dconf
elliot 1868    1 0 11:25 tty2 00:00:00 /usr/lib/ibus/ibus-x11 --kill-daemon
elliot 1871 1365 0 11:25    ? 00:00:00 /usr/lib/ibus/ibus-portal
.
.
.
```

The first column of the output lists the usernames of the process owners. The third column of the output lists the **parent process identifiers** (**PPIDs**). Well, what the heck is a parent process?

Parent process versus child process

A parent process is a process that has started one or more child processes. A perfect example will be your terminal and your bash shell; when you open your terminal, your bash shell is started as well.

To get the PID of a process, you can use the `pgrep` command followed by the process name:

```
pgrep process_name
```

For example, to get the PID of your terminal process, you can run:

```
elliot@ubuntu-linux:~$ pgrep terminal
10009
```

The PID of my terminal is `10009`. Now, let's get the PID of the bash process:

```
elliot@ubuntu-linux:~$ pgrep bash
10093
```

The PID of my bash shell is `10093`. Now, you can get the information of your bash process by using the `-p` option followed by the bash PID:

```
elliot@ubuntu-linux:~$ ps -fp 10093
UID      PID   PPID  C  STIME TTY    TIME    CMD
elliot 10093 10009  0  13:37 pts/1 00:00:00 bash
```

You can see from the output that the PPID of my bash process is equal to the PID of my terminal process. This proves that the terminal process has started the bash process. In this case, the bash process is referred to as the child process of the terminal process:

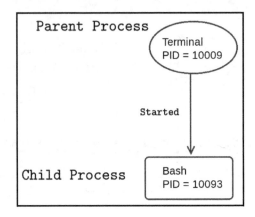

Figure 1: Parent process versus child process

The top command is a very useful command that you can use to view processes' information in real time. You can check its man page to learn how to use it:

```
elliot@ubuntu-linux:~$ man top
```

The output for the preceding command is shown in the following screenshot:

```
top - 14:11:49 up  2:48,   2 users,   load average: 0.00, 0.00,
Tasks: 178 total,   1 running, 144 sleeping,   1 stopped,   0
%Cpu(s):   0.3 us,   0.3 sy,   0.0 ni, 99.0 id,   0.0 wa,   0.0 hi,
KiB Mem :  4039720 total,  2300344 free,   939660 used,    7997
KiB Swap:   969960 total,   969960 free,        0 used.  28315

  PID USER      PR  NI    VIRT    RES    SHR S %CPU %MEM
 1385 elliot    20   0  442196  94152  44012 S  0.3  2.3
 1835 elliot    20   0 3049584 349108  94900 S  0.3  8.6
10194 elliot    20   0  110076   3516   2500 S  0.3  0.1
10301 elliot    20   0   49112   3800   3124 S  0.3  0.1
10321 elliot    20   0   48884   3696   3076 R  0.3  0.1
    1 root      20   0  159952   9196   6688 S  0.0  0.2
    2 root      20   0       0      0      0 S  0.0  0.0
    4 root       0 -20       0      0      0 I  0.0  0.0
    6 root       0 -20       0      0      0 I  0.0  0.0
    7 root      20   0       0      0      0 S  0.0  0.0
    8 root      20   0       0      0      0 I  0.0  0.0
    9 root      20   0       0      0      0 I  0.0  0.0
   10 root      rt   0       0      0      0 S  0.0  0.0
   11 root      rt   0       0      0      0 S  0.0  0.0
   12 root      20   0       0      0      0 S  0.0  0.0
```

Figure 2: The top command

Foreground versus background processes

There are two types of processes in Linux:

- Foreground processes

- Background processes

A foreground process is a process that is attached to your terminal. You have to wait for a foreground process to finish before you can continue using your terminal.

On the other hand, a background process is a process that is not attached to your terminal, and so you can use your terminal while a background process is running.

The `yes` command outputs any string that follows it repeatedly until killed:

```
elliot@ubuntu-linux:~$ whatis yes
yes (1)                    - output a string repeatedly until killed
```

For example, to output the word `hello` repeatedly on your terminal, you can run the command:

```
elliot@ubuntu-linux:~$ yes hello
hello
hello
hello
hello
hello
hello
hello
hello
hello
hello
  .
  .
  .
```

Notice that it will keep running, and you can't do anything else on your terminal; this is a prime example of a foreground process. To claim back your terminal, you need to kill the process. You can kill the process by hitting the *Ctrl + C* key combination as follows:

```
hello
hello
hello
hello
hello
^C
elliot@ubuntu-linux:~$
```

As soon as you hit *Ctrl + C*, the process will be killed, and you can continue using your terminal. Let's do another example; you can use the `firefox` command to start up Firefox from your terminal:

```
elliot@ubuntu-linux:~$ firefox
```

The Firefox browser will start, but you will not be able to do anything on your terminal until you close Firefox; this is another example of a foreground process. Now, hit *Ctrl + C* to kill the Firefox process so you can claim back your terminal.

You can start up Firefox as a background process by adding the ampersand character as follows:

```
elliot@ubuntu-linux:~$ firefox &
[1] 3468
elliot@ubuntu-linux:~$
```

Firefox is now running as a background process, and you can continue using your terminal without having to close Firefox.

Sending signals to processes

You can interact and communicate with processes via signals. There are various signals, and each signal serves a different purpose. To list all available signals, you can run the `kill -L` command:

```
elliot@ubuntu-linux:~$ kill -L
 1) SIGHUP	 2) SIGINT	 3) SIGQUIT	 4) SIGILL	 5) SIGTRAP
 6) SIGABRT	 7) SIGBUS	 8) SIGFPE	 9) SIGKILL	10) SIGUSR1
11) SIGSEGV	12) SIGUSR2	13) SIGPIPE	14) SIGALRM	15) SIGTERM
16) SIGSTKFLT	17) SIGCHLD	18) SIGCONT	19) SIGSTOP	20) SIGTSTP
21) SIGTTIN	22) SIGTTOU	23) SIGURG	24) SIGXCPU	25) SIGXFSZ
26) SIGVTALRM	27) SIGPROF	28) SIGWINCH	29) SIGIO	30) SIGPWR
```

```
31) SIGSYS 34) SIGRTMIN 35) SIGRTMIN+1 36) SIGRTMIN+2 37) SIGRTMIN+3
38) SIGRTMIN+4 39) SIGRTMIN+5 40) SIGRTMIN+6 41) SIGRTMIN+7 42) SIGRTMIN+8
43) SIGRTMIN+9 44) SIGRTMIN+10 45) SIGRTMIN+11 46) SIGRTMIN+12 47)
SIGRTMIN+13
48) SIGRTMIN+14 49) SIGRTMIN+15 50) SIGRTMAX-14 51) SIGRTMAX-13 52)
SIGRTMAX-12
53) SIGRTMAX-11 54) SIGRTMAX-10 55) SIGRTMAX-9 56) SIGRTMAX-8 57)
SIGRTMAX-7
58) SIGRTMAX-6 59) SIGRTMAX-5 60) SIGRTMAX-4 61) SIGRTMAX-3 62) SIGRTMAX-2
63) SIGRTMAX-1 64) SIGRTMAX
```

Notice that every signal has a numeric value. For example, 19 is the numeric value for the SIGSTOP signal.

To see how signals work, let's first start Firefox as a background process:

```
elliot@ubuntu-linux:~$ firefox &
[1] 4218
```

Notice that the PID of Firefox is 4218 on my system. I can kill (terminate) Firefox by sending a SIGKILL signal as follows:

```
elliot@ubuntu-linux:~$ kill -SIGKILL 4218
[1]+ Killed                 firefox
```

This will immediately shut down Firefox. You can also use the numeric value of the SIGKILL signal instead:

```
elliot@ubuntu-linux:~$ kill -9 4218
```

In general, the syntax for the kill command is as follows:

```
kill -SIGNAL PID
```

Let's start Firefox again as a background process:

```
elliot@ubuntu-linux:~$ firefox &
[1] 4907
```

Notice that the PID of Firefox is 4907 on my system. Now go ahead and start playing a YouTube video on Firefox. After you have done that, go back to your terminal and send the SIGSTOP signal to Firefox:

```
elliot@ubuntu-linux:~$ kill -SIGSTOP 4907
```

You will notice that Firefox becomes unresponsive and your YouTube video is stopped; no problem – we can fix that by sending the SIGCONT signal to Firefox:

```
elliot@ubuntu-linux:~$ kill -SIGCONT 4907
```

This will resurrect Firefox, and your YouTube video will now resume.

So far, you have learned three signals:

- SIGKILL: Terminates a process
- SIGSTOP: Stops a process
- SIGCONT: Continues a process

You can use process names instead of process identifiers with the pkill command. For example, to close your terminal process, you can run the command:

```
elliot@ubuntu-linux:~$ pkill -9 terminal
```

Now let's do something funny; open your terminal and run the command:

```
elliot@ubuntu-linux:~$ pkill -SIGSTOP terminal
```

Haha! Your terminal is now frozen. I will let you handle that!

There are many other signals that you can send to processes; check the following man page to understand the use of each signal:

```
elliot@ubuntu-linux:~$ man signal
```

Working with process priority

Each process has a priority that is determined by the niceness scale, which ranges from **-20** to **19**. The lower the nice value, the higher the priority of a process, so a nice value of **-20** gives the highest priority to a process. On the other hand, a nice value of **19** gives the lowest priority to a process:

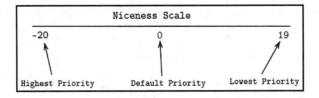

Figure 3: The Niceness Scale

You might be asking yourself: *Why do we care about a process priority?* The answer is efficiency! Your CPU is like a waiter in a busy restaurant. An efficient waiter goes around all the time to ensure that all the customers are happily served. Similarly, your CPU allocates time to all processes running on your system. A process with a high priority gets a lot of attention from the CPU. On the other hand, a process with a low priority doesn't get as much attention from the CPU.

Viewing a process priority

Start Firefox as a background process:

```
elliot@ubuntu-linux:~$ firefox &
  [1] 6849
```

You can use the `ps` command to view a process' nice value:

```
elliot@ubuntu-linux:~$ ps -o nice -p 6849
NI
0
```

My Firefox process has a nice value of **0**, which is the default value (average priority).

Setting priorities for new processes

You can use the `nice` command to start a process with your desired priority. The general syntax of the `nice` command goes as follows:

```
nice -n -20 →19 process
```

Let's say you are about to upgrade all the packages on your system; it would be wise to give such a process the highest priority possible. To do that, you can run the following command as the `root` user:

```
root@ubuntu-linux:~# nice -n -20 apt-get upgrade
```

Changing a process priority

You can use the `renice` command to change the priority of a running process. We have already seen that Firefox was running with a default process priority of zero; let's change Firefox's priority and give it the lowest priority possible:

```
root@ubuntu-linux:~# renice -n 19 -p 6849
6849 (process ID) old priority 0, new priority 19
```

Cool! Now I hope Firefox will not be very slow for me; after all, I just told my CPU not to give much attention to Firefox!

The /proc directory

Every process in Linux is represented by a directory in `/proc`. For example, if your Firefox process has a PID of `6849`, then the directory `/proc/6849` will represent the Firefox process:

```
root@ubuntu-linux:~# pgrep firefox
6849
root@ubuntu-linux:~# cd /proc/6849
root@ubuntu-linux:/proc/6849#
```

Inside a process' directory, you can find a lot of valuable and insightful information about the process. For example, you will find a soft link named `exe` that points to the process' executable file:

```
root@ubuntu-linux:/proc/6849# ls -l exe
lrwxrwxrwx 1 elliot elliot 0 Nov 21 18:02 exe -> /usr/lib/firefox/firefox
```

You will also find the `status` file, which stores various pieces of information about a process; these include the process state, the PPID, the amount of memory used by the process, and so on:

```
root@ubuntu-linux:/proc/6849# head status
Name: firefox
Umask: 0022
State: S (sleeping) Tgid: 6849
Ngid: 0
Pid: 6849
PPid: 1990
TracerPid: 0
Uid: 1000 1000 1000 1000
Gid: 1000 1000 1000 1000
```

The `limits` file displays the current limits set for the process:

```
root@ubuntu-linux:/proc/7882# cat limits
Limit                     Soft Limit      Hard Limit      Units
Max cpu time              unlimited       unlimited       seconds
Max file size             unlimited       unlimited       bytes
Max data size             unlimited       unlimited       bytes
Max stack size            8388608         unlimited       bytes
Max core file size        0               unlimited       bytes
Max resident set          unlimited       unlimited       bytes
Max processes             15599           15599           processes
Max open files            4096            4096            files
Max locked memory         16777216        16777216        bytes
Max address space         unlimited       unlimited       bytes
Max file locks            unlimited       unlimited       locks
Max pending signals       15599           15599           signals
Max msgqueue size         819200          819200          bytes
Max nice priority         0               0
Max realtime priority     0               0
Max realtime timeout      unlimited       unlimited       us
```

The `fd` directory will show you all the files that the process is currently using on your system:

```
root@ubuntu-linux:/proc/6849# cd fd
root@ubuntu-linux:/proc/6849/fd# ls -l | tail
lrwx------ 1 elliot elliot 64 Nov 21 18:12 83 -> /home/elliot/.mozilla/firefox/places.sqlite-wal
lr-x------ 1 elliot elliot 64 Nov 21 18:12 84 -> /home/elliot/.mozilla/firefox/wkgfiatj.default
/favicons.sqlite
lrwx------ 1 elliot elliot 64 Nov 21 18:12 85 -> /home/elliot/.mozilla/firefox/wkgfiatj.default
/favicons.sqlite-wal
lrwx------ 1 elliot elliot 64 Nov 21 18:12 86 -> /home/elliot/.mozilla/firefox/wkgfiatj.default
/content-prefs.sqlite
lrwx------ 1 elliot elliot 64 Nov 21 18:12 88 -> /home/elliot/.mozilla/firefox/wkgfiatj.default
/webappsstore.sqlite
lr-x------ 1 elliot elliot 64 Nov 21 18:12 89 -> /usr/lib/firefox/browser/features
/formautofill@mozilla.org.xpi
lr-x------ 1 elliot elliot 64 Nov 21 18:12 9 -> /dev/shm/org.mozilla.ipc.6849.5 (deleted)
lrwx------ 1 elliot elliot 64 Nov 21 18:12 90 -> /home/elliot/.mozilla/firefox/wkgfiatj.default
/webappsstore.sqlite-wal
lr-x------ 1 elliot elliot 64 Nov 21 18:12 92 -> /home/elliot/.mozilla/firefox/wkgfiatj.default
/webappsstore.sqlite
lrwx------ 1 elliot elliot 64 Nov 21 18:12 93 -> /home/elliot/.mozilla/firefox/wkgfiatj.default
/webappsstore.sqlite-wal
```

Figure 4: fd directory

You can also use the `lsof` command to list all the files a process is using:

```
root@ubuntu-linux:~# lsof -p 6849 | tail
lsof: WARNING: can't stat() fuse.gvfsd-fuse file system /run/user/1000/gvfs
      Output information may be incomplete.
firefox 6849 elliot  164u   unix 0xffff918255ae1c00       0t0  77045 type=SEQPACKET
firefox 6849 elliot  165u   unix 0xffff918255ae1800       0t0  77046 type=SEQPACKET
firefox 6849 elliot  166r    REG             0,23      58086     48 /dev/shm/org.mozilla.ipc.6849.41
firefox 6849 elliot  168u   unix 0xffff918255ae2000       0t0  77049 type=STREAM
firefox 6849 elliot  170r    REG             0,23      21518     49 /dev/shm/org.mozilla.ipc.6849.42
firefox 6849 elliot  172r    REG             0,23        170     50 /dev/shm/org.mozilla.ipc.6849.43
firefox 6849 elliot  174r    REG             0,23       1918     51 /dev/shm/org.mozilla.ipc.6849.44
firefox 6849 elliot  176r    REG             0,23       1772     52 /dev/shm/org.mozilla.ipc.6849.45
firefox 6849 elliot  178r    REG             0,23      20920     53 /dev/shm/org.mozilla.ipc.6849.46
firefox 6849 elliot  180r    REG             0,23       5808     54 /dev/shm/org.mozilla.ipc.6849.47
```

Figure 5: lsof command

Knowledge check

For the following exercises, open up your Terminal and try to solve the following tasks:

1. List the process ID of your running terminal.
2. List the parent process ID of your running terminal.
3. Use the `kill` command to close your terminal.
4. Start Firefox as a background process.
5. Change Firefox's priority to a maximum priority.

14
The Power of Sudo

In this chapter, you will learn how to give permissions to non-root users on the system so they can run privileged commands. In real life, the system administrator should not give the root password to any user on the system. However, some users on the system may need to run privileged commands; now, the question is: *how can non-root users run privileged commands without getting root access to the system?* Well, let me show you!

Examples of privileged commands

You would find most of the commands that require root privileges in the directories /sbin and /usr/sbin. Let's switch to user smurf:

```
elliot@ubuntu-linux:~$ su - smurf
Password:
smurf@ubuntu-linux:~$
```

Now let's see if smurf can add a new user to the system:

```
smurf@ubuntu-linux:~$ useradd bob
useradd: Permission denied.
```

User smurf gets a permission denied error. That's because the useradd command is a privileged command. OK fine! Let's try installing the terminator package, which is a pretty cool Terminal emulator I must say:

```
smurf@ubuntu-linux:~$ apt-get install terminator
E: Could not open lock file /var/lib/dpkg/lock-frontend - open
 (13: Permission denied)
E: Unable to acquire the dpkg frontend lock (/var/lib/dpkg/lock-frontend),
are you root?
```

Again! User smurf is getting an error. Life is not fun without root, I hear you saying.

Granting access with sudo

User `smurf` is now very sad as he can't add user `bob` or install the `terminator` package on the system. You can use the `visudo` command to grant user `smurf` the permissions to run the two privileged commands he wants.

Run the `visudo` command as the root user:

```
root@ubuntu-linux:~# visudo
```

This will open up the file `/etc/sudoers` so you can edit it:

```
# This file MUST be edited with the 'visudo' command as root.
#
# Please consider adding local content in /etc/sudoers.d/ instead of
# directly modifying this file.
#
# See the man page for details on how to write a sudoers file.
#
Defaults          env_reset
Defaults          mail_badpass
# Host alias specification
# User alias specification
# Cmnd alias specification
# User privilege specification
root              ALL=(ALL:ALL) ALL
# Members of the admin group may gain root privileges
%admin            ALL=(ALL) ALL
# Allow members of group sudo to execute any command
%sudo             ALL=(ALL:ALL) ALL
# See sudoers(5) for more information on "#include" directives:
#includedir /etc/sudoers.d
```

All the lines that begin with the hash characters are comments, so only focus on these lines:

```
root    ALL=(ALL:ALL) ALL
%admin ALL=(ALL) ALL
%sudo   ALL=(ALL:ALL) ALL
```

The first line `root ALL=(ALL:ALL) ALL` is a rule that grants user `root` the permission to run all the commands on the system.

We can now add a rule to grant user `smurf` the permission to run the `useradd` command. The syntax specification for a rule in the `/etc/sudoers` file is as follows:

```
user hosts=(user:group) commands
```

Now add the following rule to the `/etc/sudoers` file:

```
smurf     ALL=(ALL)        /usr/sbin/useradd
```

The `ALL` keyword means no restrictions. Notice that you also have to include the full path of the commands. Now, save and exit the file then switch to user `smurf`:

```
root@ubuntu-linux:~# su - smurf
smurf@ubuntu-linux:~$
```

Now precede the `useradd` command with `sudo` as follows:

```
smurf@ubuntu-linux:~$ sudo useradd bob
[sudo] password for smurf:
smurf@ubuntu-linux:~$
```

It will prompt user `smurf` for his password; enter it, and just like that! User `bob` is added:

```
smurf@ubuntu-linux:~$ id bob
uid=1005(bob) gid=1005(bob) groups=1005(bob)
smurf@ubuntu-linux:~$
```

Cool! So `smurf` can now add users to the system; however, he still can't install any packages on the system:

```
smurf@ubuntu-linux:~$ sudo apt-get install terminator
Sorry, user smurf is not allowed to execute '/usr/bin/apt-get install
terminator' as root on ubuntu-linux.
```

Now let's fix that. Switch back to the root user and run the `visudo` command to edit the `sudo` rule for user `smurf`:

```
smurf ALL=(ALL) NOPASSWD: /usr/sbin/useradd, /usr/bin/apt-get install
terminator
```

Notice that I also added `NOPASSWD` so that `smurf` doesn't get prompted to enter his password. I also added the command to install the `terminator` package. Now, save and exit then switch back to user `smurf` and try to install the `terminator` package:

```
smurf@ubuntu-linux:~$ sudo apt-get install terminator
Reading package lists... Done
Building dependency tree
```

```
Reading state information... Done
The following packages were automatically installed and are no longer
required:
  gsfonts-x11 java-common
Use 'sudo apt autoremove' to remove them.
The following NEW packages will be installed:
    terminator
```

Success! Notice that the sudo rule grants smurf permission only to install the terminator package. He will get an error if he tries to install any other package:

```
smurf@ubuntu-linux:~$ sudo apt-get install cmatrix
Sorry, user smurf is not allowed to execute '/usr/bin/apt-get install
cmatrix'
as root on ubuntu-linux.
```

User and command aliases

You can use user aliases to reference multiple users in the /etc/sudoers file. For example, you can create a user alias MANAGERS that includes userssmurf and bob as follows:

```
User_Alias MANAGERS = smurf,bob
```

You can use a command alias to group multiple commands together. For example, you can create a command alias USER_CMDS that includes the commands useradd, userdel, and usermod:

```
Cmnd_Alias USER_CMDS = /usr/sbin/useradd, /usr/sbin/userdel,
/usr/sbin/usermod
```

Now you can use both aliases:

```
MANAGERS ALL=(ALL) USER_CMDS
```

to grant users smurf and bob the permission to run the commands useradd, userdel, and usermod.

Group privileges

You can also specify groups in the /etc/sudoers file. The group name is preceded by the percentage character as follows:

```
%group hosts=(user:group) commands
```

The following rule will grant the `developers` group permission to install any package on the system:

```
%developers ALL=(ALL) NOPASSWD: /usr/bin/apt-get install
```

The following rule will grant the `developers` group permission to run any command on the system:

```
%developers ALL=(ALL) NOPASSWD: ALL
```

Listing user privileges

You can use the command `sudo -lU` to display a list of the `sudo` commands a user can run:

```
sudo -lU username
```

For example, you can run the command:

```
root@ubuntu-linux:~# sudo -lU smurf
Matching Defaults entries for smurf on ubuntu-linux:
    env_reset, mail_badpass

User smurf may run the following commands on ubuntu-linux:
    (ALL) NOPASSWD: /usr/sbin/useradd, /usr/bin/apt-get install terminator
```

to list all the `sudo` commands that can be run by user `smurf`.

If a user is not allowed to run any `sudo` commands, the output of the command `sudo-lU` will be as follows:

```
root@ubuntu-linux:~# sudo -lU rachel
User rachel is not allowed to run sudo on ubuntu-linux.
```

visudo versus /etc/sudoers

You may have noticed that I used the command `visudo` to edit the file `/etc/sudoers`, and you might ask yourself a very valid question: why not just edit the file `/etc/sudoers` directly without using `visudo`? Well, I will answer your question in a practical way.

First, run the `visudo` command and add the following line:

```
THISLINE=WRONG
```

Now try to save and exit:

```
root@ubuntu-linux:~# visudo
>>> /etc/sudoers: syntax error near line 14 <<<
What now?
Options are:
  (e)dit sudoers file again
 e(x)it without saving changes to sudoers file
  (Q)uit and save changes to sudoers file (DANGER!)
What now?
```

As you can see, the `visudo` command detects an error, and it specifies the line number where the error has occurred.

Why is this important? Well, if you saved the file with an error in it, all the `sudo` rules in `/etc/sudoers` will not work! Let's hit Q to save the changes and then try to list the `sudo` commands that can be run by user `smurf`:

```
What now? Q
root@ubuntu-linux:~# sudo -lU smurf
>>> /etc/sudoers: syntax error near line 14 <<<
sudo: parse error in /etc/sudoers near line 14
sudo: no valid sudoers sources found, quitting
sudo: unable to initialize policy plugin
```

We get an error, and all the `sudo` rules are now broken! Go back and run the `visudo` command to remove the line that contains the error.

If you directly edit the file `/etc/sudoers` without using the `visudo` command, it will not check for syntax errors and this may lead to catastrophic consequences, as you saw. So the rule of thumb here: always use `visudo` when editing the `/etc/sudoers` file.

Knowledge check

For the following exercises, open up your Terminal and try to solve the following tasks:

1. Add a `sudo` rule so that user `smurf` can run the `fdisk` command.
2. Add a `sudo` rule so that the `developers` group can run the `apt-get` command.
3. List all the `sudo` commands of user `smurf`.

What's Wrong with the Network?

15

We all get furious when there is something wrong with the network. There is no fun in this world without being connected to the internet. In this chapter, you will learn the basics of Linux networking. You will also learn how to check network connectivity between two hosts, and gain a practical understanding of how DNS works and much more!

Testing network connectivity

An easy way to check whether you have internet access on your Linux machine is by trying to reach any remote host (server) on the internet. This can be done by using the `ping` command. In general, the syntax of the `ping` command is as follows:

```
ping [options] host
```

For example, to test whether you can reach `google.com`, you can run the following command:

```
root@ubuntu-linux:~# ping google.com
PING google.com (172.217.1.14) 56(84) bytes of data.
64 bytes from iad23s25-in-f14.1e100.net (172.217.1.14): icmp_seq=1 ttl=55
time=38.7 ms
64 bytes from iad23s25-in-f14.1e100.net (172.217.1.14): icmp_seq=2 ttl=55
time=38.7 ms
64 bytes from iad23s25-in-f14.1e100.net (172.217.1.14): icmp_seq=3 ttl=55
time=40.4 ms
64 bytes from iad23s25-in-f14.1e100.net (172.217.1.14): icmp_seq=4 ttl=55
time=36.6 ms
64 bytes from iad23s25-in-f14.1e100.net (172.217.1.14): icmp_seq=5 ttl=55
time=40.8 ms
64 bytes from iad23s25-in-f14.1e100.net (172.217.1.14): icmp_seq=6 ttl=55
time=38.6 ms
```

```
64 bytes from iad23s25-in-f14.1e100.net (172.217.1.14): icmp_seq=7 ttl=55
time=38.9 ms
64 bytes from iad23s25-in-f14.1e100.net (172.217.1.14): icmp_seq=8 ttl=55
time=37.1 ms
^C
--- google.com ping statistics ---
8 packets transmitted, 8 received, 0% packet loss, time 66ms
rtt min/avg/max/mdev = 36.555/38.724/40.821/1.344 ms
```

The `ping` command sends a packet (unit of data) called an **ICMP echo request** to the specified host and waits for the host to send back a packet called an **ICMP echo reply** to confirm that it did receive the initial packet. If the host replies as we see in our example, then it proves that we were able to reach the host. This is like you sending a package to your friend's house and waiting for your friend to send you a text to confirm that they received it.

Notice that without any options, the `ping` command keeps sending packets continuously, and it won't stop until you hit *Ctrl + C*.

You can use the `-c` option to specify the number of packets you want to send to a host. For example, to only send three packets to `google.com`, you can run the following command:

```
root@ubuntu-linux:~# ping -c 3 google.com
PING google.com (172.217.1.14) 56(84) bytes of data.

64 bytes from iad23s25-in-f14.1e100.net (172.217.1.14): icmp_seq=1 ttl=55
time=39.3 ms
64 bytes from iad23s25-in-f14.1e100.net (172.217.1.14): icmp_seq=2 ttl=55
time=49.7 ms
64 bytes from iad23s25-in-f14.1e100.net (172.217.1.14): icmp_seq=3 ttl=55
time=40.8 ms

--- google.com ping statistics ---
3 packets transmitted, 3 received, 0% packet loss, time 59ms rtt
min/avg/max/mdev = 39.323/43.267/49.708/4.595 ms
```

If you are not connected to the internet, you will get the following output from the `ping` command:

```
root@ubuntu-linux:~# ping google.com
ping: google.com: Name or service not known
```

Listing your network interfaces

You can list the available network interfaces on your system by viewing the contents of the `/sys/class/net` directory:

```
root@ubuntu-linux:~# ls /sys/class/net
eth0 lo wlan0
```

I have three network interfaces on my system:

1. `eth0`: The Ethernet interface
2. `lo`: The loopback interface
3. `wlan0`: The Wi-Fi interface

Notice that, depending on your computer's hardware, you may get different names for your network interfaces.

The ip command

You can also use the `ip link show` command to view the available network interfaces on your system:

```
root@ubuntu-linux:~# ip link show
1: lo: <LOOPBACK,UP,LOWER_UP> mtu 65536 qdisc noqueue state UNKNOWN mode
DEFAULT group default qlen 1000
    link/loopback 00:00:00:00:00:00 brd 00:00:00:00:00:00
2: eth0: <NO-CARRIER,BROADCAST,MULTICAST,UP> mtu 1500 qdisc pfifo_fast
state DOWN mode DEFAULT group default qlen 1000
    link/ether f0:de:f1:d3:e1:e1 brd ff:ff:ff:ff:ff:ff
3: wlan0: <BROADCAST,MULTICAST,UP,LOWER_UP> mtu 1500 qdisc mq state UP mode
DORMANT group default qlen 1000
    link/ether 10:0b:a9:6c:89:a0 brd ff:ff:ff:ff:ff:ff
```

The nmcli command

Another method that I prefer is using the `nmcli` device status command:

```
root@ubuntu-linux:~# nmcli device status
DEVICE TYPE STATE CONNECTION
wlan0 wifi      connected   SASKTEL0206-5G
```

```
eth0   ethernet   unavailable --
lo     loopback   unmanaged   --
```

You can see the connection status of each network interface in the output. I am currently connected to the internet through my Wi-Fi interface.

Checking your IP address

Without a cell phone number, you can't call any of your friends; similarly, your computer needs an IP address to connect to the internet. There are many different ways you can use to check your machine's IP address. You can use the old-school (yet still popular) `ifconfig` command followed by the name of your network interface that is connected to the internet:

```
root@ubuntu-linux:~# ifconfig wlan0
wlan0: flags=4163<UP,BROADCAST,RUNNING,MULTICAST> mtu 1500
        inet 172.16.1.73 netmask 255.255.255.0 broadcast 172.16.1.255
        inet6 fe80::3101:321b:5ec3:cf9 prefixlen 64 scopeid 0x20<link>
        ether 10:0b:a9:6c:89:a0 txqueuelen 1000 (Ethernet)
        RX packets 265 bytes 27284 (26.6 KiB)
        RX errors 0 dropped 0 overruns 0 frame 0
        TX packets 165 bytes 28916 (28.2 KiB)
        TX errors 0 dropped 0 overruns 0 carrier 0 collisions 0
```

You can also use the -a option to list all network interfaces:

```
root@ubuntu-linux:~# ifconfig -a
eth0: flags=4099<UP,BROADCAST,MULTICAST> mtu 1500
        ether f0:de:f1:d3:e1:e1 txqueuelen 1000 (Ethernet)
        RX packets 0 bytes 0 (0.0 B)
        RX errors 0 dropped 0 overruns 0 frame 0
        TX packets 0 bytes 0 (0.0 B)
        TX errors 0 dropped 0 overruns 0 carrier 0 collisions 0
        device interrupt 20 memory 0xf2500000-f2520000

lo: flags=73<UP,LOOPBACK,RUNNING> mtu 65536
        inet 127.0.0.1 netmask 255.0.0.0
        inet6 ::1 prefixlen 128 scopeid 0x10<host>
        loop txqueuelen 1000 (Local Loopback)
        RX packets 4 bytes 156 (156.0 B)
        RX errors 0 dropped 0 overruns 0 frame 0
        TX packets 4 bytes 156 (156.0 B)
        TX errors 0 dropped 0 overruns 0 carrier 0 collisions 0

wlan0: flags=4163<UP,BROADCAST,RUNNING,MULTICAST> mtu 1500
        inet 172.16.1.73 netmask 255.255.255.0 broadcast 172.16.1.255
```

```
inet6 fe80::3101:321b:5ec3:cf9 prefixlen 64 scopeid 0x20<link>
ether 10:0b:a9:6c:89:a0 txqueuelen 1000 (Ethernet)
RX packets 482 bytes 45500 (44.4 KiB)
RX errors 0 dropped 0 overruns 0 frame 0
TX packets 299 bytes 57788 (56.4 KiB)
TX errors 0 dropped 0 overruns 0 carrier 0 collisions 0
```

You can see from the output that I am only connected to the internet through my Wi-Fi interface (`wlan0`), and my IP address is `172.16.1.73`.

> **WHAT IS LOOPBACK?**
> Loopback (or `lo`) is a virtual interface that your computer uses to communicate with itself; it is mainly used for troubleshooting purposes. The IP address of the loopback interface is `127.0.0.1`, and if you want to ping yourself! Go ahead and ping `127.0.0.1`.

You can also use the newer `ip` command to check your machine's IP address. For example, you can run the `ip address show` command to list and show the status of all your network interfaces:

```
root@ubuntu-linux:~# ip address show
1: lo: <LOOPBACK,UP,LOWER_UP> mtu 65536 qdisc noqueue state UNKNOWN
    link/loopback 00:00:00:00:00:00 brd 00:00:00:00:00:00
    inet 127.0.0.1/8 scope host lo
        valid_lft forever preferred_lft forever
    inet6 ::1/128 scope host
        valid_lft forever preferred_lft forever
2: eth0: <NO-CARRIER,BROADCAST,MULTICAST,UP> mtu 1500 qdisc pfifo_fast
state
        DOWN link/ether f0:de:f1:d3:e1:e1 brd ff:ff:ff:ff:ff:ff
3: wlan0: <BROADCAST,MULTICAST,UP,LOWER_UP> mtu 1500 qdisc mq state
    UP link/ether 10:0b:a9:6c:89:a0 brd ff:ff:ff:ff:ff:ff
    inet 172.16.1.73/24 brd 172.16.1.255 scope global dynamic
      noprefixroute wlan0 valid_lft 85684sec preferred_lft 85684sec
    inet6 fe80::3101:321b:5ec3:cf9/64 scope link noprefixroute
      valid_lft forever preferred_lft forever
```

Checking your gateway address

Your computer grabs an IP address from a **router**; this router is also referred to as the **default gateway** as it connects you to the outside world (internet). Those routers are everywhere; they are at your house, coffee shops, schools, hospitals, and so on.

You can check the IP address of your default gateway by running any of the following commands:

- `route -n`
- `netstat -rn`
- `ip route`

Let's start with the first command, `route -n`:

```
root@ubuntu-linux:~# route -n Kernel IP routing table
Destination Gateway       Genmask       Flags  Metric Ref Use Iface
0.0.0.0     172.16.1.254  0.0.0.0       UG     600    0   0 wlan0
172.16.1.0  0.0.0.0       255.255.255.0 U      600    0   0 wlan0
```

You can see from the output that my default gateway IP address is `172.16.1.254`. Now let's try the second command, `netstat -rn`:

```
root@ubuntu-linux:~# netstat -rn
Kernel IP routing table
Destination    Gateway       Genmask       Flags  MSS Window irtt Iface
0.0.0.0        172.16.1.254  0.0.0.0       UG     0   0      0    wlan0
172.16.1.0     0.0.0.0       255.255.255.0 U      0   0      0    wlan0
```

The output almost looks identical. Now the output differs a little bit with the third command, `ip route`:

```
root@ubuntu-linux:~# ip route
default via 172.16.1.254 dev wlan0 proto dhcp metric 600
172.16.1.0/24 dev wlan0 proto kernel scope link src 172.16.1.73 metric 600
```

The default gateway IP address is displayed on the first line: default via `172.16.1.254`. You should also be able to ping your default gateway:

```
root@ubuntu-linux:~# ping -c 2 172.16.1.254
PING 172.16.1.254 (172.16.1.254) 56(84) bytes of data.
64 bytes from 172.16.1.254: icmp_seq=1 ttl=64 time=1.38 ms
64 bytes from 172.16.1.254: icmp_seq=2 ttl=64 time=1.62 ms

--- 172.16.1.254 ping statistics ---
2 packets transmitted, 2 received, 0% packet loss, time 3ms rtt
min/avg/max/mdev = 1.379/1.501/1.624/0.128 ms
```

Flying with traceroute

You are now ready to leave your house to go to work. You must go through different streets that eventually lead to your destination, right? Well, this is very similar to when you try to reach a host (website) on the internet; there is a route that you take that starts with your default gateway and ends with your destination.

You can use the `traceroute` command to trace the route to any destination. The general syntax of the `traceroute` command is as follows:

```
traceroute destination
```

For example, you can trace the route from your machine to `google.com` by running the following command:

```
root@ubuntu-linux:~# traceroute google.com
traceroute to google.com (172.217.1.14), 30 hops max, 60 byte packets
 1 172.16.1.254 (172.16.1.254) 15.180 ms 15.187 ms 15.169 ms
 2 207-47-195-169.ngai.static.sasknet.sk.ca (207.47.195.169) 24.059 ms
 3 142.165.0.110 (142.165.0.110) 50.060 ms 54.305 ms 54.903 ms
 4 72.14.203.189 (72.14.203.189) 53.720 ms 53.997 ms 53.948 ms
 5 108.170.250.241 (108.170.250.241) 54.185 ms 35.506 ms 108.170.250.225
 6 216.239.35.233 (216.239.35.233) 37.005 ms 35.729 ms 38.655 ms
 7 yyz10s14-in-f14.1e100.net (172.217.1.14) 41.739 ms 41.667 ms 41.581 ms
```

As you can see, my machine took seven trips (hops) to reach my final destination, `google.com`. Notice the first hop is my default gateway, and the last hop is the destination.

The `traceroute` command comes in handy when you are troubleshooting connectivity issues. For example, it may take you a very long time to reach a specific destination; in this case, `traceroute` can help you detect any points of failure on the path to your destination.

Breaking your DNS

Every website (destination) on the internet must have an IP address. However, we humans are not very good with numbers so we have invented the **Domain Name System** (**DNS**). The primary function of the DNS is that it associates a name (domain name) with an IP address; this way, we don't need to memorize IP addresses while browsing the internet ... thank God for the DNS!

Every time you enter a domain name on your browser, the DNS translates (resolves) the domain name to its corresponding IP address. The IP address of your DNS server is stored in the file `/etc/resolv.conf`:

```
root@ubuntu-linux:~# cat /etc/resolv.conf
# Generated by NetworkManager
nameserver 142.165.200.5
```

I am using the DNS server `142.165.200.5`, which is provided by my **Internet Service Provider (ISP)**. You can use the `nslookup` command to see DNS in action. The general syntax of the `nslookup` command is as follows:

```
nslookup domain_name
```

The `nslookup` command uses DNS to obtain the IP address of a domain name. For example, to get the IP address of `facebook.com`, you can run the following command:

```
root@ubuntu-linux:~# nslookup facebook.com
Server:   142.165.200.5
Address:  142.165.200.5#53

Non-authoritative answer:
Name: facebook.com
Address: 157.240.3.35
Name: facebook.com
Address: 2a03:2880:f101:83:face:b00c:0:25de
```

Notice it displayed the IP address of my DNS server in the first line of the output. You can also see the IP address `157.240.3.35` of `facebook.com`.

You can also ping `facebook.com`:

```
root@ubuntu-linux:~# ping -c 2 facebook.com
PING facebook.com (157.240.3.35) 56(84) bytes of data.
64 bytes from edge-star-mini-shv-01-sea1.facebook.com (157.240.3.35):
icmp_seq=1 ttl=55 time=34.6 ms
64 bytes from edge-star-mini-shv-01-sea1.facebook.com (157.240.3.35):
icmp_seq=2 ttl=55 time=33.3 ms

--- facebook.com ping statistics ---

2 packets transmitted, 2 received, 0% packet loss, time 2ms
rtt min/avg/max/mdev = 33.316/33.963/34.611/0.673 ms
```

Now let's break things! My mum once told me that I have to break things so I can understand how they work. Let's see what life is without DNS by emptying the file `/etc/resolv.conf`:

```
root@ubuntu-linux:~# echo > /etc/resolv.conf
root@ubuntu-linux:~# cat /etc/resolv.conf

root@ubuntu-linux:~#
```

Now let's do `nslookup` on `facebook.com`:

```
root@ubuntu-linux:~# nslookup facebook.com
```

You will see that it hangs as it is unable to resolve domain names anymore. Now let's try to ping `facebook.com`:

```
root@ubuntu-linux:~# ping facebook.com
ping: facebook.com: Temporary failure in name resolution
```

You get the error message `Temporary failure in name resolution`, which is a fancy way of saying that your DNS is broken! However, you can still ping `facebook.com` by using its IP address:

```
root@ubuntu-linux:~# ping -c 2 157.240.3.35
PING 157.240.3.35 (157.240.3.35) 56(84) bytes of data.
64 bytes from 157.240.3.35: icmp_seq=1 ttl=55 time=134 ms
64 bytes from 157.240.3.35: icmp_seq=2 ttl=55 time=34.4 ms

--- 157.240.3.35 ping statistics ---
2 packets transmitted, 2 received, 0% packet loss, time 2ms
rtt min/avg/max/mdev = 34.429/84.150/133.872/49.722 ms
```

Let's fix our DNS, but this time we will not use the DNS server of our ISP; instead, we will use Google's public DNS server `8.8.8.8`:

```
root@ubuntu-linux:~# echo "nameserver 8.8.8.8" > /etc/resolv.conf
root@ubuntu-linux:~# cat /etc/resolv.conf
nameserver 8.8.8.8
```

Now let's do an `nslookup` on `facebook.com` again:

```
root@ubuntu-linux:~# nslookup facebook.com Server: 8.8.8.8
Address: 8.8.8.8#53

Non-authoritative answer:
Name: facebook.com
Address: 31.13.80.36
Name: facebook.com
Address: 2a03:2880:f10e:83:face:b00c:0:25de
```

Notice that my active DNS is now changed to `8.8.8.8`. I also got a different IP address for `facebook.com`, and that's because Facebook is running on many different servers located in various regions of the world.

Changing your hostname

Every website has a domain name that uniquely identifies it over the internet; similarly, a computer has a hostname that uniquely identifies it over a network.

Your computer's hostname is stored in the file `/etc/hostname`:

```
root@ubuntu-linux:~# cat /etc/hostname
ubuntu-linux
```

You can use hostnames to reach other computers in the same network (subnet). For example, I have another computer with the hostname `backdoor` that is currently running, and I can ping it:

```
root@ubuntu-linux:~# ping backdoor
PING backdoor (172.16.1.67) 56(84) bytes of data.
64 bytes from 172.16.1.67 (172.16.1.67): icmp_seq=1 ttl=64 time=3.27 ms
64 bytes from 172.16.1.67 (172.16.1.67): icmp_seq=2 ttl=64 time=29.3 ms
64 bytes from 172.16.1.67 (172.16.1.67): icmp_seq=3 ttl=64 time=51.4 ms
^C
--- backdoor ping statistics ---
3 packets transmitted, 3 received, 0% packet loss, time 20ms
rtt min/avg/max/mdev = 3.272/27.992/51.378/19.662 ms
```

Notice that backdoor is on the same network (subnet) and has an IP address of 172.16.1.67. I can also ping myself:

```
root@ubuntu-linux:~# ping ubuntu-linux
PING ubuntu-linux (172.16.1.73) 56(84) bytes of data.
64 bytes from 172.16.1.73 (172.16.1.73): icmp_seq=1 ttl=64 time=0.025 ms
64 bytes from 172.16.1.73 (172.16.1.73): icmp_seq=2 ttl=64 time=0.063 ms
^C
--- ubuntu-linux ping statistics ---
2 packets transmitted, 2 received, 0% packet loss, time 14ms
rtt min/avg/max/mdev = 0.025/0.044/0.063/0.019 ms
```

That's a smart way of displaying your computer's IP address – simply ping yourself!

You can use the hostnamectl command to view and set your computer's hostname:

```
root@ubuntu-linux:~# hostnamectl
     Static hostname: ubuntu-linux
           Icon name: computer-vm
             Chassis: vm
          Machine ID: 106fd80252e541faafa4e54a250d1216
             Boot ID: c5508514af114b4b80c55d4267c25dd4
      Virtualization: oracle
    Operating System: Ubuntu 18.04.3 LTS
              Kernel: Linux 4.15.0-66-generic
        Architecture: x86-64
```

To change your computer's hostname, you can use the hostnamectl set-hostname command followed by the new hostname:

```
hostnamectl set-hostname new_hostname
```

For example, you can change the hostname of your computer to myserver by running the following command:

```
root@ubuntu-linux:~# hostnamectl set-hostname myserver
root@ubuntu-linux:~# su -
root@myserver:~#
```

Keep in mind that you need to open a new shell session so that your shell prompt displays the new hostname. You can also see that the file /etc/hostname is updated as it contains the new hostname:

```
root@ubuntu-linux:~# cat /etc/hostname
myserver
```

Restarting your network interface

It's probably an abused method, but sometimes doing a restart is the quickest fix to many computer-related troubles! I myself am guilty of overusing the restart solution for most of my computer problems.

You can use the ifconfig command to bring down (disable) a network interface; you have to follow the network interface name with the down flag as follows:

```
ifconfig interface_name down
```

For example, I can bring down my Wi-Fi interface, wlan0, by running the following command:

```
root@myserver:~# ifconfig wlan0 down
```

You can use the up flag to bring up (enable) a network interface:

```
ifconfig interface_name up
```

For example, I can bring back up my Wi-Fi interface by running the following command:

```
root@myserver:~# ifconfig wlan0 up
```

You may also want to restart all your network interfaces at the same time. This can be done by restarting the NetworkManager service as follows:

```
root@myserver:~# systemctl restart NetworkManager
```

Now it's time to test your understanding of Linux networking with a lovely knowledge-check exercise.

Knowledge check

For the following exercises, open up your Terminal and try to solve the following tasks:

1. Change your hostname to `darkarmy`.
2. Display the IP address of your default gateway.
3. Trace the route from your machine to `www.ubuntu.com`.
4. Display the IP address of your DNS.
5. Display the IP address of `www.distrowatch.com`.
6. Bring down your Ethernet interface.
7. Bring your Ethernet interface back up.

16
Bash Scripting Is Fun

To complete a specific task in Linux, you will often find yourself running the same set of commands over and over again. This process can waste a lot of your precious time. In this chapter, you will learn how to create bash scripts so that you can be much more efficient in Linux.

Creating simple scripts

Our first bash script will be a simple script that will output the line "Hello Friend!" to the screen. In Elliot's home directory, create a file named `hello.sh` and insert the following two lines:

```
elliot@ubuntu-linux:~$ cat hello.sh
#!/bin/bash
echo "Hello Friend!"
```

Now we need to make the script executable:

```
elliot@ubuntu-linux:~$ chmod a+x hello.sh
```

And finally, run the script:

```
elliot@ubuntu-linux:~$ ./hello.sh
Hello Friend!
```

Congratulations! You have now created your first bash script! Let's take a minute here and discuss a few things; every bash script must do the following:

- `#!/bin/bash`
- Be executable

You have to insert `#!/bin/bash` at the first line of any bash script; the character sequence `#!` is referred to as a shebang or hashbang and is followed by the path of the bash shell.

The PATH variable

You may have noticed that I used `./hello.sh` to run the script; you will get an error if you omit the leading `./`:

```
elliot@ubuntu-linux:~$ hello.sh
hello.sh: command not found
```

The shell can't find the command `hello.sh`. When you run a command on your terminal, the shell looks for that command in a set of directories that are stored in the PATH variable.

You can use the `echo` command to view the contents of your PATH variable:

```
elliot@ubuntu-linux:~$ echo $PATH
/usr/local/sbin:/usr/local/bin:/usr/sbin:/usr/bin:/sbin:/bin
```

The colon character separates the path of each of the directories. You don't need to include the full path of any command or script (or any executable) that resides in these directories. All the commands you have learned so far reside in `/bin` and `/sbin`, which are both stored in your PATH variable. As a result, you can run the `pwd` command:

```
elliot@ubuntu-linux:~$ pwd
/home/elliot
```

There is no need to include its full path:

```
elliot@ubuntu-linux:~$ /bin/pwd
/home/elliot
```

The good news is that you can easily add a directory to your PATH variable. For example, to add `/home/elliot` to your PATH variable, you can use the `export` command as follows:

```
elliot@ubuntu-linux:~$ export PATH=$PATH:/home/elliot
```

Now you don't need the leading `./` to run the `hello.sh` script:

```
elliot@ubuntu-linux:~$ hello.sh
Hello Friend!
```

It will run because the shell is now looking for executable files in the `/home/elliot` directory as well:

```
elliot@ubuntu-linux:~$ echo $PATH
/usr/local/sbin:/usr/local/bin:/usr/sbin:/usr/bin:/sbin:/bin:/home/elliot
```

Alright! Now let's create a few more bash scripts. We will create a script named `hello2.sh` that prints out "Hello Friend!" then displays your current working directory:

```
elliot@ubuntu-linux:~$ cat hello2.sh
#!/bin/bash
echo "Hello Friend!"
pwd
```

Now let's run it:

```
elliot@ubuntu-linux:~$ hello2.sh
-bash: /home/elliot/hello2.sh: Permission denied
```

Shoot! I forgot to make it executable:

```
elliot@ubuntu-linux:~$ chmod a+x hello2.sh
elliot@ubuntu-linux:~$ ./hello2.sh
Hello Friend!
/home/elliot
```

Reading user input

Let's create a better version of our `hello.sh` script. We will let the user input his/her name and then we will greet the user; create a script named `greet.sh` with the following lines:

```
elliot@ubuntu-linux:~$ cat greet.sh
#!/bin/bash
echo "Please enter your name:"
read name
echo "Hello $name!"
```

Now make the script executable and then run it:

```
elliot@ubuntu-linux:~$ chmod a+x greet.sh
elliot@ubuntu-linux:~$ ./greet.sh
Please enter your name:
```

When you run the script, it will prompt you to enter your name; I entered `Elliot` as my name:

```
elliot@ubuntu-linux:~$ ./greet.sh
Please enter your name:
Elliot
Hello Elliot!
```

The script greeted me with "Hello Elliot!". We used the `read` command to get the user input, and notice in the `echo` statement, we used a dollar sign, `$`, to print the value of the variable `name`.

Let's create another script that reads a filename from the user and then outputs the size of the file in bytes; we will name our script `size.sh`:

```
elliot@ubuntu-linux:~$ cat size.sh
#!/bin/bash
echo "Please enter a file path:"
read file
filesize=$(du -bs $file| cut -f1)
echo "The file size is $filesize bytes"
```

And never forget to make the script executable:

```
elliot@ubuntu-linux:~$ chmod a+x size.sh
```

Now let's run the script:

```
elliot@ubuntu-linux:~$ size.sh
Please enter a file path
/home/elliot/size.sh
The file size is 128 bytes
```

I used `size.sh` as the file path, and the output was 128 bytes; is that true? Let's check:

```
elliot@ubuntu-linux:~$ du -bs size.sh
128 size.sh
```

Indeed it is; notice in the script the following line:

```
filesize=$(du -bs $file| cut -f1)
```

It stores the result of the command `du -bs $file | cut -f1` in the variable `filesize`:

```
elliot@ubuntu-linux:~$ du -bs size.sh | cut -f1
128
```

Also notice that the command `du -bs $file cut -f1` is surrounded by parentheses and a dollar sign (on the left); this is called command substitution. In general, the syntax of command substitution goes as follows:

```
var=$(command)
```

The result of the `command` will be stored in the variable `var`.

Passing arguments to scripts

Instead of reading input from users, you can also pass arguments to a bash script. For example, let's create a bash script named `size2.sh` that does the same thing as the script `size.sh`, but instead of reading the file from the user, we will pass it to the script `size2.sh` as an argument:

```
elliot@ubuntu-linux:~$ cat size2.sh
#!/bin/bash
filesize=$(du -bs $1| cut -f1)
echo "The file size is $filesize bytes"
```

Now let's make the script executable:

```
elliot@ubuntu-linux:~$ chmod a+x size2.sh
```

Finally, you can run the script:

```
elliot@ubuntu-linux:~$ size2.sh /home/elliot/size.sh
The file size is 128 bytes
```

You will get the same output as `size.sh`. Notice that we provided the file path `/home/elliot/size.sh` as an argument to the script `size2.sh`.

We only used one argument in the script `size2.sh`, and it is referenced by `$1`. You can pass multiple arguments as well; let's create another script `size3.sh` that takes two files (two arguments) and outputs the size of each file:

```
elliot@ubuntu-linux:~$ cat size3.sh #!/bin/bash
filesize1=$(du -bs $1| cut -f1)
filesize2=$(du -bs $2| cut -f1)
echo "$1 is $filesize1 bytes"
echo "$2 is $filesize2 bytes"
```

Now make the script executable and run it:

```
elliot@ubuntu-linux:~$ size3.sh /home/elliot/size.sh /home/elliot/size3.sh
/home/elliot/size.sh is 128 bytes
/home/elliot/size3.sh is 136 bytes
```

Awesome! As you can see, the first argument is referenced by `$1`, and the second argument is referenced by `$2`. So in general:

```
bash_script.sh argument1 argument2 argument3 ...
                   $1          $2          $3
```

Using the if condition

You can add intelligence to your bash script by making it behave differently in different scenarios. To do that, we use the conditional `if` statement.

In general, the syntax of the `if condition` is as follows:

```
if [ condition is true ]; then
    do this ...
fi
```

For example, let's create a script `empty.sh` that will examine whether a file is empty or not:

```
elliot@ubuntu-linux:~$ cat empty.sh
#!/bin/bash
filesize=$(du -bs $1 | cut -f1)
if [ $filesize -eq 0 ]; then
echo "$1 is empty!"
fi
```

Now let's make the script executable and also create an empty file named `zero.txt`:

```
elliot@ubuntu-linux:~$ chmod a+x empty.sh
elliot@ubuntu-linux:~$ touch zero.txt
```

Now let's run the script on the file `zero.txt`:

```
elliot@ubuntu-linux:~$ ./empty.sh zero.txt
zero.txt is empty!
```

As you can see, the script correctly detects that `zero.txt` is an empty file; that's because the test condition is true in this case as the file `zero.txt` is indeed zero bytes in size:

```
if [ $filesize -eq 0 ];
```

We used `-eq` to test for equality. Now if you run the script on a non-empty file, there will be no output:

```
elliot@ubuntu-linux:~$ ./empty.sh size.sh
elliot@ubuntu-linux:~$
```

We need to modify the script `empty.sh` so that it displays an output whenever it's passed a non-empty file; for that, we will use the `if-else` statement:

```
if [ condition is true ]; then
    do this ...
else
```

```
        do this instead ...
    fi
```

Let's edit the `empty.sh` script by adding the following `else` statement:

```
elliot@ubuntu-linux:~$ cat empty.sh
#!/bin/bash
filesize=$(du -bs $1 | cut -f1)
if [ $filesize -eq 0 ]; then
echo "$1 is empty!"
else
echo "$1 is not empty!"
fi
```

Now let's rerun the script:

```
elliot@ubuntu-linux:~$ ./empty.sh size.sh
size.sh is not empty!
elliot@ubuntu-linux:~$ ./empty.sh zero.txt
zero.txt is empty!
```

As you can see, it now works perfectly!

You can also use the `elif` (**else-if**) statement to create multiple test conditions:

```
if [ condition is true ]; then
    do this ...
elif [ condition is true]; then
    do this instead ...
fi
```

Let's create a script `filetype.sh` that detects a file type. The script will output whether a file is a regular file, a soft link, or a directory:

```
elliot@ubuntu-linux:~$ cat filetype.sh
#!/bin/bash
file=$1
if [ -f $1 ]; then
echo "$1 is a regular file"
elif [ -L $1 ]; then
echo "$1 is a soft link"
elif [ -d $1 ]; then
echo "$1 is a directory"
fi
```

Now let's make the script executable and also create a soft link to /tmp named tempfiles:

```
elliot@ubuntu-linux:~$ chmod a+x filetype.sh
elliot@ubuntu-linux:~$ ln -s /tmp tempfiles
```

Now run the script on any directory:

```
elliot@ubuntu-linux:~$ ./filetype.sh /bin
/bin is a directory
```

It correctly detects that /bin is a directory. Now run the script on any regular file:

```
elliot@ubuntu-linux:~$ ./filetype.sh zero.txt
zero.txt is a regular file
```

It correctly detects that zero.txt is a regular file. Finally, run the script on any soft link:

```
elliot@ubuntu-linux:~$ ./filetype.sh tempfiles
tempfiles is a soft link
```

It correctly detects that tempfiles is a soft link.

The following man page contains all the test conditions:

```
elliot@ubuntu-linux:~$ man test
```

So NEVER memorize! Utilize and make use of the man pages.

Looping in bash scripts

The ability to loop is a very powerful feature of bash scripting. For example, let's say you want to print out the line "Hello world" 20 times on your terminal; a naive approach would be to create a script that has 20 echo statements. Luckily, looping offers a smarter solution.

Using the for loop

The for loop has a few different syntaxes. If you are familiar with C++ or C programming, then you will recognize the following for loop syntax:

```
for ((initialize ; condition ; increment)); do
// do something
done
```

Using the aforementioned C-style syntax; the following `for` loop will print out "Hello World" twenty times:

```
for ((i = 0 ; i < 20 ; i++)); do
    echo "Hello World"
done
```

The loop initializes the integer variable `i` to 0, then it tests the condition (`i < 20`); if true, it then executes the line echo "Hello World" and increments the variable `i` by one, and then the loop runs again and again until `i` is no longer less than 20.

Now let's create a script `hello20.sh` that has the `for` loop we just discussed:

```
elliot@ubuntu-linux:~$ cat hello20.sh
#!/bin/bash
for ((i = 0 ; i < 20 ; i++)); do
    echo "Hello World"
done
```

Now make the script executable and run it:

```
elliot@ubuntu-linux:~$ chmod a+x hello20.sh
elliot@ubuntu-linux:~$ hello20.sh
Hello World
Hello World
Hello World
Hello World
Hello World
Hello World
Hello World
Hello World
Hello World
Hello World
Hello World
Hello World
Hello World
Hello World
Hello World
Hello World
Hello World
Hello World
Hello World
Hello World
```

It outputs the line "Hello World" twenty times as we expected. Instead of the C-style syntax, you can also use the range syntax with the `for` loop:

```
for i in {1..20}; do
    echo "Hello World"
done
```

This will also output "Hello World" 20 times. This range syntax is particularly useful when working with a list of files. To demonstrate, create the following five files:

```
elliot@ubuntu-linux:~$ touch one.doc two.doc three.doc four.doc five.doc
```

Now let's say we want to rename the extension for all five files from `.doc` to `.document`. We can create a script `rename.sh` that has the following `for` loop:

```
#!/bin/bash
for i in /home/elliot/*.doc; do
    mv $i $(echo $i | cut -d. -f1).document
done
```

Make the script executable and run it:

```
#!/bin/bash
elliot@ubuntu-linux:~$ chmod a+x rename.sh
elliot@ubuntu-linux:~$ ./rename.sh
elliot@ubuntu-linux:~$ ls *.document
five.document four.document one.document three.document two.document
```

As you can see, it renamed all the files with the `.doc` extension to `.document`. Now imagine if you wanted to do this for a million files. If you don't know bash scripting, you would probably spend ten years doing it. We should all thank the Linux Gods for bash scripting.

Using the while loop

The `while` loop is another popular and intuitive loop. The general syntax for a `while` loop is as follows:

```
while [ condition is true ]; do
   // do something
done
```

For example, we can create a simple script `numbers.sh` that prints the numbers from one to ten:

```
elliot@ubuntu-linux:~$ cat numbers.sh
#!/bin/bash
number=1
while [ $number -le 10 ]; do
echo $number
number=$(($number+1))
done
```

Make the script executable and run it:

```
elliot@ubuntu-linux:~$ chmod a+x numbers.sh
elliot@ubuntu-linux:~$ ./numbers.sh
1
2
3
4
5
6
7
8
9
10
```

The script is simple to understand; we first initialized the variable number to 1:

```
number=1
```

Then we created a test condition that will keep the while loop running as long as the variable number is less than or equal to 10:

```
while [ $number -le 10 ]; do
```

Inside the body of the while loop, we first print out the value of the variable number, and then we increment it by one. Notice that to evaluate an arithmetic expression, it needs to be within double parentheses as $((arithmetic-expression)):

```
echo $number
number=$(($number+1))
```

Now it's time for some fun! We will create a number guessing game. But before we do that, let me introduce you to a pretty cool command. You can use the shuffle command `shuf` to generate random permutations. For example, to generate a random permutation of the numbers between 1 and 10, you can run the following command:

```
elliot@ubuntu-linux:~$ shuf -i 1-10
1
6
5
2
10
8
3
9
7
4
```

Keep in mind that my output will most likely be different from your output because it is random! There is a one in a million chance that you will have the same output as me.

Now we can use the `-n` option to select one number out of the permutation. This number will be random as well. So to generate a random number between 1 and 10, you can run the following command:

```
elliot@ubuntu-linux:~$ shuf -i 1-10 -n 1
6
```

The output will be a random number between 1 and 10. The `shuf` command will play a key role in our game. We will generate a random number between 1 and 10, and then we will see how many tries it will take the user (player) to guess the random number correctly.

Here is our lovely handcrafted script `game.sh`:

```
elliot@ubuntu-linux:~$ cat game.sh
#!/bin/bash
random=$(shuf -i 1-10 -n 1) #generate a random number between 1 and 10.
echo "Welcome to the Number Guessing Game"
echo "The lucky number is between 1 and 10."
echo "Can you guess it?"
tries=1
while [ true ]; do
echo -n "Enter a Number between 1-10: "
read number
if [ $number -gt $random ]; then
echo "Too high!"
elif [ $number -lt $random ]; then
echo "Too low!"
```

```
else
echo "Correct! You got it in $tries tries"
break #exit the loop
fi
tries=$(($tries+1))
done
```

Now make the script executable and run it to start the game:

```
elliot@ubuntu-linux:~$ chmod a+x game.sh
elliot@ubuntu-linux:~$ game.sh
Welcome to the Number Guessing Game
The lucky number is between 1 and 10.
Can you guess it?
Enter a Number between 1-10: 4
Too low!
Enter a Number between 1-10: 7
Too low!
Enter a Number between 1-10: 9
Too high!
Enter a Number between 1-10: 8
Correct! You got it in 4 tries
```

It took me four tries in my first attempt at the game; I bet you can easily beat me!
Let's go over our game script line by line. We first generate a random number between 1 and 10 and assign it to the variable `random`:

```
random=$(shuf -i 1-10 -n 1) #generate a random number between 1 and 10.
```

Notice that you can add comments in your bash script as I did here by using the hash character, followed by your comment.

We then print three lines that explain the game to the player:

```
echo "Welcome to the Number Guessing Game"
echo "The lucky number is between 1 and 10."
echo "Can you guess it?"
```

Next, we initialize the variable `tries` to 1 so that we can keep track of how many guesses the player took:

```
tries=1
```

We then enter the game loop:

```
while [ true ]; do
```

Notice the test condition `while [ true ]` will always be `true`, and so the loop will keep running forever (infinite loop).

The first thing we do in the game loop is that we ask the player to enter a number between 1 and 10:

```
echo -n "Enter a Number between 1-10: "
read number
```

We then test to see if the number the player has entered is greater than, less than, or equal to the `random` number:

```
if [ $number -gt $random ]; then
echo "Too high!"
elif [ $number -lt $random ]; then
echo "Too low!"
else
echo "Correct! You got it in $tries tries"
break #exit the loop
fi
```

If `number` is bigger than `random`, we tell the player that the guess is too high to make it easier for the player to have a better guess next time. Likewise, if `number` is smaller than `random`, we tell the player the guess is too low. Otherwise, if it is a correct guess, then we print the total number of tries the player exhausted to make the correct guess, and we break from the loop.

Notice that you need the `break` statement to exit from the infinite loop. Without the `break` statement, the loop will run forever.

Finally, we increment the number of `tries` by 1 for each incorrect guess (high or low):

```
tries=$(($tries+1))
```

I have to warn you that this game is addictive! Especially when you play it with a friend to see who will get the correct guess in the least number of tries.

Using the until loop

Both the `for` and `while` loops run as long as the test condition is `true`. On the flip side, the `until` loop keeps running as long as the test condition is `false`. That's to say, it stops running as soon as the test condition is `true`.

The general syntax of an until loop is as follows:

```
until [condition is true]; do
  [commands]
done
```

For example, we can create a simple script 3x10.sh that prints out the first ten multiples of 3:

```
elliot@ubuntu-linux:~$ cat 3x10.sh
#!/bin/bash
counter=1
until [ $counter -gt 10 ]; do
echo $(($counter * 3))
counter=$(($counter+1))
done
```

Now make the script executable and then run it:

```
elliot@ubuntu-linux:~$ chmod a+x 3x10.sh
elliot@ubuntu-linux:~$ 3x10.sh
3
6
9
12
15
18
21
24
27
30
```

The script is easy to understand, but you might scratch your head a little bit trying to understand the test condition of the until loop:

```
until [ $counter -gt 10 ]; do
```

The test condition basically says: "until counter is greater than 10, keep running!"

Notice that we can achieve the same result with a while loop that has the opposite test condition. You simply negate the test condition of the until loop and you will get the while loop equivalent:

```
while [ $counter -le 10 ]; do
```

In mathematics, the opposite (negation) of greater than (>) is less than or equal to (≤). A lot of people forget the equal to part. Don't be one of those people!

Bash script functions

When your scripts get bigger and bigger, things can get very messy. To overcome this problem, you can use bash functions. The idea behind functions is that you can reuse parts of your scripts, which in turn produces better organized and readable scripts.

The general syntax of a bash function is as follows:

```
function_name () {
<commands>
}
```

Let's create a function named `hello` that prints out the line "Hello World". We will put the `hello` function in a new script named `fun1.sh`:

```
elliot@ubuntu-linux:~$ cat fun1.sh
#!/bin/bash

hello () {
echo "Hello World"
}

hello      # Call the function hello()
hello      # Call the function hello()
hello      # Call the function hello()
```

Now make the script executable and run it:

```
elliot@ubuntu-linux:~$ chmod a+x fun1.sh
elliot@ubuntu-linux:~$ ./fun1.sh
Hello World
Hello World
Hello World
```

The script outputs the line "Hello World" three times to the terminal. Notice that we called (used) the function `hello` three times.

Passing function arguments

Functions can also take arguments the same way a script can take arguments. To demonstrate, we will create a script `math.sh` that has two functions `add` and `sub`:

```
elliot@ubuntu-linux:~$ cat math.sh
#!/bin/bash
```

```
add () {
echo "$1 + $2 =" $(($1+$2))
}

sub () {
echo "$1 - $2 =" $(($1-$2))
}

add 7 2
sub 7 2
```

Make the script executable and then run it:

```
elliot@ubuntu-linux:~$ chmod a+x math.sh
elliot@ubuntu-linux:~$ ./math.sh
7 + 2 = 9
7 - 2 = 5
```

The script has two functions `add` and `sub`. The `add` function calculates and outputs the total of any given two numbers. On the other hand, the `sub` function calculates and outputs the difference of any given two numbers.

No browsing for you

We will conclude this chapter with a pretty cool bash script `noweb.sh` that makes sure no user is having fun browsing the web on the Firefox browser:

```
elliot@ubuntu-linux:~$ cat noweb.sh
#!/bin/bash

shutdown_firefox() {
killall firefox 2> /dev/null
}

while [ true ]; do
shutdown_firefox
sleep 10 #wait for 10 seconds
done
```

Now open Firefox as a background process:

```
elliot@ubuntu-linux:~$ firefox &
[1] 30436
```

Finally, make the script executable and run the script in the background:

```
elliot@ubuntu-linux:~$ chmod a+x noweb.sh
elliot@ubuntu-linux:~$ ./noweb.sh &
[1] 30759
```

The moment you run your script, Firefox will shut down. Moreover, if you run the script as the `root` user, none of the system users will be able to enjoy Firefox!

Knowledge check

For the following exercises, open up your terminal and try to solve the following tasks:

1. Create a bash script that will display the calendar of the current month.
2. Modify your script so it displays the calendar for any year (passed as an argument).
3. Modify your script so it displays the calendar for all the years from 2000 to 2020.

17
You Need a Cron Job

In this chapter, you will learn how to automate boring tasks in Linux by using cron jobs, which is one of the most useful and powerful utilities in Linux. Thanks to cron jobs, Linux system administrators can rest on the weekend and enjoy their vacation with their beloved ones. Cron jobs allow you to schedule tasks to run at a specific time. With cron jobs, you can schedule to run backups, monitor system resources, and much more.

Our first cron job

The following diagram shows you the typical format for a cron job:

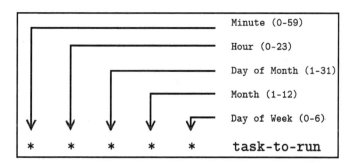

Figure 1: A cron job format

Cron jobs are user-specific, and so each user has their own list of cron jobs. For example, the user elliot can run the command crontab -l to display his their of cron jobs:

```
elliot@ubuntu-linux:~$ crontab -l
no crontab for elliot
```

Currently, the user elliot doesn't have any cron jobs.

Let's go ahead and create Elliot's first cron job. We will create a cron job that will run every minute, and it will simply append the line "A minute has passed." to the file `/home/elliot/minutes.txt`.

You can run the command `crontab -e` to edit or create cron jobs:

```
elliot@ubuntu-linux:~$ crontab -e
```

Now add the following line and then save and exit:

```
* * * * * echo "A minute has passed." >> /home/elliot/minutes.txt
```

After you exit, you will see the message: "crontab: installing new crontab":

```
elliot@ubuntu-linux:~$ crontab -e
crontab: installing new crontab
```

Finally, the user `elliot` can list their cron jobs to verify that the new cron job is scheduled:

```
elliot@ubuntu-linux:~$ crontab -l
* * * * * echo "A minute has passed." >> /home/elliot/minutes.txt
```

Now, wait for a few minutes and then check the contents of the file `/home/elliot/minutes.txt`:

```
elliot@ubuntu-linux:~$ cat /home/elliot/minutes.txt
A minute has passed.
A minute has passed.
A minute has passed.
A minute has passed.
A minute has passed.
```

I waited five minutes, and then I viewed the file to see that the line "A minute has passed." was added five times to the file `minutes.txt`, so I know the cron job is working fine.

Run every five minutes

Let's create another cron job that will run every five minutes. For example, you may want to create a cron job that checks the load average on your system every five minutes.

Run the command `crontab -e` to add a new cron job:

```
elliot@ubuntu-linux:~$ crontab -e
```

Now add the following line and then save and exit:

```
*/5 * * * * uptime >> /home/elliot/load.txt
```

Finally, let's view the list of installed cron jobs to verify that the new cron job is scheduled:

```
elliot@ubuntu-linux:~$ crontab -e
crontab: installing new crontab
elliot@ubuntu-linux:~$ crontab -l
* * * * * echo "A minute has passed" >> /home/elliot/minutes.txt
*/5 * * * * uptime >> /home/elliot/load.txt
```

Now we can see there are two cron jobs installed for the user `elliot`.

Hang around for five or ten minutes and then check the contents of the file `/home/elliot/load.txt`. If you don't have a stopwatch, run the command `sleep 300` and wait until it finishes:

```
elliot@ubuntu-linux:~$ sleep 300
```

I made myself some green tea, and then came back after ten minutes and viewed the file `/home/elliot/load.txt`:

```
elliot@ubuntu-linux:~$ cat /home/elliot/load.txt
14:40:01 up 1 day, 5:13, 2 users, load average: 0.41, 0.40, 0.37
14:45:01 up 1 day, 5:18, 2 users, load average: 0.25, 0.34, 0.35
```

The cron job ran twice in those ten minutes as expected; I recommend you check the file `/home/elliot/load.txt` again in twenty-four hours, and you will see a pretty lovely report for your system load average throughout the day.

More cron examples

You can also schedule your cron job to run at multiple time intervals. For example, the following cron job will run every hour on Sunday at the minutes 5, 20, and 40:

```
5,20,40 * * * sun task-to-run
```

You can also specify a time range. For example, a cron job that will run at 6:30 PM on `weekdays` (Monday -> Friday) will have the following format:

```
30 18 * * 1-5 task-to-run
```

Notice that `0` is Sunday, `1` is Monday, and so on.

To see more cron examples, you can check the fifth section of the `crontab` man page:

```
elliot@ubuntu-linux:~$ man 5 crontab
```

Automating system patching

As a Linux system administrator, you get to patch (update) systems quite often. And sometimes, it may drive you insane as production servers are scheduled to update at unpleasant times, like midnight on the weekends, `04:00` AM, `02:00` AM, etc. It would be nice to automate such a hectic task and get more sleep, right?

Let's switch to the `root` user and then create a bash script named `auto_patch.sh`

in `/root`:

```
root@ubuntu-linux:~# cat auto_patch.sh
#!/bin/bash
apt-get -y update
apt-get -y upgrade
shutdown -r now
```

Notice that the script `auto_patch.sh` is tiny; only three lines. We have used the `-y` option with the `apt-get` commands, which automatically answers `Yes` to all prompts during the system update; this is important because you will not be sitting in front of the computer while the script is running!

Now make the script executable:

```
root@ubuntu-linux:~# chmod +x auto_patch.sh
```

Finally, you need to schedule a cron job to run the `auto_patch.sh` script. Let's assume the system is scheduled to update on Saturday at 01:00 AM. In this case, you can create the following cron job:

```
0 1 * * sat /root/auto_patch.sh
```

Keep in mind that `auto_patch.sh` will never be deployed on any real server. I was only opening your mind to the concept of automation. You need to edit `auto_patch.sh` to check for command exit codes as it's naive to expect that everything will go smoothly without any errors. A good system administrator always creates robust scripts that handle all kinds of expected errors.

Running a job once

You have to remove the `auto_patch.sh` cron job sometime after it runs, or else it will keep updating the system every week! For this, there exists another utility called `at` for that sole purpose; that is, to schedule to run a job just once.

We first need to install the `at` package:

```
root@ubuntu-linux:~# apt-get -y install at
```

Now you can schedule to run the `auto_patch.sh` script this coming Saturday at `01:00` AM with the following command:

```
root@ubuntu-linux:~# at 01:00 AM Sat -f /root/patch.sh
```

Remember, `at` jobs only run once, so after Saturday, the `auto_patch.sh` script will not run again.

You can learn more about `at` by reading its man page:

```
root@ubuntu-linux:~# man at
```

Knowledge check

For the following exercises, open up your terminal and try to solve the following tasks:

1. Create a cron job for the root user that will run every 10 minutes. The cron job will simply append the line "10 minutes have passed!" to the file `/root/minutes.txt`.
2. Create a cron job for the root user that will run every Christmas (`25th of December at 1 AM`). The cron job will simply append the line "Merry Christmas!" to the file `/root/holidays.txt`.

18
Archiving and Compressing Files

In this chapter, you will learn how to put a group of files together into a single archive. You will also learn how to compress an archive file using various compression methods.

Creating an archive

Let's create a backup for all the bash scripts in the /home/elliot directory. As the root user, create a directory named backup in /root:

```
root@ubuntu-linux:~# mkdir /root/backup
```

To create an archive, we use the tape archive command tar. The general syntax to create an archive is as follows:

```
tar -cf archive_name files
```

The -c option is the shorthand notation of --create, which creates the archive. The -f option is the shorthand notation of --file, which specifies the archive name.

Now let's create an archive named scripts.tar in /root/backup for all the bash scripts in /home/elliot. To do that, we first change to the /home/elliot directory:

```
root@ubuntu-linux:~# cd /home/elliot
root@ubuntu-linux:/home/elliot#
```

Then we run the command:

```
root@ubuntu-linux:/home/elliot# tar -cf /root/backup/scripts.tar *.sh
```

This will create the archive file `scripts.tar` in `/root/backup`, and there will be no command output:

```
root@ubuntu-linux:/home/elliot# ls -l /root/backup/scripts.tar
-rw-r--r-- 1 root root 20480 Nov 1 23:12 /root/backup/scripts.tar
```

We could have also added the verbose option –v to see the files that are being archived:

```
root@ubuntu-linux:/home/elliot# tar -cvf /root/backup/scripts.tar *.sh
3x10.sh
detect.sh
empty.sh
filetype.sh
fun1.sh
game.sh
hello20.sh
hello2.sh
hello3.sh
hello.sh
math.sh
mydate.sh
noweb.sh
numbers.sh
rename.sh
size2.sh
size3.sh
size.sh
```

Viewing archive contents

You may want to see the contents of an archive. To do that, you can use the –t option along with the –f option followed by the archive you wish to view:

```
tar -tf archive
```

For example, to view the contents of the archive `scripts.tar` that we just created, you can run the command:

```
root@ubuntu-linux:/home/elliot# tar -tf /root/backup/scripts.tar
3x10.sh
detect.sh
empty.sh
filetype.sh
fun1.sh
game.sh
hello20.sh
```

```
hello2.sh
hello3.sh
hello.sh
math.sh
mydate.sh
noweb.sh
numbers.sh
rename.sh
size2.sh
size3.sh
size.sh
```

As you can see, it listed all the files in the `scripts.tar` archive.

Extracting archive files

You may also want to extract files from an archive. To demonstrate, let's create a directory named `myscripts` in `/root`:

```
root@ubuntu-linux:/# mkdir /root/myscripts
```

To extract files from an archive, we use the `-x` option along with the `-f` option, followed by the archive name. Then, we use the `-C` option followed by the destination directory as follows:

```
tar -xf archive -C destination
```

So to extract all the files in the `scripts.tar` archive to the `/root/myscripts` directory, you can run the following command:

```
root@ubuntu-linux:/# tar -xf /root/backup/scripts.tar -C /root/myscripts
```

The `-x` option is the shorthand notation of `--extract`, which extracts the files from the archive. We also used the `-C` option, which basically changes to the `/root/myscripts` directory before carrying out any operation, and thus the files are extracted to `/root/myscripts` instead of the current directory.

Now let's verify that the files were indeed extracted to the `/root/myscripts` directory:

```
root@ubuntu-linux:/# ls /root/myscripts
3x10.sh
empty.sh
fun1.sh
hello20.sh
hello3.sh
```

```
math.sh
noweb.sh
rename.sh
size3.sh
detect.sh
filetype.sh
game.sh
hello2.sh
hello.sh
mydate.sh
numbers.sh
size2.sh
size.sh
```

And sure enough, we see all our bash scripts in the `/root/myscripts` directory!

Compressing with gzip

Grouping files in an archive doesn't save disk space on its own. We would need to compress an archive to save disk space. Numerous compression methods are available for us to use on Linux. However, we are only going to cover the three most popular compression methods.

The most popular compression method on Linux is arguably `gzip`, and the upside is that it's really fast. You can compress an archive file with `gzip` by using the `-z` option with the `tar` command as follows:

```
tar -czf compressed_archive archive_name
```

So to compress the `scripts.tar` archive into a `gzip`-compressed archive named `scripts.tar.gz`, you first need to change to the `/root/backup` directory and then run the following command:

```
root@ubuntu-linux:~/backup# tar -czf scripts.tar.gz scripts.tar
```

Now if you list the contents of the `backup` directory, you will see the newly created `gzip`-compressed archive `scripts.tar.gz`:

```
root@ubuntu-linux:~/backup# ls
scripts.tar scripts.tar.gz
```

The magic happened by using the `-z` option, which compressed the archive with the `gzip` compression method. And that's it! Notice how it's very similar to creating an archive: we just added the `-z` option – that's the only difference.

Now let's run the `file` command on both archives:

```
root@ubuntu-linux:~/backup# file scripts.tar
scripts.tar: POSIX tar archive (GNU)
root@ubuntu-linux:~/backup# file scripts.tar.gz
scripts.tar.gz: gzip compressed data, last modified: Sat Nov 2 22:13:44
2019,
from Unix
```

As you can see, the `file` command detects the type of both archives. Now let's compare the size (in bytes) of both archives:

```
root@ubuntu-linux:~/backup# du -b scripts.tar scripts.tar.gz
20480 scripts.tar
1479 scripts.tar.gz
```

The compressed archive `scripts.tar.gz` is way smaller in size as we expected compared to the uncompressed archive `scripts.tar`. If you want to extract the files in the compressed archive `scripts.tar.gz` to `/root/myscripts`, you can run:

```
root@ubuntu-linux:~/backup# tar -xf scripts.tar.gz -C /root/myscripts
```

Notice it is exactly the same as the way that you would extract the contents of an uncompressed archive.

Compressing with bzip2

`bzip2` is another popular compression method used on Linux. On average, `bzip2` is slower than `gzip`; however, `bzip2` does a better job of compressing files to smaller sizes.

You can compress an archive with `bzip2` compression by using the `-j` option with the `tar` command as follows:

```
tar -cjf compressed_archive archive_name
```

Notice the only difference here is that we use the `-j` option for `bzip2` compression instead of `-z` for `gzip` compression.

So to compress the `scripts.tar` archive into a `bzip2`-compressed archive named `scripts.tar.bz2`, you first need to change to the `/root/backup` directory and then run the following command:

```
root@ubuntu-linux:~/backup# tar -cjf scripts.tar.bz2 scripts.tar
```

Now if you list the contents of the `backup` directory, you will see the newly created `bzip2`-compressed archive `scripts.tar.bz2`:

```
root@ubuntu-linux:~/backup# ls
scripts.tar scripts.tar.bz2 scripts.tar.gz
```

Let's run the `file` command on the `bzip2`-compressed archive `scripts.tar.bz2`:

```
root@ubuntu-linux:~/backup# file scripts.tar.bz2
scripts.tar.bz2: bzip2 compressed data, block size = 900k
```

It correctly detects the type of compression method used for the archive `scripts.tar.bz2`. Awesome – now let's compare the size (in bytes) of the `gzip`-compressed archive `scripts.tar.gz` and the `bzip2`-compressed archive `scripts.tar.bz2`:

```
root@ubuntu-linux:~/backup# du -b scripts.tar.bz2 scripts.tar.gz
1369 scripts.tar.bz2
1479 scripts.tar.gz
```

Notice that the `bzip2`-compressed archive `scripts.tar.bz2` is smaller than the `gzip`-compressed archive `scripts.tar.gz`. If you want to extract the files in the compressed archive `scripts.tar.bz2` to `/root/myscripts`, you can run:

```
root@ubuntu-linux:~/backup# tar -xf scripts.tar.bz2 -C /root/myscripts
```

Notice it is exactly the same as the way that you would extract the contents of a `gzip`-compressed archive.

Compressing with xz

The `xz` compression method is yet another popular compression method used on Linux. On average, `xz` compression does the best job out of all three compression methods in reducing (compressing) the file sizes.

You can compress an archive with xz compression by using the `-J` option with the `tar` command as follows:

```
tar -cJf compressed_name archive_name
```

Notice here we use the uppercase letter `J` with `xz` compression. So to compress the `scripts.tar` archive into an `xz`-compressed archive named `scripts.tar.xz`, you first need to change to the `/root/backup` directory and then run the following command:

```
root@ubuntu-linux:~/backup# tar -cJf scripts.tar.xz scripts.tar
```

Now if you list the contents of the `backup` directory, you will see the newly created `xz`-compressed archive `scripts.tar.xz`:

```
root@ubuntu-linux:~/backup# ls
scripts.tar scripts.tar.bz2 scripts.tar.gz scripts.tar.xz
```

Let's run the file command on the `xz`-compressed archive `scripts.tar.xz`:

```
root@ubuntu-linux:~/backup# file scripts.tar.xz
scripts.tar.xz: XZ compressed data
```

It correctly detects the type of compression method used for the archive `scripts.tar.xz`.

Measuring performance

You can use the `time` command to measure the time it takes a command (or a program) to finish executing. The general syntax for the `time` command is as follows:

```
time command_or_program
```

For example, to measure how long it takes for the `date` command to finish executing, you can run the following command:

```
root@ubuntu-linux:~# time date
Sun Nov 3 16:36:33 CST 2019

real 0m0.004s
user 0m0.003s
sys 0m0.000s
```

It just took four milliseconds to run the `date` command on my system; this is quite fast!

The `gzip` compression method is the fastest of all three compression methods; well, let's see if I am lying or telling the truth! Change to the `/root/backup` directory:

```
root@ubuntu-linux:~# cd /root/backup
root@ubuntu-linux:~/backup#
```

Now let's see how long it takes to create a `gzip`-compressed archive file for all the files in `/boot`:

```
root@ubuntu-linux:~/backup# time tar -czf boot.tar.gz /boot
real 0m4.717s
user 0m4.361s
sys 0m0.339s
```

On my system, it took `gzip` 4.717 seconds to run! Now let's measure the time it takes to create a `bzip2`-compressed archive of the same directory `/boot`:

```
root@ubuntu-linux:~/backup# time tar -cjf boot.tar.bz2 /boot
real 0m19.306s
user 0m18.809s
sys    0m0.359s
```

It took `bzip2` an enormous `19.306` seconds to run! You can see how `gzip` compression is much faster than `bzip2`. Now let's see the time it takes to create an `xz`-compressed archive of the same directory `/boot`:

```
root@ubuntu-linux:~/backup# time tar -cJf boot.tar.xz /boot
real 0m53.745s
user 0m52.679s
sys    0m0.873s
```

It almost took `xz` a full minute! We can conclude that `gzip` is definitely the fastest of all three compression methods we have discussed.

Finally, let's check the size (in bytes) of the three compressed archives:

```
root@ubuntu-linux:~/backup# du -b boot.*
97934386 boot.tar.bz2
98036178 boot.tar.gz
94452156 boot.tar.xz
```

As you can see, `xz` did the best job of compressing the files. `bzip2` claimed second place, and `gzip` came in last.

Knowledge check

For the following exercises, open up your Terminal and try to solve the following tasks:

1. Create a `gzip` archive named `var.tar.gz` in `/root` for all the files in `/var`.
2. Create a `bzip2` archive named `tmp.tar.bz2` in `/root` for all the files in `/tmp`.
3. Create an `xz` archive named `etc.tar.xz` in `/root` for all the files in `/etc`.

19
Create Your Own Commands

Sometimes, you may be having a hard time remembering one command. Other times, you will find yourself running a very long command over and over again, and that drives you insane. In this chapter, you will learn how you can make your *own* commands, because you are the real boss.

Your first alias

Let's assume that you always forget that the command `free -h` displays the memory information of your system:

```
elliot@ubuntu-linux:~$ free -h
              total        used        free      shared  buff/cache   available
Mem:           3.9G        939M        2.2G        6.6M        752M        2.7G
Swap:          947M          0B        947M
```

You may be asking yourself: "Why can't I just type `memory` to display the memory information instead of `free -h`?". Well, you certainly can do that by creating an `alias`.

The `alias` command instructs the shell to replace one string (word) with another. Well, how is this useful? Let me show you; if you run the following command:

```
elliot@ubuntu-linux:~$ alias memory="free -h"
```

Then every time you enter `memory`, your shell will replace it with `free -h`:

```
elliot@ubuntu-linux:~$ memory
              total        used        free      shared  buff/cache   available
Mem:           3.9G        936M        2.2G        6.6M        756M        2.7G
Swap:          947M          0B        947M
```

Wow! So now you have achieved your dream! You can create an alias for any Linux command that you are having trouble remembering. Notice that the general format of the `alias` command is as follows:

```
alias alias_name="command(s)_to_run"
```

One alias for multiple commands

You can use a semicolon to run multiple commands on the same line. For example, to create a new directory named `newdir` and change to `newdir` all at once, you can run the following command:

```
elliot@ubuntu-linux:~$ mkdir newdir; cd newdir
elliot@ubuntu-linux:~/newdir$
```

So you use a semicolon to separate each command. In general, the syntax for running multiple commands on the same line is as follows:

```
command1; command2; command3; command4; ....
```

We often like to check the calendar and the date at the same time, right? For that, we will create an alias named `date` so that every time we run `date`, it will run both the `date` and `calendar` commands:

```
elliot@ubuntu-linux:~$ alias date="date;cal"
```

Now let's run `date` and see what's up:

```
elliot@ubuntu-linux:~$ date
Mon Nov  4 13:34:04 CST 2019
    November 2019
Su Mo Tu We Th Fr Sa
                1  2
 3  4  5  6  7  8  9
10 11 12 13 14 15 16
17 18 19 20 21 22 23
24 25 26 27 28 29 30
```

Notice here that we used the alias name `date`, which is already the name of an existing command; this is completely fine with aliases.

Listing all aliases

You should also know that aliases are user-specific. So the aliases created by `elliot` will not work for user `smurf`; take a look:

```
elliot@ubuntu-linux:~$ su - smurf
Password:
smurf@ubuntu-linux:~$ date
Mon Nov 4 13:33:36 CST 2019
smurf@ubuntu-linux:~$ memory
Command 'memory' not found, did you mean:
    command 'lmemory' from deb lmemory
Try: apt install <deb name>
```

As you can see, `smurf` can't use the aliases of user `elliot`. So every user has their own set of aliases. Now, let's exit back to user `elliot`:

```
smurf@ubuntu-linux:~$ exit
logout
elliot@ubuntu-linux:~$ memory
          total     used     free     shared   buff/cache   available
Mem:      3.9G      937M     2.0G     6.6M     990M         2.7G
Swap:     947M      0B       947M
```

You can run the `alias` command to list all the aliases that can be used by the currently logged-in user:

```
elliot@ubuntu-linux:~$ alias
alias date='date;cal'
alias egrep='egrep --color=auto'
alias fgrep='fgrep --color=auto'
alias grep='grep --color=auto'
alias l='ls -CF'
alias la='ls -A'
alias ll='ls -alF'
alias ls='ls --color=auto'
alias memory='free -h'
```

Creating a permanent alias

So far, we have been creating temporary aliases; that is, the two aliases of `memory` and `date` that we created are temporarily and only valid for the current Terminal session. These two aliases will vanish as soon as you close your Terminal.

Open a new Terminal session, then try and run the two aliases we have created:

```
elliot@ubuntu-linux:~$ date
Mon Nov 4 13:43:46 CST 2019
elliot@ubuntu-linux:~$ memory

Command 'memory' not found, did you mean:
    command 'lmemory' from deb lmemory
Try: sudo apt install <deb name>
```

As you can see, they are gone! They are not even in your list of aliases anymore:

```
elliot@ubuntu-linux:~$ alias
alias egrep='egrep --color=auto'
alias fgrep='fgrep --color=auto'
alias grep='grep --color=auto'
alias l='ls -CF'
alias la='ls -A'
alias ll='ls -alF'
alias ls='ls --color=auto'
```

To create a permanent alias for a user, you need to include it in the hidden `.bashrc` file in the user's home directory. So to permanently add our two aliases back, you have to add the following two lines at the very end of the `/home/el- liot/.bashrc` file:

```
alias memory = "free -h"
alias date = "date;cal"
```

You can do it by running the following two `echo` commands:

```
elliot@ubuntu-linux:~$ echo 'alias memory="free -h"' >>
/home/elliot/.bashrc
elliot@ubuntu-linux:~$ echo 'alias date="date;cal"' >> /home/elliot/.bashrc
```

After you add both aliases to the `/home/elliot/.bashrc` file, you need to run the `source` command on the `/home/elliot/.bashrc` file for the change to take effect in the current session:

```
elliot@ubuntu-linux:~$ source /home/elliot/.bashrc
```

Now you can use your two aliases, `memory` and `date`, forever without worrying that they will disappear after you close your current Terminal session:

```
elliot@ubuntu-linux:~$ memory
              total        used        free      shared   buff/cache   available
Mem:           3.8G        233M        3.3G        672K         282M        3.4G
Swap:            0B          0B          0B
elliot@ubuntu-linux:~$ date
Mon Nov  4 13:35:59 CST 2019
    November 2019
Su Mo Tu We Th Fr Sa
                1  2
 3  4  5  6  7  8  9
10 11 12 13 14 15 16
17 18 19 20 21 22 23
24 25 26 27 28 29 30
```

Removing an alias

Let's create another temporary alias named lastline that will display the last line in a file:

```
elliot@ubuntu-linux:~$ alias lastline="tail -n 1"
```

Now let's try our new alias on the /home/elliot/.bashrc file:

```
elliot@ubuntu-linux:~$ lastline /home/elliot/.bashrc
alias date="date;cal"
```

Alright! It works well. Now, if you wish to delete the alias, then you can run the unalias command followed by the alias name:

```
elliot@ubuntu-linux:~$ unalias lastline
```

So now the lastline alias has been deleted:

```
elliot@ubuntu-linux:~$ lastline /home/elliot/.bashrc
lastline: command not found
```

You can also use the unalias command to temporarily deactivate a permanent alias. For example, if you run the following command:

```
elliot@ubuntu-linux:~$ unalias memory
```

Now, the permanent alias `memory` will not work in the current Terminal session:

```
elliot@ubuntu-linux:~$ memory

Command 'memory' not found, did you mean:
    command 'lmemory' from deb lmemory
Try: sudo apt install <deb name>
```

However, the alias `memory` will come back in a new Terminal session. To remove a permanent alias, you need to remove it from the `.bashrc` file.

Some useful aliases

Now let's create some useful aliases that will make our life much more enjoyable while working on the Linux command line.

A lot of people hate to remember all the `tar` command options, so let's make it easy for these people then. We will create an alias named `extract` that will extract files from an archive:

```
elliot@ubuntu-linux:~$ alias extract="tar -xvf"
```

You can try the alias on any archive, and it will work like a charm.

Similarly, you can create an alias named `compress_gzip` that will create a gzip-compressed archive:

```
elliot@ubuntu-linux:~$ alias compress_gzip="tar -czvf"
```

You may also want to create an alias named `soft` that will create soft links:

```
elliot@ubuntu-linux:~$ alias soft="ln -s"
```

You can use the soft alias to create a soft link named `logfiles` that points to the `/var/logs` directory:

```
elliot@ubuntu-linux:~$ soft /var/logs logfiles
elliot@ubuntu-linux:~$ ls -l logfiles
lrwxrwxrwx 1 elliot elliot 9 Nov 4 15:08 logfiles -> /var/logs
```

Now let's create an alias named `LISTEN` that will list all the listening ports on your system:

```
elliot@ubuntu-linux:~$ alias LISTEN="netstat -tulpen| grep -i listen"
```

Now let's try and run the `LISTEN` alias:

```
elliot@ubuntu-linux:~$ LISTEN
tcp    0    0 127.0.0.53:53    0.0.0.0:*    LISTEN
tcp    0    0 0.0.0.0:22       0.0.0.0:*    LISTEN
tcp    0    0 127.0.0.1:631    0.0.0.0:*    LISTEN
tcp    0    0 127.0.0.1:25     0.0.0.0:*    LISTEN
tcp6   0    0 :::22            :::*         LISTEN
tcp6   0    0 ::1:631          :::*         LISTEN
tcp6   0    0 ::1:25           :::*         LISTEN
```

This is pretty cool! Let's create one final alias, `sort_files`, that will list all the files in the current directory sorted by size (in descending order):

```
alias sort_files="du -bs * | sort -rn"
```

Now let's try and run the `sort_files` alias:

```
elliot@ubuntu-linux:~$ sort_files
9628732 Downloads
2242937 Pictures
65080 minutes.txt
40393 load.txt
32768 dir1
20517 Desktop
20480 small
8192 hackers
476 game.sh
168 practise.txt
161 filetype.sh
142 noweb.sh
108 3x10.sh
92 rename.sh
92 numbers.sh
88 detect.sh
74 hello3.sh
66 fun1.sh
59 hello20.sh
37 hello2.sh
33 hello.sh
17 mydate.sh
16 honey
9 logs
6 softdir1
0 empty
```

As you can see, the files in the current directory are listed in descending order of size (that is, the biggest first). This will prove to be particularly useful when you are doing some cleaning on your system and you want to inspect which files are occupying the most space.

Adding safety nets

You can also use aliases to protect against dumb mistakes. For example, to protect against removing important files by mistake, you can add the following alias:

```
elliot@ubuntu-linux:~$ alias rm="rm -i"
```

Now you will be asked to confirm each time you attempt to remove a file:

```
elliot@ubuntu-linux:~$ rm *
rm: remove regular file '3x10.sh'?
```

Go crazy with aliases

You can also have some fun with aliases and make users go crazy; take a look at this alias:

```
elliot@ubuntu-linux:~$ alias nano="vi"
```

Now when user `elliot` tries to open the `nano` editor, the `vi` editor will open instead! User `elliot` can overcome this dilemma by typing in the full path of the `nano` editor. Here is another funny alias:

```
elliot@ubuntu-linux:~$ alias exit="echo No I am not exiting ..."
```

Now look what will happen when user `elliot` tries to exit the Terminal:

```
elliot@ubuntu-linux:~$ exit
No I am not exiting ...
elliot@ubuntu-linux:~$ exit
No I am not exiting ...
```

I will let you deal with this by yourself; I am evil like that! Haha.

Knowledge check

For the following exercises, open up your Terminal and try to solve the following tasks:

1. Create a temporary alias called `ins` for the `apt-get install` command.
2. Create a temporary alias called `packages` for the `dpkg -l` command.
3. Create a permanent alias called `clean` that will remove all the files in the `/tmp` directory.

20
Everyone Needs Disk Space

In this chapter, you will learn how to manage your hard disk in Linux. You will learn how to create new partitions on your drive. Then you will learn how to create and mount filesystems. Finally, you will learn how to use LVM to create logical volumes.

Where are your devices?

As we all know by now, a file represents everything in Linux, and devices are no exception. All your devices are located inside the /dev directory; this includes your keyboard, mouse, terminal, hard disk, USB devices, CD-ROM, and so on.

The terminal you are working on right now is, in fact, a device. If you run the w command, you will see the name of the terminal you are connected to in the second column of the output.

```
elliot@ubuntu-linux:~$ w
11:38:59 up 17 min, 1 user, load average: 0.00, 0.00, 0.02
USER    TTY       FROM            LOGIN@  IDLE  JCPU  PCPU  WHAT
elliot  pts/0     172.16.1.67     11:22   0.00s 0.06s 0.00s w
```

In my case, it is pts/0; **pts** is short for **pseudoterminal** slave. Now, this terminal is represented by the file /dev/pts/0:

```
elliot@ubuntu-linux:~$ ls -l /dev/pts/0
crw------- 1 elliot tty 136, 0 Nov 7 11:40 /dev/pts/0
```

I will echo the line Hello Friend to /dev/pts/0 and pay close attention to what will happen:

```
elliot@ubuntu-linux:~$ echo "Hello Friend" > /dev/pts/0
Hello Friend
```

As you can see, `Hello Friend` got printed to my terminal! Now you can play that game with other users on your system. You can run the `w` command to figure out which terminal they are using and then start sending them messages!

Where is your hard disk?

To know which file represents your hard disk; you need to run the command `lsblk`, which is short for **list block**:

```
elliot@ubuntu-linux:~$ lsblk
NAME      MAJ:MIN  RM SIZE RO  TYPE MOUNTPOINT
sda        8:0      0   20G 0  disk
| sda1     8:1      0   20G 0  part /
sr0       11:0      1 1024M 0  rom
```

From the output, I can see that the name of my hard disk device is **sda**, which is short for **SCSI Disk A**. Now you need to understand that depending on the type of your hard disk drive, you may get a different name. `Figure 1` summarizes Linux naming strategies for different types of hard drives:

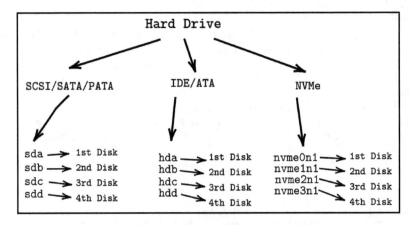

Figure 1: Hard disk naming in Linux

So from the output of the `lsblk` command, you can conclude that I only have one disk (`sda`) on my virtual machine. Now we don't want to play with this disk as it contains the root filesystem, so let's add another disk to our virtual machine for learning purposes.

Adding disks to your virtual machine

There are a few steps you need to follow to successfully add a new disk to your virtual machine. You have to follow these steps in this specific order:

1. Shut down your virtual machine.
2. Go to **Virtual Machine Settings** | **Storage** | **Create new Disk**.
3. Start your virtual machine.

So the first step is pretty simple; shut down your virtual machine because you cannot add a new disk to your virtual machine while it is still running. For the second step, you need to go to your virtual machine settings, then click on storage and then select your disk controller, right-click, and then create a new disk as shown in Figure 2:

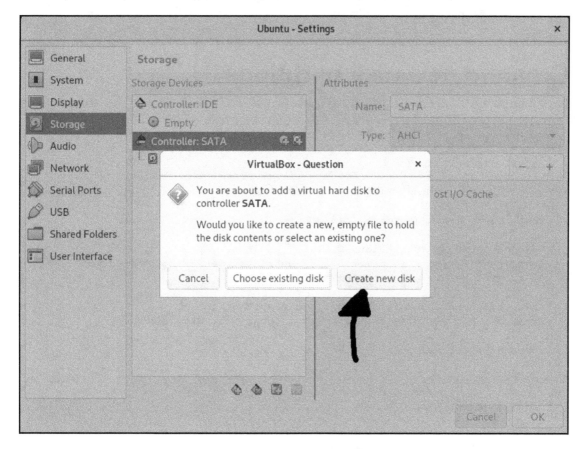

Figure 2: Creating a new disk on your virtual machine

You will then be asked to choose the size for your new disk. You can select any size you want. I have an abundance of disk space on my host machine, so I will add a 10 GB disk to my virtual machine. After you are done, the last step is to start up your virtual machine again.

You should be able to see your new disk as soon as your virtual machine starts:

```
elliot@ubuntu-linux:~$ lsblk
NAME      MAJ:MIN RM SIZE  RO TYPE MOUNTPOINT
sda          8:0   0  20G   0  disk
| sda1       8:1   0  20G   0  part /
sdb         8:16   0  10G   0  disk
sr0        11:0    1 1024M  0  rom
```

My new disk got the name `sdb` because it is the second disk on my virtual machine, and you can also see that its size is 10 GB.

Creating new disk partitions

Now let's play with the new disk that we just created. The first thing you may want to do is to create a new partition. To create a new partition, we use the `fdisk` command followed by the disk name:

```
fdisk [options] device
```

So to create a new partition on the /dev/sdb disk; you can run the following command:

```
root@ubuntu-linux:~# fdisk /dev/sdb

Welcome to fdisk (util-linux 2.31.1).
Changes will remain in memory only, until you decide to write them.
Be careful before using the write command.

Device does not contain a recognized partition table.
Created a new DOS disklabel with disk identifier 0xb13d9b6a.

Command (m for help):
```

This opens up the `fdisk` utility. If you are unsure what to do; you can enter `m` for help:

```
Command (m for help): m
Help:
  DOS (MBR)
   a   toggle a bootable flag
   b   edit nested BSD disklabel
```

```
c   toggle the dos compatibility flag

Generic
d   delete a partition
F   list free unpartitioned space l list known partition types
n   add a new partition
p   print the partition table t change a partition type
v   verify the partition table
i   print information about a partition

Save & Exit
w   write table to disk and exit
q   quit without saving changes

Create a new label
g   create a new empty GPT partition table
G   create a new empty SGI (IRIX) partition table
o   create a new empty DOS  partition table
s   create a new empty Sun partition table
```

We want to create a new partition so enter n:

```
Command (m for help): n
Partition type
    p primary (0 primary, 0 extended, 4 free)
    e extended (container for logical partitions)
Select (default p):
```

It will then ask you if you want a primary partition or an extended partition. We would accept the default selection (primary) so just hit *Enter*:

```
Using default response p.
Partition number (1-4, default 1):
```

It will then ask you to select a partition number. We will also accept the default, which is partition number 1, so just hit *Enter*. Notice that you can create up to four primary partitions on a given disk:

```
Partition number (1-4, default 1):
First sector (2048-20971519, default 2048):
```

You will then be prompted to choose the sector you would want your new partition to start at; hit *Enter* to accept the default (2048):

```
First sector (2048-20971519, default 2048):
Last sector, +sectors or +size{K,M,G,T,P} (2048-20971519, default
20971519):
```

Now you will be asked to choose the size of your new partition; I want a 2 GB partition so I would type +2G and then hit *Enter*:

```
Last sector, +sectors or +size{K,M,G,T,P} (2048-20971519, default
20971519): +2G

Created a new partition 1 of type 'Linux' and of size 2 GiB.
Command (m for help):
```

Finally, you have to save the configuration by hitting w:

```
Command (m for help): w
The partition table has been altered.
Calling ioctl() to re-read partition table.
Syncing disks.
```

Now you can run lsblk to see the new partition you just created:

```
root@ubuntu-linux:~# lsblk
NAME      MAJ:MIN RM SIZE  RO TYPE MOUNTPOINT
sda         8:0   0  20G    0  disk
| sda1      8:1   0  20G    0  part /
sdb         8:16  0  10G    0  disk
| sdb1      8:17  0  2G     0  part
sr0        11:0   1 1024M   0  rom
```

You can see the 2 GB partition sdb1 is listed under sdb. You can also use the -l option with the fdisk command to print out the partition table of your disk:

```
root@ubuntu-linux:~# fdisk -l /dev/sdb
Disk /dev/sdb: 10 GiB, 10737418240 bytes, 20971520 sectors
Units: sectors of 1 * 512 = 512 bytes
Sector size (logical/physical): 512 bytes / 512 bytes
I/O size (minimum/optimal): 512 bytes / 512 bytes
Disklabel type: dos
Disk identifier: 0xb13d9b6a

Device     Boot Start    End Sectors  Size Id Type
/dev/sdb1       2048 4196351 4194304   2G  83 Linux
```

Creating new filesystems

I cannot start creating files and directories on my /dev/sdb1 partition just yet; first, I need to create a filesystem. A filesystem basically dictates how data is organized and stored on a disk (or partition). A good analogy would be passengers on an airplane; flight companies can't just let the passengers (data) seat themselves in an airplane (partition); it would be a total mess.

There are many different types of filesystems available on Linux. It is important to note that ext4 and xfs are the most commonly used filesystems. Figure 3 shows you only a few of the available filesystems that are supported on Linux:

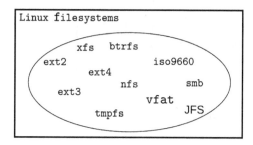

Figure 3: Linux filesystems

You can read the description of each Linux filesystem type in the filesystems man page:

```
root@ubuntu-linux:~# man filesystems
```

To create a filesystem, we use the mkfs command, which is short for make filesystem. The general syntax for the mkfs command is as follows:

```
mkfs --type [fstype] disk_or_partition
```

Now let's create an ext4 filesystem on our new partition /dev/sdb1:

```
root@ubuntu-linux:~# mkfs --type ext4 /dev/sdb1
mke2fs 1.44.1 (24-Mar-2018)
Creating filesystem with 524288 4k blocks and 131072 inodes
Filesystem UUID: 61d947bb-0cd1-41e1-90e0-c9895b6de428
Superblock backups stored on blocks:
32768, 98304, 163840, 229376, 294912

Allocating group tables: done
Writing inode tables: done
Creating journal (16384 blocks): done
Writing superblocks and filesystem accounting information: done
```

We have created an `ext4` filesystem on our partition `/dev/sdb1`. We can verify our work by running the `file -s` command on the `/dev/sdb1` partition:

```
root@ubuntu-linux:~# file -s /dev/sdb1
/dev/sdb1: Linux rev 1.0 ext4 filesystem data,
UUID=61d947bb-0cd1-41e1-90e0-c9895b6de428 (extents) (64bit) (large files)
(huge files)
```

As you can see, it displays that there is an `ext4` filesystem on the `/dev/sdb1` partition.

You can use the `wipefs` command to remove (wipe out) a filesystem. For example, if you want to remove the `ext4` filesystem that we just created on `/dev/sdb1`, you can run the following command:

```
root@ubuntu-linux:~# wipefs -a /dev/sdb1
/dev/sdb1: 2 bytes were erased at offset 0x00000438 (ext4): 53 ef
```

Now if you rerun `file -s` on the `/dev/sdb1` partition, you will see there is no filesystem signature:

```
root@ubuntu-linux:~# file -s /dev/sdb1
/dev/sdb1: data
```

Let's recreate an `ext4` filesystem on `/dev/sdb1` and keep it this time around:

```
root@ubuntu-linux:~# mkfs --type ext4 /dev/sdb1
mke2fs 1.44.1 (24-Mar-2018)
Creating filesystem with 524288 4k blocks and 131072 inodes
Filesystem UUID: 811aef62-d9ca-4db3-b305-bd896d1c8545
Superblock backups stored on blocks:
32768, 98304, 163840, 229376, 294912

Allocating group tables: done
Writing inode tables: done
Creating journal (16384 blocks): done
Writing superblocks and filesystem accounting information: done
```

Mounting filesystems

We have created an `ext4` filesystem on the partition `/dev/sdb1`. Now we need to mount our filesystem somewhere in the Linux directory tree.

WHAT IS MOUNTING?

Mounting refers to the process of attaching any filesystem or any storage device (like USB flash drives, CDs, etc.) to a directory.

But why do we need to mount? I mean we have just created an `ext4` filesystem on the 2 GB partition `/dev/sdb1`. Can't we just start creating files in `/dev/sdb1`? The answer is a big FAT NO! Remember, `/dev/sdb1` is only a file that represents a partition.

To mount a filesystem, we use the mount command as follows:

```
mount filesystem mount_directory
```

So let's assume we are going to use the filesystem `/dev/sdb1` to store our games. In this case, let's create a new directory `/games`:

```
root@ubuntu-linux:~# mkdir /games
```

Now the only thing left is to mount our filesystem `/dev/sdb1` on the `/games` directory:

```
root@ubuntu-linux:/# mount /dev/sdb1 /games
```

We can verify our work by running the `lsblk` command:

```
root@ubuntu-linux:~# lsblk
NAME    MAJ:MIN  RM SIZE RO TYPE MOUNTPOINT
sda      8:0      0  20G  0  disk
| sda1   8:1      0  20G  0  part /
sdb      8:16     0  10G  0  disk
| sdb1   8:17     0   2G  0  part /games
sr0      11:0     1 1024M 0  rom
```

As you can see, `/dev/sdb1` is indeed mounted on `/games`.

You can also use the `mount` command by itself to list all the mounted filesystems on your system. For example, to verify that `/dev/sdb1` is mounted on `/games`, you can run the following command:

```
root@ubuntu-linux:/# mount | grep sdb1
/dev/sdb1 on /games type ext4 (rw,relatime,data=ordered)
```

We now have 2 GB available for us to use in `/games` and you can use the `df` command to display the filesystem disk space usage:

```
root@ubuntu-linux:~# df -h /games
Filesystem      Size Used Avail Use% Mounted on
/dev/sdb1       2.0G 6.0M 1.8G   1%  /games
```

Now let's create three files in /games:

```
root@ubuntu-linux:~# cd /games
root@ubuntu-linux:/games# touch game1 game2 game3
```

Unmounting filesystems

You can also unmount (the reverse of mounting) a filesystem. As you may have guessed, unmounting refers to the process of detaching a filesystem or a storage device. To unmount a filesystem, you can use umount as follows:

```
umount filesystem
```

Change to the /games directory and try to unmount the /dev/sdb1 filesystem:

```
root@ubuntu-linux:/games# umount /dev/sdb1
umount: /games: target is busy.
```

Oops! It is saying that the target is busy! That's because I am inside the mount point /games; I will back up one directory and then try again:

```
root@ubuntu-linux:/games# cd ..
root@ubuntu-linux:/# umount /dev/sdb1
```

This time it worked! You have to be careful and never unmount a filesystem or any storage device while it is actively being used; otherwise, you may lose data!

Now let's verify the filesystem /dev/sdb1 is indeed unmounted:

```
root@ubuntu-linux:/# lsblk
NAME    MAJ:MIN RM SIZE  RO TYPE MOUNTPOINT
sda       8:0    0 20G    0  disk
| sda1    8:1    0 20G    0  part /
sdb       8:16   0 10G    0  disk
| sdb1    8:17   0 2G     0  part
sr0      11:0    1 1024M  0  rom
root@ubuntu-linux:/# mount | grep sdb1
```

Yup! It is definitely unmounted! Now let's list the contents of the /games directory:

```
root@ubuntu-linux:/# ls /games
```

Nothing! But do not panic or worry! The three files we created still exist in the `/dev/sdb1` filesystem. We need to mount the filesystem again, and you will see the files:

```
root@ubuntu-linux:~# mount /dev/sdb1 /games
root@ubuntu-linux:~# ls /games
game1 game2 game3 lost+found
```

Permanently mounting filesystems

The `mount` command only mounts a filesystem temporarily; that is, filesystems mounted with the `mount` command won't survive a system reboot. If you want to mount a filesystem permanently, then you need to include it in the filesystem table file `/etc/fstab`.

Each entry (or line) in `/etc/fstab` represents a different filesystem, and each line consists of the following six fields:

- `filesystem`
- `mount_dir`
- `fstype`
- `mount_options`
- `dump`
- `check_fs`

So, for example, to mount our `/dev/sdb1` filesystem on `/games` permanently, you need to include the following line in `/etc/fstab`:

```
/dev/sdb1 /games ext4 defaults 0 0
```

You should add the line to the end of the `/etc/fstab` file:

```
root@ubuntu-linux:~# tail -1 /etc/fstab
/dev/sdb1    /games ext4    defaults    0    0
```

Now let's unmount `/dev/sdb1`:

```
root@ubuntu-linux:~# umount /dev/sdb1
```

Finally, you can now mount `/dev/sdb1` permanently by running:

```
root@ubuntu-linux:~# mount /dev/sdb1
```

Notice we did not specify a mount destination this time; that's because the mount destination is already specified in the /etc/fstab file. You can use the -a option with the mount command:

```
root@ubuntu-linux:~# mount -a
```

To mount all the filesystems that are included in /etc/fstab. It is also used to check for syntax errors. For example, if you made a typo in /etc/fstab and wrote /dev/sdx1 instead of /dev/sdb1, it will show you the following error:

```
root@ubuntu-linux:~# mount -a
mount: /games: special device /dev/sdx1 does not exist.
```

All the mounts specified in /etc/fstab are permanent and they will survive a system reboot. You may also refer to the fstab man page for more information on /etc/fstab:

```
root@ubuntu-linux:~# man fstab
```

Running out of space

Let's create huge files that would consume all the available disk space in /games.

A fast way to create big files in Linux is by using the dd command. To demonstrate, let's first change to the /games directory:

```
root@ubuntu-linux:~# cd /games
root@ubuntu-linux:/games#
```

Now you can run the following command to create a 1 GB file named bigGame:

```
root@ubuntu-linux:/games# dd if=/dev/zero of=bigGame bs=1G count=1
1+0 records in
1+0 records out
1073741824 bytes (1.1 GB, 1.0 GiB) copied, 1.44297 s, 744 MB/s
```

We have now already used more than half of the available space in /games:

```
root@ubuntu-linux:/games# df -h /games
Filesystem      Size Used Avail Use% Mounted on
/dev/sdb1       2.0G 1.1G 868M  55%  /games
```

Now let's attempt to create another file named `bigFish` of size 3 GB:

```
root@ubuntu-linux:/games# dd if=/dev/zero of=bigFish bs=1G count=3
dd: error writing 'bigFish': No space left on device
1+0 records in
0+0 records out
1016942592 bytes (1.0 GB, 970 MiB) copied, 1.59397 s, 638 MB/s
```

We got an error as we ran out of space:

```
root@ubuntu-linux:/games# df -h /games
Filesystem      Size Used Avail Use% Mounted on
/dev/sdb1       2.0G 2.0G  0    100% /games
```

Now we can't even create a tiny file with the word `Hello` in it:

```
root@ubuntu-linux:/games# echo Hello > greeting.txt
-su: echo: write error: No space left on device
```

Corrupting and fixing filesystems

In some unfortunate situations, you may run into an issue where your system will not boot because of a corrupted filesystem. In this case, you have to fix your filesystem so your system boots properly. I will show you how you can corrupt a filesystem, and then I will show you how you can repair it.

An easy way to corrupt a filesystem is by writing random data to it.

The following command will surely corrupt your `/dev/sdb1` filesystem:

```
root@ubuntu-linux:/games# dd if=/dev/urandom of=/dev/sdb1 count=10k
```

Your `/dev/sdb1` filesystem is now corrupted! If you don't believe me, unmount it and then try to mount it back again:

```
root@ubuntu-linux:~# umount /dev/sdb1
```

OK, it unmounted successfully! Let's see if it will mount:

```
root@ubuntu-linux:~# mount /dev/sdb1 /games
mount: /games: wrong fs type, bad option, bad superblock on /dev/sdb1,
missing codepage or helper program, or other error.
```

As you can see, it fails to mount as it spits out an error message.

Congrats! Your filesystem is corrupted. What can we do now? Well, we can certainly fix it!

You can use the file system check command `fsck` to check and repair filesystems. So let's run `fsck` on our corrupted filesystem:

```
root@ubuntu-linux:~# fsck /dev/sdb1
fsck from util-linux 2.31.1
e2fsck 1.44.1 (24-Mar-2018)
/dev/sdb1 was not cleanly unmounted, check forced.
fsck.ext4: Inode checksum does not match inode while reading bad blocks
inode
This doesn't bode well, but we'll try to go on...
Pass 1: Checking inodes, blocks, and sizes
Inode 1 seems to contain garbage. Clear<y>?
```

As you can see, it states that the filesystem contains garbage data and asks if you want to clear the errors. You can hit *Y*, but it will keep asking you again and again for every single inode it is fixing! You can avoid that by using the -y option, which answers an automatic yes to all prompts during the repair process:

```
root@ubuntu-linux:~# fsck -y /dev/sdb1
```

When you run it, you will see a lot of numbers running down on your screen. Do not worry! It is fixing your corrupted filesystem. It is basically going through thousands of inodes.

After it finishes, you can rerun `fsck` to verify the filesystem is now clean:

```
root@ubuntu-linux:~# fsck /dev/sdb1
fsck from util-linux 2.31.1
e2fsck 1.44.1 (24-Mar-2018)
/dev/sdb1: clean, 11/131072 files, 9769/524288 blocks
```

Amazing! Now let's try to mount it:

```
root@ubuntu-linux:~# mount /dev/sdb1 /games
```

It mounted this time around. Mission accomplished! We have successfully fixed the filesystem.

LVM to the rescue

When you run out of space on a filesystem, things can get very ugly. We already ran out of space in /games, and there is no easy solution that exists for adding more space using standard partitioning. Luckily, **Logical Volume Manager** (**LVM**) offers a better alternative for managing filesystems.

Installing the LVM package

Before we start playing with LVM, first, we need to install the `lvm2` package:

```
root@ubuntu-linux:~# apt-get install lvm2
```

After the installation is complete, you can run the `lvm version` command to verify the installation is successful:

```
root@ubuntu-linux:~# lvm version
  LVM version:     2.02.176(2) (2017-11-03)
  Library version: 1.02.145 (2017-11-03)
  Driver version:  4.37.0
```

Three layers of abstraction

To understand how LVM works, you first need to visualize it. LVM is like a cake that is made up of three layers, as shown in `Figure 4`.

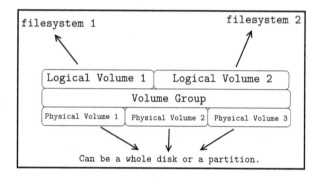

Figure 4: Visualizing LVM

Physical volumes construct the first (base layer) of the LVM cake. Physical volumes can either be whole disks (`/dev/sdb`, `/dev/sdc`, etc) or partitions (`/dev/sdb2`, `/dev/sdc3`, etc).

The **Volume Group** layer is the second and biggest layer in the LVM cake, and it sits on top of the **Physical Volume** layer. A volume group can span multiple physical volumes; that is, one volume group can be composed of one or more physical volumes.

The **Logical Volume** layer makes up the third and last layer in the LVM cake. Multiple logical volumes can belong to the same volume group, as shown in `Figure 4`. Finally, you can create filesystems on logical volumes.

Creating physical volumes

The recipe for creating physical volumes is pretty simple; you only need a disk or a partition. We have already created a 2 GB partition /dev/sdb1. Now go ahead and create three more partitions under /dev/sdb, each of size 2 GB.

This is what the end result should look like:

```
root@ubuntu-linux:~# lsblk
NAME       MAJ:MIN  RM  SIZE  RO  TYPE MOUNTPOINT
sda         8:0     0   20G   0   disk
| sda1      8:1     0   20G   0   part /
sdb         8:16    0   10G   0   disk
| sdb1      8:17    0    2G   0   part /games
| sdb2      8:18    0    2G   0   part
| sdb3      8:19    0    2G   0   part
| sdb4      8:20    0    2G   0   part
sr0        11:0     1  1024M  0   rom
```

To create a physical volume, we use the pvcreate command followed by a disk or a partition:

```
pvcreate disk_or_partition
```

We are going to create three physical volumes: /dev/sdb2, /dev/sdb3, and /dev/sdb4. You can create all three with one command:

```
root@ubuntu-linux:~# pvcreate /dev/sdb2 /dev/sdb3 /dev/sdb4
  Physical volume "/dev/sdb2" successfully created.
  Physical volume "/dev/sdb3" successfully created.
  Physical volume "/dev/sdb4" successfully created.
```

Cool stuff! You can also use the pvs command to list all physical volumes:

```
root@ubuntu-linux:~# pvs
  PV         VG Fmt  Attr PSize PFree
  /dev/sdb2     lvm2 --- 2.00g 2.00g
  /dev/sdb3     lvm2 --- 2.00g 2.00g
  /dev/sdb4     lvm2 --- 2.00g 2.00g
```

Alright! Everything looks good so far.

Creating volume groups

One volume group can span multiple physical volumes. So let's create a volume group that would consist of the two physical volumes: /dev/sdb2 and /dev/sdb3.

To create a volume group, we use the vgcreate command followed by the name of the new volume group and then the physical volumes:

```
vgcreate vg_name PV1 PV2 PV3 ...
```

Let's create a volume group named myvg that would span /dev/sdb2 and /de- v/sdb3:

```
root@ubuntu-linux:~# vgcreate myvg /dev/sdb2 /dev/sdb3
  Volume group "myvg" successfully created
```

Awesome! You can also use the vgs command to list all volume groups:

```
root@ubuntu-linux:~# vgs
  VG    #PV #LV #SN Attr   VSize VFree
  myvg   2   0   0 wz--n- 3.99g 3.99g
```

Notice that the size of the volume group myvg is equal to 4 GB, which is the total size of /dev/sdb2 and /dev/sdb3.

Creating logical volumes

We can now create logical volumes on top of our mvg volume group.

To create a logical volume, we use the lvcreate command followed by the size of the logical volume, the name of the logical volume, and finally, the volume group name:

```
lvcreate --size 2G --name lv_name vg_name
```

Let's create a logical volume named mybooks of size 2 GB:

```
root@ubuntu-linux:~# lvcreate --size 2G --name mybooks myvg
  Logical volume "mybooks" created.
```

Now create another logical volume named myprojects of size 500 MB:

```
root@ubuntu-linux:~# lvcreate --size 500M --name myprojects myvg
  Logical volume "myprojects" created.
```

You can use the `lvs` command to list all logical volumes:

```
root@ubuntu-linux:~# lvs
  LV          VG    Attr        LSize Pool Origin Data% Meta% Move Log
  mybooks     myvg  -wi-a----- 2.00g
  myprojects myvg  -wi-a----- 500.00m
```

One final step remains, which is creating filesystems on our logical volumes.

Your logical volumes are represented in the device mapper directory `/dev/mapper`:

```
root@ubuntu-linux:~# ls /dev/mapper
myvg-mybooks myvg-myprojects
```

Let's create an `ext4` filesystem on our `mybooks` logical volume:

```
root@ubuntu-linux:~# mkfs --type ext4 /dev/mapper/myvg-mybooks
mke2fs 1.44.1 (24-Mar-2018)
Creating filesystem with 524288 4k blocks and 131072 inodes
Filesystem UUID: d1b43462-6d5c-4329-b027-7ee2ecebfd9a
Superblock backups stored on blocks:
32768, 98304, 163840, 229376, 294912

Allocating group tables: done
Writing inode tables: done
Creating journal (16384 blocks): done
Writing superblocks and filesystem accounting information: done
```

Similarly, we can create an `ext4` filesystem on our `myprojects` logical volume:

```
root@ubuntu-linux:~# mkfs --type ext4 /dev/mapper/myvg-myprojects
mke2fs 1.44.1 (24-Mar-2018)
Creating filesystem with 512000 1k blocks and 128016 inodes
Filesystem UUID: 5bbb0826-c845-4ef9-988a-d784cc72f258
Superblock backups stored on blocks:
8193, 24577, 40961, 57345, 73729, 204801, 221185, 401409

Allocating group tables: done
Writing inode tables: done
Creating journal (8192 blocks): done
Writing superblocks and filesystem accounting information: done
```

We have to mount both filesystems somewhere so we will create two new directories, `/books` and `/projects`:

```
root@ubuntu-linux:~# mkdir /books /projects
```

Now we can mount both filesystems:

```
root@ubuntu-linux:~# mount /dev/mapper/myvg-mybooks /books
root@ubuntu-linux:~# mount /dev/mapper/myvg-myprojects /projects
```

We can check the last two lines of the mount command output:

```
root@ubuntu-linux:~# mount | tail -n 2
/dev/mapper/myvg-mybooks on /books type ext4 (rw,relatime,data=ordered)
/dev/mapper/myvg-myprojects on /projects type ext4
(rw,relatime,data=ordered)
```

Indeed! Both filesystems are mounted.

To summarize; these are the steps that you need to follow to create LVM logical volumes:

1. Create a physical volume(s).
2. Create a volume group(s).
3. Create a logical volume(s).
4. Create a filesystem(s) on the logical volume(s).
5. Mount the filesystem(s).

Pretty easy, right?

Extending logical volumes

Now comes the moment of appreciation. After all the hard work you have put in so far, you will see why LVM is such a big deal in Linux.

Let's consume all the available space in /books. Notice we only have 2 GB to use:

```
root@ubuntu-linux:~# df -h /books
Filesystem                 Size Used Avail Use% Mounted on
/dev/mapper/myvg-mybooks 2.0G 6.0M 1.8G   1% /books
```

Change to the /books directory and create a 1 GB file named book1 as follows:

```
root@ubuntu-linux:/books# dd if=/dev/zero of=book1 bs=1G count=1
1+0 records in
1+0 records out
1073741824 bytes (1.1 GB, 1.0 GiB) copied, 1.47854 s, 726 MB/s
```

Now create another file `book2` of size 900 MB:

```
root@ubuntu-linux:/books# dd if=/dev/zero of=book2 bs=900M count=1
1+0 records in
1+0 records out
943718400 bytes (944 MB, 900 MiB) copied, 1.34533 s, 701 MB/s
```

We are now running out of space! You will get an error if you attempt to create a 100 MB file:

```
root@ubuntu-linux:/books# dd if=/dev/zero of=book3 bs=100M count=1 dd:
error writing 'book3': No space left on device
1+0 records in
0+0 records out
6103040 bytes (6.1 MB, 5.8 MiB) copied, 0.0462688 s, 132 MB/s
```

We are now officially out of disk space in `/books`:

```
root@ubuntu-linux:/books# df -h /books
Filesystem                 Size Used Avail Use% Mounted on
/dev/mapper/myvg-mybooks 2.0G 2.0G  0     100% /books
```

Here comes LVM to our rescue. We do have some disk space left on our `myvg` volume group, so we can extend the size of our logical volumes and thus the size of our filesystems:

```
root@ubuntu-linux:/books# vgs
  VG    #PV #LV #SN  Attr VSize VFree
  myvg 2    2   0 wz--n- 3.99g 1.50g
```

We precisely have 1.5 GB of disk space left on `myvg`. We can now use the `lvextend` command to add 1 GB to our `/dev/mapper/myvg-mybooks` logical volume:

```
root@ubuntu-linux:/books# lvextend -r --size +1G /dev/mapper/myvg-mybooks
  Size of logical volume myvg/mybooks changed from 2.00 GiB (512 extents)
to
    3.00 GiB (768 extents).
  Logical volume myvg/mybooks successfully resized.
resize2fs 1.44.1 (24-Mar-2018)
Filesystem at /dev/mapper/myvg-mybooks is mounted on /books; on-line
resizing required
old_desc_blocks = 1, new_desc_blocks = 1
The filesystem on /dev/mapper/myvg-mybooks is now 786432 (4k) blocks long.
```

The `-r` option is essential as it resizes the filesystem along with the logical volume. We can now see that our `mybooks` logical volume has grown from 2 GB to 3 GB:

```
root@ubuntu-linux:/books# lvs
  LV            VG    Attr LSize     Pool Origin Data% Meta% Move Log
```

```
Cpy%Sync Convert
   mybooks    myvg -wi-ao---- 3.00g
   myprojects myvg -wi-ao---- 500.00m
```

Consequently, we have gained more disk space in /books:

```
root@ubuntu-linux:/books# df -h /books
Filesystem                 Size Used Avail Use% Mounted on
/dev/mapper/myvg-mybooks 2.9G 1.9G 865M  70% /books
```

Now let's check how much disk size we have remaining in our myvg volume group:

```
root@ubuntu-linux:/books# vgs
   VG   #PV #LV #SN Attr   VSize VFree
   myvg 2    2   0  wz--n- 3.99g 516.00m
```

Let's go all out and extend our myprojects logical volume to take up all the remaining space left in myvg:

```
root@ubuntu-linux:~# lvextend -r -l +100%FREE /dev/mapper/myvg-myprojects
   Size of logical volume myvg/myprojects changed from 516.00 MiB (129
extents)
      to 1016.00 MiB (254 extents).
   Logical volume myvg/myprojects successfully resized.
resize2fs 1.44.1 (24-Mar-2018)
Filesystem at /dev/mapper/myvg-myprojects is mounted on /projects;
The filesystem on /dev/mapper/myvg-myprojects is now 1040384 (1k) blocks
long
```

Notice that the size of our myprojects logical volume has increased and eaten up all that's left in myvg:

```
root@ubuntu-linux:~# lvs
   LV             VG     Attr     LSize     Pool Origin Data% Meta% Move Log
Cpy%Sync Convert
   mybooks    myvg -wi-ao---- 3.00g
   myprojects myvg -wi-ao---- 1016.00m
root@ubuntu-linux:~# vgs
   VG   #PV #LV #SN Attr   VSize VFree
   myvg 2    2   0  wz--n- 3.99g 0
```

Now we can't extend our logical volumes as the myvg volume group ran out of space. Try to add 12 MB to our mybooks logical volume, and you will get an error message:

```
root@ubuntu-linux:~# lvextend -r --size +12M /dev/mapper/myvg-mybooks
   Insufficient free space: 3 extents needed, but only 0 available
```

Extending volume groups

We can only extend our logical volumes if we have available space on the volume group. Now how do we extend a volume group? We simply add a physical volume to it!

Remember, I left out the one physical volume /dev/sdb4 that I didn't add to the volume group myvg. Now it's time to add it!

To extend a volume group, we use the vgextend command followed by the volume group name and then the physical volumes you wish to add. So to add the physical volume dev/sdb4 to our myvg volume group, you can run the command:

```
root@ubuntu-linux:~# vgextend myvg /dev/sdb4
    Volume group "myvg" successfully extended
```

Now we have added a whole 2 GB to our myvg volume group:

```
root@ubuntu-linux:~# vgs
  VG    #PV #LV #SN Attr    VSize VFree
  myvg 3    2    0   wz--n- <5.99g <2.00g
```

How amazing is that? You can now extend either of your two logical volumes as we added more disk space to the volume group. We should all take a moment to appreciate the power and flexibility of Linux LVM.

Now it's time for the last knowledge check exercise in the book. I am sure you will miss them!

Knowledge check

For the following exercises, open up your Terminal and try to solve the following tasks:

1. Add a new 1 GB disk to your virtual machine.
2. Create three 250 MB partitions on your new disk.
3. Use your three new partitions to create three physical volumes.
4. Create a volume group named bigvg that spans all your three physical volumes.
5. Create a logical volume named biglv of size 500 MB.
6. Create an ext4 filesystem on the biglv logical volume.
7. Mount your filesystem on the /mnt/wikileaks directory.

21
echo "Goodbye My Friend"

I want to congratulate you on finishing reading the book and learning over 116 Linux commands. I hope you have enjoyed reading it as much as I have enjoyed writing it! Linux surely requires a curious brain, and I bet you are very courageous to give Linux a shot. I once read a quote that said, "Linux is user-friendly — it's just choosy about who its friends are," so I now welcome you to the elite Linux club.

Where to go next?

You now may be wondering, "where do I go from here?"; most people ask the same question after learning a new skill, and here are my two cents on what to do after learning Linux:

- Put your new skill to work! If you don't keep practicing what you have learned, you will eventually lose it.
- Validate your skill! Employers will surely love it if you have a Linux certification, such as the Linux Foundation LFCS/LFCE certifications or Red Hat RHCSA/RHCE certifications.
- Make money! Linux is in huge demand; start applying for Linux jobs.
- Become a Linux kernel developer! If you are a programmer or you want to become one, you might want to consider learning about the Linux kernel, and maybe one day you can become a Linux kernel contributor.
- Learn another skill! You have now learned Linux; you might want to learn about cloud computing, cybersecurity, or computer networking. It really depends on what your end goal is and your areas of interest.

Keep in touch

You can connect with me on LinkedIn. Also, do not hesitate to send me an email if you ever want to enroll in any of my Udemy courses; I will be more than happy to send you a free coupon!

Assessments

Knowledge check 1

1. `cal 2023`
2. `free -h`
3. `ls /home/elliot`
4. `passwd`
5. echo "Mr.Robot is an awesome TV show!"

True or false

1. False
2. False
3. True
4. False
5. True

Knowledge check 2

1. `ls -l /var/log`
2. `cat /etc/hostname`
3. `touch file1 file2 file3`
4. `ls -a /home/elliot`
5. `mkdir /home/elliot/fsociety`

True or false

1. False
2. False
3. True
4. False
5. True

Knowledge check 3

1. `head -n 2 facts.txt`
2. `tail -n 1 facts.txt`
3. `tac facts.txt`
4. `vi facts.txt`
5. `:q`

Knowledge check 4

1. `touch hacker1 hacker2 hacker3`
2. `mkdir Linux Windows Mac`
3. `touch Linux/cool`
4. `touch Windows/boring`
5. `touch Mac/expensive`
6. `cp hacker1 hacker2 /tmp`
7. `cp -r Windows Mac/tmp`
8. `mv hacker3 /tmp`
9. `mv Linux /tmp`
10. `rm Mac/expensive`
11. `rmdir Mac`
12. `rm -r Windows`
13. `rm hacker2`
14. `mv hacker1 hacker01`

True or false

1. False
2. False
3. True
4. False
5. True

Knowledge check 5

1. `type echo`
2. `which uptime`
3. `whatis mkdir`
4. `man mv`
5. `apropos calendar`
6. `help history`

True or false

1. False
2. False
3. True
4. True

Knowledge check 6

1. `ls -id /var/log`
2. `stat /boot`
3. `mkdir coins`
4. `ln -s coins currency`
5. `touch coins/silver coins/gold`
6. `touch currency/bronze`
7. `ls coins currency`

8. `ln beverages drinks`
9. `rm beverages`
10. `cat drinks`

True or false

1. False
2. True
3. True
4. False
5. True
6. False
7. True

Knowledge check 7

1. `su root`
2. `passwd root`
3. `su - elliot`
4. `su`

True or false

1. True
2. True
3. False

Knowledge check 8

1. `useradd -u 333 abraham`
2. `groupadd admins`
3. `usermod -aG admins abraham`
4. `chgrp admins /home/abraham`
5. `chmod g=r /home/abraham`

True or false

1. True
2. False
3. False

Knowledge check 9

1. `head -n 5 facts.txt / tail -n 1`
2. `free > system.txt`
3. `lscpu >> system.txt`
4. `rmdir /var 2> error.txt`

Knowledge check 10

1. `du -b /etc/hostname`
2. `cut -d: -f1 /etc/group`
3. `wc -l /etc/services`
4. `grep bash /etc/passwd`
5. `uptime / tr [:lower:] [:upper:]`

Knowledge check 11

1. `locate boot.log`
2. `find / -size +50M`
3. `find / -size +70M -size -100M`
4. `find / -user smurf`
5. `find / -group developers`

Knowledge check 12

1. `apt-get install tmux`
2. `apt-cache depends vim`
3. `apt-get install cowsay`
4. `apt-get purge cowsay`
5. `apt-get update then run apt-get upgrade`

Knowledge check 13

1. `pgrep terminal`
2. `ps -fp pid_of_terminal`
3. `kill -9  pid_of_terminal`
4. `firefox &`
5. `renice -n -20 pid_of_firefox`

Knowledge check 14

1. `smurf ALL=(ALL) /sbin/fdisk`
2. `%developers ALL=(ALL) /usr/bin/apt-get`
3. `sudo -lU smurf`

Knowledge check 15

1. `hostnamectl set-hostname darkarmy`
2. `netstat -rn or ip route`
3. `traceroute www.ubuntu.com`
4. `cat /etc/resolv.conf`
5. `nslookup www.distrowatch.com`
6. `ifconfig eth0 down`
7. `ifconfig eth0 up`

Knowledge check 16

1. ```
   #!/bin/bash
   cal
   ```

2. ```
   #!/bin/bash
   cal $1
   ```

3. ```
   #!/bin/bash
   for i in {2000..2020}; do
           cal $i
   done
   ```

Knowledge check 17

1. ```
   */10 *   *   *   *    echo "10 minutes have passed!" >>
   /root/minutes.txt
   ```
2. ```
   0 1  25  12  *    echo "Merry Christmas!" >> /root/holidays.txt
   ```

Knowledge check 18

1. `tar -cvf /root/var.tar.gz /var`
2. `tar -jvf /root/tmp.tar.bz2 /tmp`
3. `tar -Jvf /root/etc.tar.xz /etc`

Knowledge check 19

1. `alias ins="apt-get install"`
2. `alias packages="dpkg -l"`
3. Add the line
   `alias clean="rm -r /tmp/*"`
   to the end of the `.bashrc` file.
   ```

Knowledge check 20

1. Go to the **Virtual Machine Settings** > **Storage** > **Create a new Disk**.
2. `fdisk /dev/sdc`
3. `pvcreate /dev/sdc1 /dev/sdc2 /dev/sdc3`
4. `vgcreate bigvg /dev/sdc1 /dev/sdc2 /dev/sdc3`
5. `lvcreate -n ` **biglv** ` -L 500M ` **bigvg**
6. `mkfs -t ` **ext4** ` /dev/mapper/bigvg-biglv`
7. `mount ` **/dev/mapper/bigvg-biglv** ` /mnt/wikileaks`

Other Books You May Enjoy

If you enjoyed this book, you may be interested in these other books by Packt:

Hands-On Linux for Architects
Denis Salamanca and Esteban Flores

ISBN: 978-1-78953-410-8

- Study the basics of infrastructure design and the steps involved
- Expand your current design portfolio with Linux-based solutions
- Discover open source software-based solutions to optimize your architecture
- Understand the role of high availability and fault tolerance in a resilient design
- Identify the role of containers and how they improve your continuous integration and continuous deployment pipelines
- Gain insights into optimizing and making resilient and highly available designs by applying industry best practices

Mastering Linux Security and Hardening - Second Edition

Donald A. Tevault

ISBN: 978-1-83898-177-8

- Create locked-down user accounts with strong passwords
- Configure firewalls with iptables, UFW, nftables, and firewalld
- Protect your data with different encryption technologies
- Harden the secure shell service to prevent security break-ins
- Use mandatory access control to protect against system exploits
- Harden kernel parameters and set up a kernel-level auditing system
- Apply OpenSCAP security profiles and set up intrusion detection
- Configure securely the GRUB 2 bootloader and BIOS/UEFI

Leave a review - let other readers know what you think

Please share your thoughts on this book with others by leaving a review on the site that you bought it from. If you purchased the book from Amazon, please leave us an honest review on this book's Amazon page. This is vital so that other potential readers can see and use your unbiased opinion to make purchasing decisions, we can understand what our customers think about our products, and our authors can see your feedback on the title that they have worked with Packt to create. It will only take a few minutes of your time, but is valuable to other potential customers, our authors, and Packt. Thank you!

Index

www.ingramcontent.com/pod-product-compliance
Lightning Source LLC
LaVergne TN
LVHW081515050326
832903LV00025B/1499